NEW SHORT HISTORY OF THE CATHOLIC CHURCH

New Short History of the Catholic Church

NORMAN TANNER

burns & oates

Published by Burns & Oates
A Continuum imprint

The Tower Building	80 Maiden Lane
11 York Road	Suite 704
London	New York
SE1 7NX	NY 10038

www.continuumbooks.com

First published 2011

British Library Cataloguing-in-Publication Data
A catalogue record for this book is available from the British Library.

ISBN: HB: 978-0-8601-2455-9

Designed and typeset by Fakenham Photosetting
Printed and bound in India

Contents

Nihil obstat and *Imprimatur*
   Francisco J. Egana SJ, Vice-Rector, Gregorian University, Rome

Dedication

For Angela and John,
Gerard and Jenny,
with many thanks

Acknowledgements

History, especially church history, has for long been a passion in my life. So I take this opportunity to thank all who have encouraged and helped me in this charism: teachers of history at the schools of Woldingham Convent and Avisford; those at Ampleforth College, especially Thomas Charles-Edwards, William Price (headmaster), W. A. Davidson and Basil (later Cardinal) Hume; teachers and colleagues at Oxford University, especially James Campbell, Peter and Jill Lewis, James O'Higgins, and the supervisor of my doctoral thesis William Pantin; most recently, my colleagues at the Gregorian University in Rome. I am grateful to my Superiors in the Society of Jesus for fostering my studies in Church History, for the opportunities to teach in many different countries – opportunities which have greatly enriched my appreciation of the Catholic church worldwide – and for encouraging me to write. Among many editors and publishers, I thank especially Martin Redfern of Sheed and Ward, who had the courage to publish *Decrees of the Ecumenical Councils*; and Robin Baird-Smith of Continuum, who commissioned the present work and has sustained the project with fortitude and patience.

For the present book, I am indebted to all the above persons and to many more. The short Bibliography gives some indication of these extended debts. I take this opportunity to express my thanks to all those concerned. Among more particular debts, I thank Dr Frank Lawrence of Trinity College, Dublin, for help on the section on music in Chapter 3. In addition, I wish to thank the communities of the following institutions who gave me hospitality and inspiration during the research and writing of the book: the Gregorian University in Rome, Campion Hall in Oxford, the Jesuit

Theologate in Nairobi and, in India, the Papal Seminary in Pune and the Regional Seminary in Shillong.

Norman Tanner SJ
Gregorian University, Rome
20 September 2010

Notes and Abbreviations

References to publications. References to books and articles are given in the body of the text, not in footnotes. For the works referred to frequently, see Abbreviations below. Other references are given in the following form: author or first word(s) of title, as appropriate, followed by the date of publication and the pages (or numbers etc.) referred to, thus: (Baur, 1998, p. 443). The full title of the book or article can be found in the Bibliography, under the chapter in which the reference occurs.

Bible. In references to Scripture, a recognizable title of the book is given together with the chapter and verse, thus: Genesis 4.13.

Dates of birth and death. For most individuals who appear in this book, the year of birth and, in many cases, that of death is not known with certainty. The policy has been to give dates wherever possible, rather than question-marks (?) or spread-dates (1370/75), but the year indicated often indicates an approximate rather than a definite date.

Abbreviations

c.	*circa*/about
+	date of death
Decrees	*Decrees of the Ecumenical Councils*, ed. N. Tanner, 2 vols, Georgetown and London 1990. The pagination is continuous through the two volumes, therefore only the page is indicated.
DS	H. Denzinger and A. Schönmetzer (eds), *Enchiridion Symbolorum, Definitionum et Declarationum de Rebus Fidei et Morum*, 37th edn, Freiburg im Breisgau 1991.

Mansi, *Conciliorum*	J. D. Mansi and others (eds), *Sacrorum Conciliorum Nova et Amplissima Collectio*, 53 vols, 1757–1927
Migne, *PG*	J. P. Migne (ed.), *Patrologia Graeca*, 162 vols, Paris, 1857–66,
Migne, *PL*	J. P. Migne (ed.), *Patrologia Latina*, 221 vols, Paris, 1844–64,

Map: The Mediterranean World

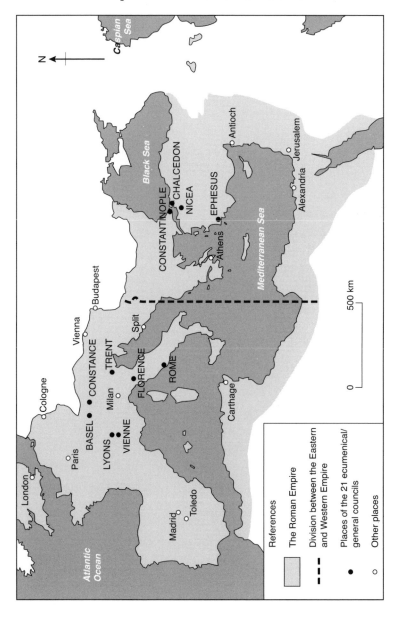

Introduction

From an early age history has been crucial for the people of God. Much of the Old Testament recounts the history of the Jewish people, while the story of Jesus and the early Church is told in the New Testament. The history of the Catholic church – the subject of this short book – forms perhaps the most fascinating story of any institution in world history. But for Catholics this history is more than just interesting, it is crucially important on account of the normative role of Tradition. That is to say, Catholics have held firmly to the belief that the Bible must be accompanied by an awareness of how its message has been lived and interpreted through the centuries, by a sense of how the contents of Scripture have been clarified by the teaching authorities within the Church and through the life, prayer, study and struggles of Christians. Tradition and the history of the Church complement the development of doctrine, they complete our understanding of Christ as the fullness of Truth and of God's revelation to us.

Fortunately, writers have come forward through the centuries to record the history of the Church and so to help us with the necessary Tradition. Eusebius of Caesarea, writing in the fourth century, is acclaimed as the 'Father of Church History'. Three centuries later Britain and France produced two church historians of the highest quality, Bede and Gregory of Tours. Church historians abounded in the Middle Ages and, with more polemical edge, throughout the period of Reformation and Counter-Reformation. The nineteenth century witnessed many advances in historical scholarship which greatly affected the writing of church history. The twentieth century has reaped the fruits of these advances through multi-volume histories of the Church as well as shorter works. The present book fits squarely into the latter category of a short history.

1

The book divides conveniently and naturally into five chapters. Chapter 1 covers the early Church of the first four centuries, the period when the boundaries of the Church mainly coincided with those of the Roman Empire. During the first three centuries persecution was never far from the Church and greatly influenced its history. The fourth century witnessed the conversion of emperor Constantine to Christianity and resulted in first freedom and then a privileged position for the Church – the establishment of Christianity as the official religion of the Empire.

Chapters 2 and 3 cover the long period of the Middle Ages, some half of the Church's history. It begins with the breakup of the Roman Empire in the West through the so-called barbarian invasions. The invaders gradually converted to Christianity and brought new life and energy to the Church in most of the western, Latin-speaking half of the former Roman Empire. There resulted, too, the evangelization and conversion of central and northern Europe. Meanwhile the eastern, Greek-speaking half of the empire, which had succeeded in warding off the barbarian invaders, became threatened by the rise of Islam from the early seventh century onwards. Gradually most of this Byzantine Empire was conquered by Muslim forces, culminating in the capture of Constantinople in 1453. In these regions Christians lived increasingly as a tolerated minority.

In 1054, the dividing date between Chapters 2 and 3, occurred the schism between eastern Christendom, with its capital in Constantinople, and western Christendom, with its capital in Rome – the schism between the Catholic and Orthodox churches which, sadly, still remains unhealed. Chapter 3 traces the story of the Catholic church in this second half of the Middle Ages. It is the longest chapter in the book. Whereas the Middle Ages are treated quite briefly and even disparagingly in many histories of the Church, in my opinion the central and late Middle Ages were an extraordinarily rich and creative period in the history of Christianity and one that is crucial for understanding subsequent developments in the Catholic church. In many respects Chapter 3 is the hinge of the whole book.

Chapter 4 covers the sixteenth to eighteenth centuries. For the Catholic church the period was greatly influenced by its response to the Protestant Reformation. The chapter might have been entitled 'The Counter-Reformation', for long the usual title for works on this period. But historians are increasingly aware that much was going on within the Catholic church that cannot be explained only as a response to Protestantism – Catholic missions beyond Europe are an obvious example. In all sorts of ways the Catholic church had its own inner dynamism during the three centuries. This book, moreover, is a history of the Catholic church in its own right, not just in its reactions to other churches. For these and other reasons the title for the period recently gaining support, Early Modern Catholicism, has been preferred – a blander but more accurate title.

The fifth and final chapter covers the last two centuries, a period when the expansion of Catholicism into a truly world religion was consolidated. The Catholic church has emerged as much the largest of all the Christian churches and communities, with over a billion members and some 17 per cent of the world's population, according to the most recent estimates. It has been a period of much energy and creativity within the Catholic church at many levels: popular religion, intellectual developments, organization and missionary endeavour. At the same time there have been plenty of challenges: the aftermath of the French Revolution; coercion and persecution; intellectual and other challenges from within the Catholic church, from other Christian churches and communities and, on a scale unseen since the early Church, from other religions and systems of thought. It has been a Church of both saints and sinners. In the last section of the chapter, developments since the second Vatican council are assessed.

Chapter 1
Pentecost to the Fourth Century

i. The Apostolic Age

When should this book begin? An obvious date is the birth of Christ, the founder of Christianity and its loadstar ever since. There is insufficient space, however, in this short history to review the life and times of Jesus Christ. The story is well known, as recorded principally in the four Gospels of Matthew, Mark, Luke and John, and the details have been investigated extensively by numerous writers. It forms, of course, the essential background, indeed the foreground, to all that will be said hereafter.

Pentecost makes a more realistic starting point, especially since this book is styled a history of the Church rather than of Christianity.

Acts of the Apostles

On Pentecost, the fiftieth day (fifty in Greek = *pentecoste*) after Christ's ascension into heaven, according to the Acts of the Apostles, the Holy Spirit descended upon the disciples gathered together in Jerusalem and transformed them, principally through the gifts of wisdom and fortitude, into an enduring church. Traditionally the day has been called the birthday of the Christian church, on account of the gift of the Holy Spirit who sustains and guides the Church, as distinct from Christmas, the birthday of Christ. It is appropriate, therefore, to begin this history with the account of Pentecost in Acts 2.1–4 and 41–2:

When the day of Pentecost had come, the disciples were all together in one place. Suddenly a sound came from heaven like

5

> *the rush of a mighty wind, and it filled all the house where they were sitting. There appeared to them tongues as of fire, distributed and resting on each one of them. They were all filled with the Holy Spirit and began to speak in other tongues, as the Spirit gave them utterance.*

Peter the apostle then preached to the multitude. As a result:

> *Those who received Peter's word were baptized, and there were added that day (to the number of believers) about three thousand souls. They devoted themselves to the apostles' teaching and fellowship, to the breaking of bread and the prayers.*

The period from Pentecost to the death of the John the Evangelist, who is usually reckoned to be the last to die of the twelve apostles chosen by Jesus Christ, has come to be called the Apostolic Age: that is, the age, after the death of Jesus, when at least one of the apostles was alive. It forms a convenient time span for the first part of this chapter. The large majority of directly relevant evidence comes from the New Testament, principally Acts of the Apostles and the letters of Paul; some additional information comes from various other sources, from both within and beyond the Christian community.

Acts of the Apostles is essentially an historical work; though one with an apologetic purpose. Indeed, the Greek word *Praxeis*, and the Latin *Acta*, which we translate as 'Acts', were commonly used in the titles of historical books. To begin this *New Short History of the Catholic Church* with Acts of the Apostles is doubly appropriate. First and most obviously, because Acts formed the most important document about the history of the Church during this early period. Secondly, to begin with Acts may give special encouragement to readers of the present book. For it shows that present-day interest in the history of the Church dovetails with that of the early Christians. For them history was informative and interesting, but it was also constitutive of the Christian message. Or, in the subsequent language of the councils of Trent and Vatican II, Tradition clarifies Scripture.

The account of Pentecost in Acts records that the multitude addressed by Peter included 'Parthians and Medes and Elamites and residents of Mesopotamia, Judea and Cappadocia, Pontus and Asia, Phrygia and Pamphylia, Egypt and the parts of Libya

belonging to Cyrene, and visitors from Rome, both Jews and prose-
lytes, Cretans and Arabians'. From among them, as a result, 'about
three thousand souls' were baptized. We can visualize the rapid
expansion of Christianity to many parts of the Roman Empire and
beyond, as those baptized returned to their own countries.

The place and timing of Christ's life within the Roman Empire
were extraordinarily favourable to the spread of Christianity, even
from a human standpoint. Christians can praise the wisdom of
Divine Providence in the choices. Good communications by land
and sea as well as relative peace within the vast empire meant
that, despite the trials of persecution, the Christian message
could be preached and practiced, and thereby grow, throughout
the Mediterranean world, and beyond it, for some four centuries
(see Map, p. xv). Essential for this expansion, too, was the depth
and sophistication of the Jewish religion, which provided for
Christianity its rich foundation.

After the account of Pentecost, the early chapters of Acts of the
Apostles focus on the spread and persecution of Christianity
among the Jewish people within the lands known to Jesus. The
story culminates with the preaching and martyrdom of Stephen,
the first Christian martyr, in Jerusalem around the year 35 and the
dramatic conversion of Paul of Tarsus on the road to Damascus.

Thereafter the account in Acts moves decisively to the wider
world, to lands and peoples beyond Judea and the Jews. Crucial to
this expansion were the difficult decisions to admit to the Christian
fold persons who were not Jews and to lift several obligations – at
least for non-Jewish converts to Christianity – regarding circum-
cision and diet: decisions that could be seen as going beyond
the explicit teachings and practice of Jesus. Peter and Paul are
represented as the key figures in these resolutions, with important
roles also played by James 'brother of the Lord' and Barnabas, the
companion of Paul. The decisions were ratified, after discussion, at
the council 'of the apostles and elders' which was held at Jerusalem
in about the year 49 (Acts, chapter 15).

After the council of Jerusalem, Paul dominates Acts. He parted
from Barnabas following a difference over their choice of colleagues,
and Timothy became his closest companion. His remarkable
missionary journeys, which had already begun before the council
of Jerusalem with visits to Cyprus and various places in modern

Turkey, took him to cities in Syria and Greece as well as to Turkey again. Paul then returned to Jerusalem where he was arrested by the Roman authorities on account of the religious disturbances he was causing. As a result, he appealed to the emperor, following his rights as a Roman citizen, and he was taken in captivity to Rome. The book concludes with the story of this eventful journey and his sojourn in Rome, without describing his death. Besides Acts, there are the surviving letters traditionally ascribed to Paul that were written to various Christian communities and individuals: two each to the Christians in Corinth and Thessalonia, one each to the Christians of Rome, Galatia, Ephesus, Philippi and Colossae, two to his companion Timothy and one to his disciple Titus. Many of these letters are long and very substantial, informative regarding both Christian theology, as preached by Paul, and the communities and individuals to whom they are addressed. Taken together, Acts and Paul's letters provide us with an exceptionally full and lively account of the development of the Church during the three decades or so after the death of Jesus.

Two quotations, both from Acts of the Apostles, must suffice to illustrate the vitality described by this early literature. The first comes from chapter 4 of Acts and portrays the early Christian community soon after Pentecost:

> Now the company of those who believed were of one heart and soul, and no one said that any of the things which he possessed was his own, but they had everything in common. And with great power the apostles gave their testimony to the resurrection of the Lord Jesus and great grace was upon them all. There was not a needy person among them, for as many as were possessors of lands or houses sold them, and brought the proceeds of what was sold and laid it at the apostles' feet; and distribution was made to each as any had need.

The portrayal may be idealistic, especially regarding common property, yet it captures something of the energy and dedication of the early Christians. The second quotation also portrays energy and commitment, novelty too within the Christian message, but also the difficulty of communicating this message, this time in the context of the preaching of Paul. It comes from chapter 17 of Acts, towards the end of Paul's ministry, and describes his speech in the Areopagus – a meeting-place near the Acropolis – in Athens:

So Paul, standing in the middle of the Areopagus, said: 'Men of Athens, I perceive that in every way you are very religious. For as I passed along, and observed the objects of your worship, I found also an altar with this inscription, "To an unknown god". What therefore you worship as unknown, this I proclaim to you. The God who made the world and everything in it, being Lord of heaven and earth, does not live in shrines made by man, nor is he served by human hands, as though he needed anything, since he himself gives to all people life and breath and every-thing ... Yet he is not far from each one of us, for "In him we live and move and have our being" ... The times of ignorance God overlooked, but now he commands everyone everywhere to repent, because he has fixed a day on which he will judge the world in righteousness by a man (Jesus Christ) whom he has appointed, and of this he has given assurance to all people by raising him from the dead.'

Other sources

The other books of the New Testament provide only limited historical information about the early Church. Letter to the Hebrews (the author is now widely considered to be someone other than Paul) and Book of Revelation (Apocalypse) are important theological treatises but give few details about the life of the early Christians. The remaining seven books (entitled: James; Jude; 1 and 2 Peter; 1, 2 and 3 John) are letters addressed to Christians in general rather than to particular churches, hence their common description as 'catholic' (meaning 'universal') letters/epistles. As a result, while they are significant as theological treatises and moral exhortations, they are short on the details of the early Christian communities. They underline, nevertheless, the liveliness and religious commitment of the early Church.

There are no other surviving works written by Christians that clearly belong to the Apostolic Age; though a few writings discussed in the second section of this chapter may have been composed towards the end of this period. The absence of other such works comes as no surprise. Christians took great pains to establish which books should be included in the New Testament. The main list (or 'canon') of these works was essentially approved during the second century AD and finalized by the fourth or fifth century. The best works were chosen, it seems, on account of their quality and, in most cases, the writer's privileged knowledge of Jesus. Certainly the books that were included, taken together, are of very high quality even from a human point of view. Other possibly contemporary writings, which were excluded from the canon, became lost.

Also excluded from the New Testament canon were a large number of 'gospels', 'acts', 'letters/epistles' and 'apocalypses' relating to the life of Jesus and the early Church which date, according to modern scholarship, from the second century onwards. They are usually called 'Apocryphal Books' because they were written after the Apostolic Age and their reliability is doubtful and, as a result of these and other factors, they were excluded from the canon. It is difficult to know what to make of them. They focus much on the strange and awkward, in contrast to the overall sobriety of the canonical books. They are essential reading for scholars of the period but they need not detain us here.

No extensive studies of the early Church by non-Christians – which might give us an outside evaluation of the movement – survive from the Apostolic Age. It seems unlikely that such works ever existed. However, a few scattered passages survive in the writings of various non-Christians from the late first and early second centuries. They provide precious independent evidence of the existence of the early Church even though the information is very limited. They may be considered here together.

The earliest passage comes from *Antiquities of the Jews*, which was written by the Jewish historian Flavius Josephus around the year 94. It provides an account of the martyrdom of James 'the brother of Jesus' in Jerusalem, probably in 62. The sentence of death was ordered by the Jewish high priest but it appears to have been an unpopular move. James's martyrdom is not mentioned in the Acts of the Apostles or elsewhere in the New Testament, but Josephus's account rings true and thus provides important independent evidence about the existence of the early Church. Josephus writes thus:

> *Ananus the High Priest assembled the Sanhedrin of judges and brought before them the brother of Jesus who was called Christ, whose name was James, and some others. When he had formed*

an accusation against them as breakers of the law, he delivered them to be stoned. But those who seemed the most equitable of the citizens, and accurate in legal matters, disliked what was done.

Two Roman historians, Tacitus in *Annales* (Annals) and Suetonius in *Vita Neronis* (Life of Nero), both writing between 110 and 120, described the persecution of Christians by the emperor Nero. Tacitus records how they were made scapegoats for the fire that ravaged Rome in 64. He acknowledged that the steadfastness of Christians under torture drew the citizens' admiration: 'All this punishment gave rise to a feeling of pity, even towards people (Christians) whose guilt merited the most exemplary punishment; for it was felt that they were being destroyed not for the public good but to gratify the cruelty of an individual (Nero).' Suetonius, too, relates the sufferings inflicted by Nero upon Christians, while describing them disparagingly as 'people adhering to a novel and mischievous superstition'.

Interesting further information is contained in an exchange of letters around the year 112 between emperor Trajan and his emissary in Bithynia (in modern Turkey), Pliny the Younger. Reporting to the emperor regarding affairs in that region, Pliny noted that Christians 'had spread not only in the cities but in the villages and rural districts as well'. He summarized their practices and lifestyle thus:

On an appointed day (Sunday?) they had been accustomed to meet before daybreak, and to recite a hymn antiphonally to Christ, as to a God, and to bind themselves by an oath, not for the commission of any crime but to abstain from theft, robbery, adultery and breach of faith, and not to deny a deposit when it was claimed. After the conclusion of this ceremony it was their custom to depart and meet again to take food (the Eucharist?).

These, then, are the principal witnesses to the Church of the first century AD: writers, principally those of the New Testament, who wrote during this time or shortly afterwards. They provide the overwhelming majority of our reliable knowledge about the early Church, after the ascension of Jesus, during this century.

Tombs of Peter and Paul

One event that comes to us from later records is the burial of the apostle Peter. Neither Peter's ministry in Rome nor his martyrdom are mentioned in Acts of the Apostles or elsewhere in the New Testament; though 'Babylon' mentioned in 1 Peter 5.13 may refer to Rome and therefore indicate Peter's presence there. Two letters, which were written by Clement of Rome and Ignatius of Antioch just before and after the year 100, refer to Peter's presence and death in the city. The first mention that his death was by crucifixion comes from Tertullian, writing in the early third century. Eusebius of Caesarea in his *Historia Ecclesiastica*, written in the early fourth century, dates this martyrdom more precisely to the persecution of emperor Nero – probably he was put to death during the persecution in 64 even though Eusebius indicates a later persecution in 68. For his tomb, we rely partly on the letter of a certain Proclus, which was reportedly written around 200 and survives in the same *Historia Ecclesiastica* of Eusebius. Proclus writes of the 'trophy' (Latin, *trophaeum*) of Peter, indicating his burial place, on the Vatican hill. We know that when emperor Constantine initiated the building of the original St Peter's church in Rome (which remains the basis of the present Church today), he chose a somewhat inconvenient site: a marsh had to be filled in and a hill excavated in order to accommodate the building. An obvious motive for accepting these inconveniences, and the one generally recognized for centuries, was to include something very special within the church's crypt, namely Peter's tomb. Subsequently, in extensive excavations in the crypt carried out in the middle of the last century, a team of archaeologists (led by professors Kirschbaum, Ferrua, Ghetti and Josi) discovered a tomb with a flagstick that seemed to correspond with Proclus's description of the *trophaeum*. Modern archaeology thus appeared to confirm the ancient tradition.

Acts of the Apostles mentions Paul's captivity in Rome but not his death there. However, the letters of Clement of Rome and Ignatius of Antioch record the death of Paul in Rome alongside that of Peter. Paul was recognized to be a Roman citizen (Acts 22.25–30) and the normal form of death penalty for Roman citizens was beheading. Tertullian states explicitly that he was beheaded. The date of his execution is usually assigned to the Neronian persecution in which Peter also perished, though some scholars date it earlier and a few later. Early evidence places the execution at 'Tre Fontane' (following the legend that Paul's head bounced three times after his execution, resulting in three fountains springing up) some three miles to the south of Rome. The tomb in which he was buried is ascribed to the crypt of the church of St Pauls outside the Walls – a location that recent excavations have corroborated. The tomb in St Pauls has recently been finely restored.

ii. Second and third centuries: continuing persecution

During these two centuries, persecution remained central to the life of the Church. It colours much of the surviving evidence of the period. It also explains many gaps in this evidence and therefore in our knowledge, inasmuch as Christians were reluctant to preserve incriminating evidence. This section begins by examining the persecutions of the period and their effects. Thereafter the main institutional developments are considered, then popular religion and some major theologians.

Persecutions

We have seen already that persecution – whether actual or threat-ening – featured prominently in the life of the Church during the first century. Much the same situation persisted through the next two centuries and into the early fourth century, when the conversion of emperor Constantine to Christianity radically altered the situation. Persecutions were intermittent and confined mostly to particular regions. Nevertheless they had a profound influence upon the history of Christianity in at least three important ways. First and most obviously, many people suffered grievously. Secondly, the possibilities for many normal forms of church life that we take for granted – for example, the establishment of church buildings – were very limited or out of the question. Thirdly, in following the example of Jesus Christ, the Christian martyrs of the time have markedly affected the history of Christianity ever since: the heroic ideal of martyrdom became established firmly in Christian tradition. As a result of these persecutions Christian life was both restricted and greatly enriched.

Many of the persecutions best known to us were conducted by Roman emperors. The attitudes of these emperors varied considerably. Thus, the emperor Trajan urged persecution somewhat as a last resort, in his reply to Pliny the Younger around 112, in contrast to the fierce and open persecution ordered half a century earlier by emperor Nero. Trajan replied to Pliny's inquiries in these words:

> *You have taken the right line, my dear Pliny, in examining the cases of those denounced to you as Christians, for no hard and fast rule can be laid down, of universal application. Christians are not to be sought out. If they are informed against, and the charge is proved, they are to be punished, with this reservation – that if any one denies that he is a Christian, and actually proves it, that is by worshipping our gods, he shall be pardoned as a result of his recantation, however suspect he may have been with respect to the past.*

During Trajan's reign Ignatius, bishop of Antioch, was condemned as a Christian and sent to Rome to be slain by beasts in the ampitheatre (traditionally identified as the Colosseum), a prospect Ignatius described with eagerness in his famous letter to the Christians in Rome:

> *Let there come on me fire and cross and conflicts with wild beasts, mangling of limbs, crushing of the whole body, grievous torments of the devil, may I but attain to Jesus Christ.*

Trajan's successors Hadrian (117–38) and Antoninus Pius (138–61) were tolerant rulers, at least officially so. Even so, it was probably during the latter's reign that there occurred the well-recorded martyrdoms of Polycarp, bishop of Smyrna, and eleven companions. Polycarp, when he refused to recant, was burnt to death in his episcopal city. The reign of Marcus Aurelius (161–180) witnessed persecutions in various places. The best known occurred in Lyons in 177, when forty-eight Christians were put to death. They included the heroic young slave-girl Blandina.

Gender and equality before God were subtly highlighted, too, in the account of the martyrdom of Perpetua and her slave Felicity in the ampitheatre of Carthage in 203. The group of martyrs included Perpetua's husband and two other men, but the narrative focuses on the two women. It seems, indeed, that the account of their time in prison together awaiting death, and of the visions they enjoyed there, was composed by Perpetua, while the gruesome story of their martyrdom was added – or touched up, since Perpetua had already foreseen the impending doom – by Tertullian. Altogether the 'Passion' is a literary masterpiece and has exercised great influence upon Christian spirituality. Felicity and Perpetua (in that order) were commemorated in the Roman canon of the Mass and they are remembered today in the first eucharistic prayer.

The middle years of the third century brought a renewed upsurge in persecutions. The short reign of emperor Decius (249–50) witnessed the first general persecution of Christians throughout the Roman Empire. He issued an edict ordering all those living within the empire to perform some act of pagan worship, such as offering a libation, or taking part in a sacrificial meal, or burning incense before a statue of the emperor. Many Christians complied with the edict, others purchased documents stating that they had complied. Others resisted. Pope Fabian was put to death at Rome, Origen the theologian was imprisoned and tortured, the priest Pionius was burned to death at Smyrna, bishop Babylas of Antioch died in prison, bishop Cyprian of Carthage went into hiding. Gallus succeeded Decius as emperor and persecution continued. Pope Cornelius was exiled to Civitavecchia and died there in 253. Emperor Valerian (253–60) initially favoured Christians but subsequently issued various edicts of persecution. As a result, pope Sixtus II and four of his deacons were put to death in the cemetery of Callistus in Rome, Cyprian of Carthage was beheaded in his city, Bishop Fructuosus and two of his deacons were executed in Tarragona in Spain. Gallienus, who succeeded his father Valerian in 260, put an end to the persecution and issued the first official declaration of tolerance for Christianity throughout the Roman Empire.

The end of the third century witnessed another renewal of fierce persecution, lasting into the early fourth century. Emperor Diocletian (284–305), towards the end of his reign, ordered a purge of soldiers in his army who refused to abandon Christianity and then moved to a much wider persecution of Christians throughout the empire. Various edicts ordered the destruction of church buildings, the burning of sacred books, the prohibition of religious services, and the obligation to offer non-Christian sacrifice. In the province of Palestine there were some eighty-four known martyrs and the Thebaid in Egypt saw mass executions of up to one hundred Christians at a time. The historian Bede dated the martyrdom of Saint Alban, protomartyr of Britain, to the reign of Diocletian; though some modern scholars argue rather for the mid or early third century. After Diocletian resigned as emperor in 305, persecution continued intermittently as various rivals fought for the succession. Peace was finally brought to Christianity – at least for a while – with Constantine's triumph over his enemies in 324.

Three comments, or questions, may conclude this section. First, to repeat, many Christians suffered horrendously. They came from many walks of life, as we have seen: men and women, young and old, slaves and soldiers, wives and popes. We do not know precisely how many individuals died – those that have been mentioned represent only a fraction of the total – but because Christians greatly valued their martyrs, so we are particularly well informed about them. The single most important source is Eusebius of Caesarea, *Historia Ecclesiastica*, but there were plenty of other, independent records: Perpetua's 'Passion' is one such example.

Secondly, there was perhaps nothing exceptional in the number of Christian martyrs. Life within the Roman Empire was brutal in many respects and capital punishment was frequent. In addition to Christians, various religious groups suffered. To mention just two cases, many Jews were put to death by the Roman authorities during the first century AD, principally within their homeland, and emperor Diocletian targeted Manichaeans as well as Christians. Christian rulers, moreover, once they had assumed power, from the fourth century onwards, could be as intolerant towards other faiths and religions as the Roman Empire had been towards Christianity. Perhaps in mitigation of the harsh attitudes of the times, we must remember that life was more communitarian that today, less individual, so that religious dissidence could be considered an affront to the whole community, not just a personal matter.

Thirdly, some historians have argued that Christian rulers behaved with even greater severity inasmuch as they demanded inner assent, at least from baptized Christians, whereas Roman authorities had required only external conformity. The behaviour of Christian rulers will be examined later, but the plea that Roman authorities acted leniently may be stretching the point; Christians who were ordered to show some external signs by worshipping an idol or a statue of the emperor would understandably view such action as requiring an inner betrayal of Christianity, not just external conformity.

Institutional developments

Persecution left an imprint upon the Church that remains today. It strengthened and enriched the early Christian community in many ways. At the same time, the reality or prospect of persecution restricted the Church's freedom and thereby limited the possibilities for institutional development. In considering these developments, the *papacy* makes an obvious starting point.

We have already indicated the special role of Peter in the early Church and his links with Rome. His ministry and martyrdom in Rome were normally mentioned alongside those of the apostle Paul in the same city. The next bishop of Rome for whom we have direct evidence was Clement of Rome, whose letter around the year 96, mentioning the death of Peter, has been noted. It may appear surprising that Clement does not clearly identify himself in the letter as the bishop of Rome. Possibly, at this early stage, after the death of Peter, there was a group of bishops who supervised the church in Rome, rather than a single bishop, and Clement was one – perhaps the senior – among them. Such a collegial arrangement in Rome is suggested by the letters of Ignatius of Antioch in the early second century. In most of his letters, Ignatius clearly identifies the bishop of the community to which the letter was addressed, but not so in the case of his letter to the church in Rome. The more monarchical concept of episcopal authority, whereby there was a single bishop in a city, seems to have originated in the East, and then spread, during the early second century, to Rome and the West. Irenaeus of Lyons provides us with the list of the bishops of Rome down to Eleutherius (174–189), though perhaps suggesting a more solitary role for the early bishops among them (after Peter and Paul) than was actually the case. Writing around 180, Irenaeus says that Peter and Paul 'committed the episcopate' to Linus who was then followed by Anacletus, Clement, Evaristus, Alexander, Sixtus 'sixth from the apostles', Telesephorus 'who was gloriously martyred', Hyginus, Pius, Anicetus, Soter and Eleutherius 'now in the twelfth place from the apostles'.

During the third century, the authority of the bishop of Rome grew beyond his city and Italy principally through the interventions of two popes, Stephen I and Dionysius/Denis. The title 'pope' – which essentially means 'father' – began to be used in the sixth century, became more official from the eighth century, and was applied exclusively to the bishop of Rome, at least in the western Church, from the eleventh century onwards. However, for the sake of simplicity, the term 'pope' will be used even for the earlier bishops of Rome, likewise 'papacy' for the institution.

Stephen I (254–7) became involved in controversies involving two sensitive issues: the return to their sees of bishops who had apostatized during persecution or were irregular in other respects, and who had repented of their failures; secondly, the validity of baptism administered by heretics. On both issues, Stephen took the softer line, allowing such bishops to be restored to their dioceses and recognizing the validity of the baptisms provided the baptizer was acting in good faith. The ensuing debate involved bishops in Spain and France as well as in north Africa and Asia. Many of them opposed Stephen's leniency, including the highly regarded Cyprian bishop of Carthage. Nevertheless the debate meant that the voice of the bishop of Rome was beginning to be heard throughout the Mediterranean world.

The intervention of pope Dionysius (260–8) involved correspondence with the bishop of Alexandria in Egypt, who was also called Dionysius. The letters touched on two important issues. First, pope Dionysius, like pope Stephen, insisted on the validity of baptism by heretics, provided it was administered correctly. Secondly, to resolve a theological controversy in which the bishop of Alexandria had become involved, pope Dionysius suggested the Greek word 'homoousios' (consubstantial) to denote the relationship between Father and Son in the Trinity – a word that was later adopted in the Nicene creed. Through this correspondence we find the authority of the bishop of Rome extending beyond Italy, to the African church, while Nicea's adoption of *homoousios* added further weight to papal foresight.

The roles of *bishops and priests* developed in various ways during the second and third centuries. Our immediate and contemporary information about these developments is limited. Most of it comes to us through the surviving accounts of bishops and priests who were martyred. So we should remember that we are mostly looking at remarkable cases, mainly bishops, such as Ignatius of Antioch, Polycarp of Smyrna and Cyprian of Carthage. More systematic and ordinary evidence is largely lacking, in good part for the obvious reason that Christian communities who were liable to be persecuted did not want to leave around incriminating evidence. Fortunately the fourth century, as the Church emerged from persecution, provides us with much valuable information that tells us, indirectly, about the situation in the earlier period.

This later evidence, as well as the fragmentary evidence from the period itself, shows that by the second half of the third century, perhaps earlier, the Church had developed a sophisticated organization, based principally upon the diocese. Christians took over the word 'diocese' from the administrative units into which the Roman Empire was divided – the empire was divided into thirteen huge 'dioceses', one of which was Britain, following the administrative reforms of the emperor Diocletian in the late third century – but the territory was much smaller. The average sized diocese in the Christian church was more like a deanery or a large parish today. Indeed, in many regions before the fourth century there was no clear distinction between 'diocese' and 'parish'. By way of comparison, today there are some 2,600 dioceses for a worldwide Catholic population of over one billion; in the year 325 somewhat, but not markedly, fewer dioceses (the precise number is unknown; dioceses were particularly numerous in north Africa) for perhaps twenty million Christians.

Arrangements varied somewhat by country or region, but a three-tiered episcopate was already apparent in the late third century: bishops of dioceses; metropolitan bishops who lived in the larger towns (metro-polis = large town) and had some authority over the bishops of the area; and the bishops of the three major sees of Rome, Alexandria and Antioch (to be joined later by Constantinople and Jerusalem, to form the 'pentarchy' of five patriarchal sees). Priests and deacons go back to New Testament times, though the distinction between priest and bishop was not always clear then. The various roles of priests and deacons as cooperators with the bishop were strengthened during the persecutions of the early Church and their responsibilities were to be further clarified during the fourth century.

Councils. The council of Jerusalem, about the year 49, has been mentioned. Councils continued to play a role in the life of the Church during the second and third centuries, though as public gatherings their frequency and freedom were severely curtailed by the threat of persecution. Mansi, *Conciliorum* (see p. xiv), the monumental collection of conciliar documents, provides most of the surviving evidence about them, and hints at their vitality, even though in most cases little information survives beyond the fact that a meeting took place. Some of the fullest information relates to the one or more councils held in Antioch in the 260s (the number and precise dates are unclear). They reveal the Church's ability to organize substantial meetings and its readiness to confront thorny issues, in this case the lifestyle and teaching of the bishop of the city, Paul of Samosata. Antioch was a major see and Paul a powerful figure. He was condemned, nevertheless, both for his inappropriate conduct – he was judged to be too close to young women and his lifestyle was too worldly – as well as for his faulty teaching on the Trinity. As a result, he was deposed from his see. A few years earlier, several important councils were held in Carthage in north Africa, presided over by Cyprian, the learned and saintly bishop of the city. These councils dealt with the delicate issues of penance required of Christians who had lapsed during persecution, and the re-baptism of schismatics. On both issues, the African councils, led by Cyprian, opposed the softer line taken by pope Stephen. The fuller flowering of church councils would come in the fourth century, when the Church emerged from persecution.

Canon law, meaning the law of the Christian community, concerned the various church institutions that have been mentioned as well as many other aspects of Christian life. Christianity had emerged from Judaism which greatly respected law, both divine and human. Order within the Christian community was emphasized in the New Testament, most notably in Matthew's gospel and some of Paul's letters. The Roman Empire, into which Christianity was born, was famous for its attention to civil law. Unsurprisingly, therefore, even during the first three centuries after Christ, when persecution prevailed and Christians led a somewhat underground life, canon law played an important role in the life of the Church. There was no universal code of canon law, such as the Catholic church has today: this was to come about only in the twentieth century. In many ways canon law then was closer in concept (though different in content) to the 'common law' prevailing today in many English-speaking countries, especially Britain and the USA. That is to say, it gave answers – always within the framework, at least in theory, of Christ's teaching in the New Testament – to particular problematic cases that emerged. It was quite eclectic in the areas it covered: liturgy, prayer and asceticism as well as more obviously legal topics.

Both the importance and the eclectic nature of early canon law are revealed by the three main works of this kind that survive from before 300: *Didache* (meaning 'Teaching', probably from Syria, *c.* 90–100, written in Greek), *Apostolic Tradition* (written in Greek, probably by Hippolytus in Rome in the early third century, though possibly from Egypt, hence the alternative title, *Egyptian Church Order*), and *Didaskalia Apostolorum* ('Teaching of the Apostles', probably from northern Syria, early third century). They treat of Scripture, notably the Sermon on the Mount in *Didache*; the freedom of Christians from Jewish observances and ceremonial law; the sacraments of Baptism and Eucharist – the core of the Catholic church's present second eucharistic prayer is already there in *Apostolic Tradition* – and the expectations of their recipients; ordination and duties of bishops, priests and deacons; marriage and the lifestyles of husbands and wives (especially in *Didaskalia*); widows and deaconesses; fasting and prayer (the text of the Our Father is given in *Didache*); penance and the reconciliation of sinners; the trials of persecution. The three works formulate, for the most part, existing regulations and practices rather than prescribe new legislation. All three were intended for use within a particular locality, rather than for the universal Church. Together they provide an insight into the joys and trials, the hopes and expectations, of the early Church.

Popular religion

We must use our imagination to enter into the daily lives of Christians during these first three centuries. The Eucharist, which came to be celebrated preferably on Sunday, the day of the Lord's resurrection, stood at the centre of the Christian's life. So much seems clear. The threat of persecution meant that churches as buildings were impractical in most places, so the Eucharist was normally celebrated in private houses or in secret places such as catacombs.

The catacombs (networks of underground passages and caves) in Rome contain many of the surviving works of Christian art from this early period. Several of them portray the Eucharist. The earliest, from the late second century, is to be found in the catacomb of Saint Callistus. Christ is symbolized as a fish: the letters that make up the Greek word for fish, ICHTHUS, were taken to represent I(esus) Ch(ristos) Th(eou) U(ios) S(oter) – Jesus Christ, Son of God, Saviour – a meaning obvious only to Christians. In the painting are two fishes, one bearing on its back loaves of bread, the other carrying beakers of wine. The eucharistic motif is clear, the art is of fine quality. The two catacombs of Priscilla and of Peter and Marcellinus contain wall-paintings portraying the Eucharist in a more realistic manner. The paintings probably date from the third century and show women (mainly) and men seated or reclining around a table, with various signs indicating the Eucharist as a meal of love (agape) and peace. Christ is again represented by a fish. Whether the women are portrayed as ministers of the Eucharist is debated.

Although catacombs were used on occasion for the celebration of the Eucharist, their primary purpose was to house the bodies of the dead. Christians paid great attention to burial, it seems. There was some tension on the issue. In Luke's gospel, the angels tell the women who came to look for Jesus on Easter day, 'Why look among the dead for someone who is alive? He is not here; he has risen' (Luke 24.5). Christ was indeed a unique case. Other people would normally have to wait before the resurrection of their bodies. Even so, since the resurrection of the body and life everlasting were key doctrines of the new Christian religion, it might be expected that attention to burial and tombs would be moderate. On the other hand, balancing these more eternal considerations, love and concern for one's brothers and sisters in Christ were human factors, rooted in this life, and included proper respect for their bodies. Some forty catacombs (each a distinct complex of passages and caves) have been discovered in and around Rome, others in Naples, Syracuse in Sicily, Malta, Milos, Syria, the region of Jerusalem, Alexandria and elsewhere in north Africa. The spaces were formed through various climatic and geological factors specific to these regions; the graves and sometimes the corpses have been preserved remarkably well. Such catacombs, however, were exceptional.

Probably most Christians were buried in cemeteries quite similar to those we know today, sometimes alongside non-Christians and sometimes in cemeteries exclusively dedicated to Christians. Many graves survive and archaeologists are constantly extending our knowledge about them. Concern for burial characterized most religions that preceded Christianity, and many of them proclaimed some hope of future life. The custom of surrounding the corpse with grave-goods was widespread. Sometimes the tombs of Christians can be identified by the recognizably Christian grave-goods, such as crucifixes, that have been found in them. Sometimes churches were built over the tombs of martyrs, after persecution ended in the fourth century. It is these tombs that are best known to us. Those of Peter and Paul have been mentioned, and churches were built over the supposed tombs of many other martyrs of the early Church. For England, the best example is the church (now the cathedral) of St Albans which was built over the tomb of Alban, the protomartyr of the country.

Baptism, the rite of initiation into Christianity, retained a central role in the life of the Church. It continued normally to be reserved for adults, though increasingly infants or children were baptized. The fuller information that survives from the fourth century, immediately after the end of the persecutions, sheds much light on the practice of baptism in the second and third centuries. The same is true of many other religious practices, about which we have little direct information from the era of persecutions. The story of popular religion, therefore, will be taken up again in the third part of this chapter.

Theologians

The second and third centuries produced some remarkable theologians, despite the trials of persecution. Indeed their roots in the realities and perplexities of life strengthen and enrich their writings. Some individuals and works have already been mentioned: Clement of Rome and Ignatius of Antioch; *Didache, Apostolic Tradition* and *Didaskalia Apostolorum*, which were theological treatises as well as works of canon law; the correspondences involving popes Stephen and Dionysius; Perpetua, whose 'Passion' was both a theological and spiritual treatise; Polycarp and Cyprian, who were writers and theologians as well as bishops and martyrs. Three theologians deserve special mention.

Justin Martyr (100–165) came from a non-Christian family in Samaria (Holy Land). After studying philosophy, he converted to Christianity and thereafter regarded himself as a teacher of both philosophy and Christianity. He taught at Ephesus and then at Rome, where he opened a Christian school and wrote 'First Apology', which was boldly addressed to the emperor Antoninus Pius and his (adopted) sons, 'Dialogue with Trypho the Jew', and 'Second Apology', which was addressed to the Roman Senate. Justin is regarded as the most important early Christian 'Apologist' in the sense that he provided an exposition and defence of Christianity for the non-Christian people of his time. He taught that Christianity is the true philosophy while recognizing that other philosophies contain shadows of the truth. He argued thus: the 'germinative' Word had sown the seed of truth in all people, and the Word then became incarnate in Christ in order to teach people the full truth and so to redeem them from the power of evil. He also wrote on baptism and Eucharist and on the relationship between the Old and New Testaments; he was ready to introduce Platonic philosophy into his defence of Christianity. Justin thus represented significant openness of Christianity to other religions and philosophies as well as readiness to dialogue with them. Around the year 165 he and some of his disciples were denounced as Christians, and on refusing to offer sacrifice they were scourged and beheaded.

Tertullian (160–225: full name, Quintus Septimus Florens Tertullianus), the son of a centurion in the Roman army, was brought up as a pagan in north Africa, probably in Carthage. He received a good education and practiced successfully as a lawyer in Rome, at the same time leading a licentious life. Following his conversion to Christianity, and change of lifestyle, he acted as a catechist in Carthage. Whether he was ordained priest is unclear. Eventually he left the Catholic church to join the Montanist sect, an apocalyptic group with pronounced ascetic tendencies. Tertullian was a prolific and provocative author, writing mainly in Latin but sometimes in Greek. He changed (or developed) his mind on various issues. He appealed for the toleration of Christianity, on the grounds that Christians were no danger to the state but good and useful citizens. On the other hand, he urged Christians to separate themselves from pagan society, to avoid contamination with its immorality and idolatry. He wrote extensively on theological topics and the Church, including the interpretation of Scripture, the Trinity, the life and teachings of Christ, and Christian discipleship. He disapproved of infant baptism and as a Montanist he wrote against Christians engaging in military service. His contribution to the 'Passion' of Perpetua and Felicity has been mentioned. The wide range and depth of his reflections, as well as his brilliant style, have ensured that Tertullian remains today one of the most widely read and influential Fathers of the Church.

Origen (185–254) paralleled, even excelled, Tertullian in the range and depth of his thought: biblical scholar, theologian and spiritual writer. He was brought up as a Christian by his devout parents in Alexandria, Egypt. During the persecution in the city in 202, in which his father was killed, he was prevented from seeking martyrdom only by his mother, who hid his clothes and so discouraged him from leaving their home. He taught in Alexandria and succeeded as head of the influential Catechetical School there. At the same time he led an ascetical life of fasting, prayer and voluntary poverty. According to Eusebius of Caesarea, he castrated himself, misinterpreting in a literal sense the recommendation in the gospel of Matthew 19.12, 'there are eunuchs who have made themselves so for the sake of the kingdom of heaven'. Origen ranged widely in his reading, including Plato and other philosophers and classical literature. He travelled, too, visiting Rome and Arabia. Subsequently he moved to Palestine and was ordained priest. He settled permanently in Caesarea around 231 and established a school which soon became famous. In 250, during the persecution of emperor Decius, he was imprisoned and tortured, and he died soon afterwards.

Origen was a prolific writer, though many of his works have perished, due principally to various condemnations of his works, or survive only in partial and somewhat unreliable Latin translations (he wrote in Greek). He was first and foremost a biblical scholar, writing commentaries on almost all the books of Scripture. He developed a threefold meaning within Scripture, literal, moral and allegorical, preferring himself the third. Some of his sermons survive and he wrote two widely read spiritual works, 'Exhortation to Martyrdom' and 'On Prayer'. His principal theological work, which survives mainly in the Latin translation, *De Principiis*, is wide ranging in its coverage and remarkable for its intuitions and depth of thought. Subordination of Son and Spirit to the Father within the Trinity, his belief in the eternity of the world, the transmigration of souls, and the final salvation of all creatures, even the devil, were doctrines that led to his various condemnations; though at the time they were still somewhat open questions. Origen retains his fascination today.

iii. Establishment of Christianity

The fourth century brought a radical change for Christianity. The effects are still with us today. The catalyst was the conversion of the emperor Constantine to Christianity. As a result of his conversion and many other factors, Christianity moved from being the religion of a persecuted minority to the official religion of the vast Roman Empire. Peace brought many possibilities for institutional developments in the Church and greatly influenced the ways in which Christians practiced their religion. Indeed *Pax Constantiniana* (Peace of Constantine) ushered in for Christianity a revolution which has had a profound effect upon world history.

Conversion of Constantine and afterwards

In 306 Constantine (+337) was acclaimed emperor by his troops in York. The most likely site of this historic event may still be visible today: within the main gateway of the *praetorium* (fort) of the Roman army in the city, which survives today within the crypt of York cathedral. After a long struggle Constantine emerged victorious over several other claimants to be emperor. A crucial event in this struggle occurred in 312, when Constantine defeated Maxentius at the battle of the Milvian Bridge near Rome. Constantine is recounted as having a vision the night before the battle, in which Christ promised him victory if he and his army would fight under the sign of the cross. He complied – precisely how the cross was borne is unclear – and duly gained the victory.

In the following year 313 Constantine reached an agreement with his co-emperor Licinius on a policy of religious freedom which was enshrined in the so-called Edict of Milan. He subsequently fell out with Licinius, who resorted to spasmodic persecutions of Christians, and it was only in 324 that Constantine won a decisive battle at Chrysopolis which left him as sole emperor.

The victory at Chrysopolis enabled Constantine to proclaim again toleration for Christianity throughout the Roman Empire. Precisely when he was baptized is disputed. According to one account, he was cured of leprosy when he allowed himself to be baptized by pope Sylvester (314–35). More likely, he was baptized only towards the end of his life by bishop Eusebius of Nicomedia (not to be confused with Eusebius of Caesarea); though he was regarded as a Christian from 312 onwards.

Constantine's successors as emperor maintained the privileged status of Christianity almost without interruption, though several of his successors in the fourth century were Arian Christians. The most serious challenge occurred during the short reign of Julian 'the Apostate', nephew of Constantine. Precocious and intellectually brilliant, Julian resisted all attempts to convert him to Christianity, preferring instead a mixture of paganism, Neoplatonism and Eleusinian mysteries. He emerged as sole emperor in 361 and set about the restoration of traditional religion within the empire, degrading Christianity and sometimes persecuting its followers. Julian died, however, two years later during a military campaign in Mesopotamia. After his death, Christianity received again its privileged status.

Another important stage in the establishment of Christianity came with the promulgation of the Theodosian Code in 438/9. This code of law, named after the emperor Theodosius II (408–50), raised Christianity from the status of favoured religion to that of the only permitted religion. Paganism was banned and heresy penalized. Though the work was done in Constantinople (where Theodosius was emperor), the Code was compiled in Latin. It was accepted as authoritative in both halves into which the empire had now divided: fully authoritative in the East (capital, Constantinople), officially but more fragmentarily so in the West (capital, Rome), where the invasions of barbarian tribes had much reduced imperial authority.

Councils of Nicea and Constantinople

The councils of Nicea I (325) and Constantinople I (381) provide rich insights into the Church of the fourth century in terms of both doctrinal development and the practice of Christianity. Indirectly, too, they tell us much about the situation of Christians in the previous two centuries. They came to be called 'ecumenical' councils, that is councils of the whole Church – the first two in the list of twenty-one councils down to Vatican II that are recognized by the Catholic church as ecumenical (see Appendix, pp. 241–2). The council of Nicea is best known for its creed. Here is the text, in English translation from the Greek original:

> *We believe in one God the Father all powerful, maker of all things both seen and unseen.*
>
> *And in one Lord Jesus Christ, the Son of God, the only-begotten begotten from the Father, that is from the substance of the Father,* God from God, light from light, *true God from true God, begotten not made, consubstantial with the Father, through whom all things came to be, both those in heaven and those on earth; for us humans and for our salvation he came down and became incarnate, became human, suffered and rose up on the third day, went up into the heavens, is coming to judge the living and the dead.*
>
> *And in the Holy Spirit.*
>
> And those who say 'there once was when he was not,' and 'before he was begotten he was not,' and that he came to be from things that were not, or from another hypostasis or substance, affirming that the son of God is subject to change or alteration – these the catholic and apostolic church anathematizes.

How did this creed come about? No official account (or minutes) of the proceedings of this council survives, so we depend on various later accounts and some guesswork. Arius was the cause of the council, this seems clear. Our knowledge about him comes largely from his opponents, those who condemned him. Here we face a fundamental problem of Church history. Especially during the first millennium AD, our knowledge of those who were condemned by the Church comes largely from the 'orthodox', those whose teachings were approved. Considerable efforts were made to destroy the works of the condemned and little evidence survives that represents them on their own terms. Church history was written by the victors.

We know that Arius was a priest and popular preacher in the capital city of north Africa, Alexandria. Like all Christians of the time, he believed in the Trinity: Father, Son and Spirit within the one God. But wishing to emphasize the oneness of God, monotheism, he more or less identified God with the Father, thereby attributing a subordinate role to the Son. His bishop, Alexander, realizing the importance of the issue, condemned his teaching at one or more diocesan councils in the early 320s. Then the emperor Constantine intervened. Having reunited the empire politically through his defeat of Licinius, he did not want it divided through a religious controversy: for, despite the censures of his bishop, Arius retained quite widespread support for his teachings, mainly in the East.

Constantine summoned the council to meet in his imperial palace at Nicea. Some 250–300 bishops attended, in addition to Constantine himself. The traditional number of 318 was first given by Athanasius towards the end of his life (*Synodal letter to the bishops of Africa*, dated 368/72, chapter 2), unexplained and after having earlier given other figures. Maybe the number alludes to the 318 servants or retainers that Abraham brought with him when he went to meet his cousin Lot (Genesis 14.14). The large majority of the bishops came from the Greek-speaking eastern half of the empire. They included bishop Alexander of Alexandria, who was accompanied by his young secretary and deacon Athanasius, and some twenty bishops from Egypt. Only half a dozen bishops came from the Latin-speaking western half of the empire. Silvester, bishop of Rome, did not come but, importantly, sent two legates as his representatives.

The council was in session for about a month (the precise dates are unclear) in the summer of 325. Arius, who was present, and his supporters were invited to speak first, it seems, and to propose a creed. Their proposed text was rejected on the grounds that it attributed a subordinate role to the Son, denied his full divinity. Other creeds – which at the time were used principally for the rite of baptism – were introduced and the council eventually settled upon one of them, adding to it various anti-Arian clauses. These additions, as we may surmise, are indicated by normal type (non-italics) in the text above. They include the entire final paragraph of anathemas and the word 'consubstantial'

(Greek, *homoousios*), which was introduced to express the Son's close relationship with the Father. This word is not found in Scripture but nevertheless the Church came to accept its introduction, thereby recognizing the role of Tradition and the need to use fresh language to express the fullness of revelation in Christ. Altogether the creed is a masterpiece of doctrine and concision.

Canons. In addition to the creed, the council of Nicea promulgated twenty canons. They dealt with a wide range of disciplinary issues and provide a wealth of information about life in the early Church. Precisely how they came to be composed and promulgated by the council remains unclear, but they were regarded as decrees of the council. They were composed in Greek and were intended primarily for the eastern Church. Their reception in the West came slowly and was due principally to Dionysius Exiguus (+526/556), who translated the decrees into Latin and included them in his *Corpus* of canon law decrees. Some of the twenty canons were based on the canons of earlier local councils, all of them appear to be responses to concrete cases. They reinforce the 'common law' nature of early canon law – judgments on particular cases – and were not intended to form a comprehensive 'code'. They are worth looking at individually.

Canon 1 deals with castration. It recognizes that men who have been castrated against their will 'by barbarians or by their masters', or for medical reasons, can be ordained to the priesthood. 'But if anyone among the clergy who is in good health has castrated himself, he should be suspended and in future no such person should be promoted.' The canon declares the sanctity of the human body. Origen's voluntary castration probably lies behind the canon, and there had been other similar cases, but now the council rules decisively against the practice.

Canons 2 to 4 also focus on the clergy. Canon 2 orders 'time and probation after baptism' before a man is ordained priest or bishop. There would be exceptions, such as Ambrose who was ordained bishop of Milan within a week of his baptism, but the norm is made clear. Canon 3 'forbids a bishop, priest or deacon to keep a woman who has been brought in to live with him, except of course his mother or sister or aunt or any person above suspicion'. The canon may have had in mind the well-known case of Paul of Samosata, already mentioned, who kept young women in his house allegedly for the purpose of spiritual direction. Why are wives not mentioned? While celibacy of the clergy was highly regarded, marriage was common, even the norm, especially in the eastern Church, which was the main focus of the council. So, probably, it was obvious that wives were permitted and would have been superfluous, indeed insulting to the wife, to mention her in the canon. A speech allegedly made at the council and attributed to bishop Paphnutius supports this interpretation. Canon 4 urges neighbouring bishops to attend the ordination of a new bishop: a wise rule, still observed today, which seeks to prevent disputed elections.

Canon 5 treats of excommunication and procedures for appeal. Provincial councils were to be held twice a year, so that excommunications imposed by individual bishops could be confirmed by the bishops of the whole province, or modified by them if the sentence seemed too harsh. The regularity of councils and procedures for appeal are impressive. They reveal a Catholic church that in many ways was more democratic and representative than today. One of the councils was to be held before Lent, the other in the autumn: both suitable times climatically, between the cold of winter and heat of summer – one among many indications of the early Church's respect for nature. The Greek word used here for Lent is *tessarakonta* meaning forty days. This is the first recorded mention of Lent lasting forty days. In the early Church the immediate preparation for Easter lasted a few days at most, it seems. Now, with persecution ended, a full and public season, in imitation of Christ's forty days fast in the desert, became possible. This rich tradition remains today.

Canons 6 and 7 treat of the episcopate and the special authority of the sees of Alexandria, Rome and Antioch. Canons 8 to 14 are concerned, in various ways, with penance and reconciliation. The persecutions of Christians, which had only recently ended, remained a burning issue. Some Christians had been martyred, others lost their property, others had compromised and so saved their lives and goods. There were, too, serious sins unconnected with persecution. These canons are both merciful and firm, skillfully offering reconciliation for fraught social and religious situations. For individuals seeking forgiveness, three stages of public penance are mentioned, all of them principally in the context of the Sunday liturgy: 'hearers' stayed for the liturgy of the Word and then departed; 'prostrators' prostrated themselves before the celebrant and the community at the offertory and then departed: 'prayers' remained throughout the eucharistic prayer but did not receive communion. Each stage lasted several years, though it might be shortened or even omitted if there was genuine repentance. Other penitential tariffs of the time mention a preliminary stage of 'weepers', who stood outside the church and 'wept' as the parishioners in good standing entered the church. The prescriptions may seem severe and too public for today. Yet some public recognition of serious sins, especially those that affect other people, may be healthy. Christians were perhaps more robust than today and readier to acknowledge their frailty as well as the need of their neighbour's forgiveness. Perhaps, too, one should appreciate a certain sense of humour and levelling in life, a Christian recognition of our equality before God. Alongside each other among the weepers and prostrators there might be, for example, army generals, businessmen, politicians, women, labourers and slaves.

Canons 15 to 18 turn to the lives of the clergy, to the new and sometimes dangerous opportunities that the end of persecution offered them. Bishops, priests and deacons should be 'stable', not moving 'recklessly' from one diocese or city to another. Men should be ordained for the diocese in which they live. Clergy should not be 'induced by greed and avarice' to become extortionate money-lenders. 'Deacons must remain within their limits, knowing that they are ministers of the bishop and subordinate to the priests'; they should sit apart from priests during the liturgy and receive the Eucharist after the bishop.

Canon 19 regulates, among various matters, the role of deacon-esses. Here they are clearly stated to be 'laity' who 'do not receive any imposition of hands'. Canon 15 of the council of Chalcedon in 451, however, speaks more clearly of the ordination of women as deacons: the key word used is *keirotonia* (*keiro* meaning 'hand' and *tonia* meaning 'laying on'). Accordingly, the Catholic church today is careful not to exclude the possibility of the ordination of women as deacons.

Finally, canon 20 treats of posture in prayer. It rules that on Sundays and during Eastertide (here called 'the season of Pentecost'), 'prayer should be offered to the Lord standing' rather than kneeling. So, we pray with our bodies as well as with our souls, and standing is particularly appropriate for celebrating resurrection – the special theme of Sundays and Eastertide. Several decrees, indeed, stress the importance and dignity of the human body; others, notably canon 5, pay attention to the natural world. Thus the doctrines of creation and incarnation infuse these very practical twenty canons of Nicea.

Half a century after the council of Nicea, the council of Constantinople in 381 proclaimed a new and improved version of the Nicene creed. This new creed was considered a development rather than a change from the creed of Nicea, thus skirting various prohibitions against changes to the earlier creed. Accordingly, it is normally called the Nicene creed rather than given the more precise title of Constantinopolitan, or Nicene-Constantinopolitan, creed. The text, in English translation from the original Greek, is as follows. The words added to the 325 creed are in normal type (non-italics); passages in the 325 creed that are missing from the creed of 381 are indicated by ^.

> *We believe in one God the Father all-powerful, maker* of heaven and earth, and *of all things both seen and unseen.*
>
> *And in one Lord Jesus Christ, the only-begotten Son of God, begotten from the Father* ^ before all the ages, ^ *light from light, true God from true God, begotten not made, consubstantial with the Father, through whom all things came to be* ^; *for us humans and for our salvation he came down* from the heavens *and became incarnate* from the Holy Spirit and the Virgin Mary, *became human*, and was crucified on our behalf under Pontius Pilate; *he suffered* and was buried *and rose up on the third day* in accordance with the Scriptures; *and he went up into the heavens* and is seated at the Father's right hand; *he is coming* again with glory *to judge the living and the dead;* his kingdom will have no end.
>
> *And in the Spirit, the holy,* the lordly and life-giving one, proceeding forth from the Father, co-worshipped and co-glorified with Father and Son, the one who spoke through the prophets.
>
> In one, holy, catholic and apostolic church. We confess one baptism for the forgiveness of sins. We look forward to a resurrection of the dead and life in the age to come. Amen.
> ^

We can only guess, for the most part, at the reasons for the omissions and additions. As with Nicea I, no minutes of the proceedings of the council survive to explain the changes. The most significant omission, from the creed of 325, is the final paragraph of anathemas. By 381 the Arian controversy was dying down, so the anathemas probably no longer seemed necessary and they were cumbersome for public recitation. Much of the paragraph's content, moreover, was elegantly incorporated into the body of the new creed – for example, by the addition of 'before all the ages' in the first sentence regarding the Son. Altogether the 381 creed flows better for recitation and is richer in content. It gives fuller treatment to both humanity and divinity in Christ and, principally in the final paragraph, to the hopes and destiny of Christians.

The Holy Spirit, too, is accorded richer treatment and full divinity in the creed of 381, in contrast to the half sentence in the creed of 325. The expansion came through the council confronting another doctrinal challenge, that of the so-called Pneumatomachi ('Enemies of the Spirit') who attributed a lesser divinity to the Spirit. Once again we may be grateful for the theological debate which produced doctrinal development. Subsequently and controversially, as we shall see, the western Church added the word *Filioque* ('and the Son') to the Latin text of the creed, so that the Spirit was said to proceed 'from the Father and the Son'.

Altogether the new creed reveals remarkable drafting skill. It remains today, almost unaltered, the most important creed for the Catholic church as well as for the Orthodox and Protestant churches – another witness to the brilliance and creativity of the early Church.

Growth of the visible Church

The councils of Nicea and Constantinople are among the most remarkable results of the peace brought to the Church in the fourth century. Such large and public assemblies of Christians would have been impossible during the previous centuries. The 'coming out' of Christianity brought many other changes.

In terms of numbers, precision is impossible. The Christian population appears to have been growing quite rapidly from around 250 onwards. Christians are estimated to have numbered some twenty million out of the Roman Empire's total population of around seventy million when *Pax Constantiniana* arrived in 324. The total population of the empire was probably much the same at the end of the fourth century as at the beginning, but Christians had increased to more than half the population, perhaps two-thirds.

Although the large majority of Christians lived within the borders of the Roman Empire, there were some important developments beyond these boundaries. To the East, king Tiridates III (298–330) of Armenia was baptized by Gregory 'the Illuminator', and Christianity became the official religion of the country, at some date before Constantine's victory over Licinius. Armenia is therefore considered to be the first Christian nation. There is the long tradition that the apostle Thomas reached India, or at least the Indus valley, and was martyred there. Other evidence, too, suggests that Christianity had penetrated quite far beyond the eastern border of the Roman Empire. Mani (+276) taught in Persia, India and elsewhere in Asia: his teaching, Manichaeism, spread far and wide both in Asia and within the Roman Empire. There were many Christian elements in his teaching, even though Mani's rejection of the material world as evil, and the resulting dualism, were quickly repudiated by the Church as heretical. Eusebius of Caesarea called him a poisonous Christian serpent, but 'Christian' nevertheless. Ethiopia, to the south of Roman Egypt, received Christianity through the officer at the royal court of Ethiopia who was baptized by Philip (Acts 8.27). Origen, writing in the third century, wrote of the evangelization of the country, while noting that the work was incomplete. A new impetus came with Frumentius (300–380), who was consecrated bishop of Axum, the capital of Ethiopia, by Athanasius, bishop of Alexandria. Frumentius is venerated in Ethiopia as St Abuna Salama (Our Father of Salvation). Probably, too, Christianity had penetrated sporadically beyond the northern and western borders of the Roman Empire.

Many churches were built during the fourth century, as a result of Christianity's new-found freedom. These churches transformed the landscape and, more importantly, the practice of the liturgy. The largest of them – and intended to be so – was St Peter's church in Rome, which was built to honour the relics of the apostle Peter. The church of St Paul's outside the Walls, on the outskirts of Rome, was built to house the relics of St Paul. Construction of St Paul's may have started during the reign of Constantine, but more probably later, with completion coming between 395 and 403 under the direction of emperor Honorius. Several other, smaller churches in Rome survive from the fourth century. Some churches were built during this century in Constantinople, the new capital of the empire, though the largest and best known, Hagia Sophia, dates from the sixth century. In other cities and towns of the Roman Empire, the remains of a number of churches survive from the fourth century. As a result of the new buildings, church services – principally the Sunday Eucharist – became much more public as well as more solemn and regulated. We have caught glimpses of these liturgies through the canons of the council of Nicea, which suggest there were sizeable congregations as well as church-like structures even before the end of the persecutions. At the same time, the tradition of house chapels and more familiar liturgies, dating from the time of persecution, continued. In England, fine examples of such chapels survive within the Roman villas at Lullingstone and Hinton St Mary – they were probably constructed in the mid or late fourth century, therefore after peace had come to the Church.

Various new lifestyles also became possible for Christians as a result of this peace. Religious orders, which came to play a huge role in the history of the Church, can trace many of their roots to the 'desert fathers' of the fourth century. The earliest of them, Paul of Thebes (227–340), fled into the Egyptian desert as a young man in order to escape persecution. According to his *Life*, written with imagination by saint Jerome, he remained a hermit in the desert for the rest of his life, living off the dates of a palm tree and food brought to him by a raven. He was visited each year by Anthony (250–356), who eventually found him close to death. Two lions, who had befriended Paul, came and dug a grave with their paws and Anthony laid his body inside. In iconography Paul is represented in old age standing under a palm-tree with a raven and two lions close by: indicative of his long and frugal life as well as his closeness to the natural and animal worlds – a rediscovery of life in the garden of Eden, before the fall of Adam and Eve. In this and other ways we find ecological concerns of today close to many Christians of the early Church. Anthony's *Life* was written by Athanasius, also with much imagination. His temptations as a hermit were accorded detailed treatment by Athanasius and were famously depicted in art by Hieronymus Bosch (1450–1516) in the painting 'Temptations of Anthony', which now adorns the Prado Museum in Madrid. The *Life* of Anthony is very realistic about the difficulties of a hermit. Indeed the eremitical and monastic ways of life came to be exalted as 'dry martyrdom', replacing the martyrdom by blood which became impossible when persecution ended: a deeper and more radical commitment to the Christian way of life, a second baptism.

Anthony later founded a community of hermits. Thus we pass from the eremitical to the monastic way of life. Pachomius (290–346), also from Egypt, developed monasticism further. He founded seven such communities for men and two for women. For them he wrote a *Rule*, the earliest monastic Rule to survive, which influenced the development of monasticism far beyond Africa. From that continent leadership in the monastic movement passed to Asia. Basil of Caesarea (330–79), also called Basil the Great, was notable as preacher and theologian and he lived for a time as a hermit before becoming bishop of his native city in modern Turkey. He wrote a *Rule* for monks, dependent in part on Pachomius, which exerted great influence and still remains today the basic monastic Rule for the Orthodox church. His sister Macrina established a flourishing religious community of women on the family estate in Pontus. She is considered the founder of female monasticism in the eastern Church. Finally, John Cassian (360–433) lived as a monk in Bethlehem, Egypt and southern France, near Marseilles, where he founded two monasteries. He collected in his two main works, 'Institutes' and 'Conferences', monastic wisdom from the various countries in which he had lived. Later, Benedict knew these works and used them in his *Rule*. Cassian thus represents an important bridge between monasticism in the three continents of Africa, Asia and Europe.

The eremetical and monastic ways of life were regarded as journeys of the soul, though they might also involve considerable physical journeying, as we have seen. Pilgrimages were both similar and different: journeys to a particular place which sprang from devotion and enriched the soul. *Pax Constantiniana* made possible, or easier, the necessary travelling as well as public devotions at the pilgrimage shrines. Helena, the mother of emperor Constantine, made a pilgrimage in 326 to the Holy Land, where she founded churches on the Mount of Olives and at Bethlehem and, according to later tradition, discovered the cross on which Christ was crucified. Towards the end of the century a devout woman, who probably came from Spain or France and is usually identified as Egeria, made an extensive pilgrimage of some three years to Egypt, the Holy Land, Edessa and Constantinople. She was assiduous in attending liturgical services and her copious observations on this and various other topics were written up into a fascinating book, *The Pilgrimage of Egeria*. In Rome, the churches of St Peter's and St Paul's were important centres for pilgrimage. Many shrines were established elsewhere.

Religious art became more public, while still remaining largely symbolic (as distinct from 'realistic'). The floor mosaics in the house-chapel at Hinton St Mary in Britain provide a fine example at the domestic level. Christ is portrayed as a clean-shaven man, with the Greek letters *Chi Rho* (Ch R) behind him, and beside him two pomegranates, symbols of eternal life. Within the same mosaic is a scene from pagan mythology, Bellephoron slaying the Chimaera, which seems to hint, like the pomegranates, at Christ's victory over death. Altogether the composition is sophisticated and beautifully executed. Some works of art survive from the new churches that were being built during the fourth century. In them Christ continues to be portrayed symbolically, principally as teacher or shepherd. Representations of the crucified Christ, and crucifixes, become common only in the seventh century.

The councils of Nicea and Constantinople reveal the liveliness of theological debate during the fourth century. Among individual theologians, Athanasius, who was bishop of Alexandria from 328 to 373, was the outstanding defender of Nicea's creed and the dominant African theologian of the century. John Chrysostom, who was bishop of Constantinople from 398 until his death in 407, was famous for his sermons – Chrysostom means 'golden mouth' – which were written down and circulated in manuscripts. The sermons focus mainly on the instruction and moral reform of Christian society and include commentaries on various books of Scripture: Genesis, Psalms, Isaiah, Matthew, John, Acts and the letters of Paul. His early work 'On the Priesthood' is a fine description of the responsibilities of the Christian minister. Always combative, he made many enemies and died in exile. He was soon regarded as a saint. Basil 'the Great', his younger brother

Gregory of Nyssa, and their contemporary Gregory of Nazianzen, are called the Cappadocian Fathers because all three were born in Cappadocia. Brilliant as both philosophers and theologians, they played a crucial role in defence of the Nicene creed and the establishment of Christian orthodoxy. They wrote widely and profoundly on many areas of theology and spirituality. Also from the East, but writing in Syriac rather than Greek, were Aphrahat, whose works include treatises on asceticism and a survey of the Christian faith, and Ephraem, who is distinguished principally as a biblical scholar and hymn-writer. Both men were born and lived outside the Roman Empire, in Persia, though Ephraem later settled in Edessa, within the empire. Augustine of Hippo (354–430), the giant of western theology, will be treated in the next chapter.

How widespread was interest in theology? A famous comment of Gregory of Nyssa suggests it was normal among Christians, not just the preserve of theologians. Visiting Constantinople soon after the council in the city in 381, Gregory observed – somewhat tongue in cheek – that when he went to change money, or to buy bread, or to visit the public baths, the money-changer, shop-assistant and bath attendant insisted on discussing with him the doctrine of the Trinity, and the relationships between the three Persons, before they would respond to his material needs (Migne, *PG*, 46, col. 557). Doctrine was recognized to involve issues crucial to Christian living and immortality, not just theological speculations about the nature of God.

A final question, was the favoured treatment that arrived in the fourth century really for the good of Christianity? Eusebius of Caesarea, the friend of Constantine and influential church historian, who came to dominate the interpretation of the period, was confident the change was for the better. Others were less sure. The canons of the first council of Nicea suggest, indeed, that freedom brought difficulties and temptations as well as benefits.

Chapter 2
Early Middle Ages: 400–1054

This long period brought notable expansion for Christianity: principally through the conversion to Christianity of the tribes who invaded the Roman Empire and, later, through further evangelization in central and northern Europe. Contraction, however, was more extensive than expansion: principally through conversions to Islam in north Africa and western Asia. We tend to think of Christianity as constantly expanding, so it is important to remember this long period of overall contraction, which extended almost to the year 1500, and to ponder the possible causes.

The first two sections of the chapter focus on this expansion and contraction. Section iii examines the ecumenical councils of the period. Four of them in succession – Ephesus to Constantinople III – played a crucial role in the development of the Church's teaching on Christ's humanity and divinity, while Nicea II provided a defence of religious art. Together these councils stand at the centre of the Tradition of the Church. Section iv studies the most significant theologians of this epoch, many of whom were present at or influenced the ecumenical councils. The schism of 1054, when Christendom split into two churches, Catholic and Orthodox, and the events that led up to this rupture, are treated in section v. Institutional developments are studied in section vi, popular religion in the last section.

The Middle Ages acquired its name because it was considered to be in the 'middle' of the 'ancient' world of Greece and Rome and the 'new' world of the sixteenth century.

i. Expansion

The tribes who invaded the western Roman Empire, from shortly before the year 400 onwards, gradually but without exception converted to Christianity. These conversions produced one of the seismic shifts in European history, indeed in world history. They resulted in a Europe that remained predominantly Christian into the twentieth century and produced, in turn, a Christian Europe that would be the powerhouse of Christianity worldwide for many centuries. They were and still are often called 'barbarian' tribes, though note that the word 'barbarian' derives not from *barba*, the Latin for beard, but because the Greeks, unable to understand their languages, claimed they could only hear them saying 'bar-bar' and so called them *barbaroi* – I will continue to use the word for the sake of convenience and with some hesitation.

Precisely why these tribes converted to Christianity remains something of a mystery. However, three factors appear to have been crucial. First, the example in this life, and the promise of eternal life, that Christ offered. Almost all religions of the Mediterranean world that we know of – for example, Mithraism or the many Egyptian religious cults – offered future life in some form. But Christianity seemed to promise everlasting life in a fuller and more coherent fashion. Added to this promise was the example of Christ's own life and the violent nature of his death. For people living in a violent and precarious world, Christianity seemed to offer the most satisfactory account of the present life, with both its joys and sufferings, and astonishing hope for the life to come. It is important to take this religious motivation seriously.

Second, the perceived link between Christianity and the Roman Empire. Here the motivation may seem puzzling. Invaders who conquer a country normally seek to impose their own religion upon the conquered land. But with the tribes who invaded the Roman Empire, the result was the other way round. The invaders embraced the prevalent religion of the people they conquered. A key to understanding this turnabout seems to be the invaders' admiration for the lifestyle of the Roman Empire, which included Christianity as its official religion. The invaders sought not to destroy the Roman Empire – even though in the event much destruction took place – but rather to be incorporated into it and hence to embrace Christianity. A revealing glimpse of the popularity of the Roman Empire in its colonies comes from Bede's, *Church History of the English People*, 1.11–12. Bede (673–735) notes that when the Roman government withdrew its troops from Britain in order to defend Rome from the barbarian invaders, the Britons pleaded with the Romans to remain.

Third, earlier contacts between the barbarian tribes and Christianity. The borders of the Roman Empire in the West were not watertight; there were contacts in both directions. In particular, many young men from east of the Rhine river were employed as mercenary soldiers in the Roman armies. Some of them converted to Christianity, most of them would have acquired some familiarity with Christianity, and many of them returned to their homelands – some presumably still Christians – on completing military service. Merchants and other people, too, crossed the border. In these various though scantily documented ways, the mass conversions of the invaders were prepared beforehand.

It was the eastern half of the empire, not the western, that suffered the first major incursion from outside. The catalyst was the movement of the Huns from central Asia into eastern Europe in the early 370s. As a result of this movement, the Huns pressed on the Goths living near the Black Sea. The Visigoths, a sub-tribe of the Goths, then started to move southwards. They crossed the imperial border in 376 and two years later their army inflicted a crushing defeat upon the Roman army at Adrianople. The eastern emperor, Valens, was killed in the battle. However, instead of attacking Constantinople, which lay close by, the Visigoths moved westwards, finally into Spain. The eastern empire was spared and pressure fell upon the West. From the early 400s onwards various other tribes crossed the border into the western empire: Ostrogoths and Lombards moved into northern Italy; Huns settled in Hungary; Vandals moved through France and Spain and finally reached north Africa; Suevi settled in north-west Spain; Franks entered Gaul, which was renamed France; Angles, Saxons and Jutes came to Britain.

Each tribe converted to Christianity as some point between the fifth and seventh centuries. At the same time, Christianity survived among the indigenous population of the former western empire, though with varying degrees of success and institutional framework. Situations were complex and varied geographically, but overall and gradually there was a mixing of old and new: the Church of the first four centuries blended with the fresh energy and creativity of the newly converted peoples.

Many of the tribes first converted to an Arian form of Christianity, even though Arianism had faded away in the East by the end of the fourth century. The teaching of a divine yet subordinate Christ evidently struck a sympathetic chord among the new arrivals in the West. The first tribal king of major importance to convert to orthodox Christianity was Clovis, king of the Franks. His conversion was due in good measure to the persuasion of his Christian wife, queen Clotilde. The traditional date for his baptism is 496, though a somewhat later date is possible. Through his energetic rule and success in war, and his alliance with Catholic bishops and other church authorities, Clovis did much for the establishment of Christianity as the official religion throughout most of modern France. Our knowledge of the evangelization of France during his reign and the following century comes to us principally through Gregory of Tours' (538–94), *Historia Francorum* (History of the Franks).

In Spain, the decisive events came about during the reign of king Recared, who was king of the Visigoths from 586 to 601. The country had been divided between orthodox Christians, descendants of the original population, and Arian Christians, who belonged to the conquering Visigoth tribe. Recared was baptized as an orthodox Christian in 587 and two years later the king's action was ratified at a national church council, Toledo III. This was the council that first introduced the word *Filioque* ('and from the Son') into the Nicene creed – thus changing, 'the Spirit ... proceeding from the Father' to 'the Spirit ... proceeding from the Father and the Son' – in order to emphasize the Son's full divinity within the Trinity and so to counter residual Arianism. Recared's baptism and the council of Toledo led to the religious unification of the Iberian peninsula and a remarkable Christian renaissance lasting until the Muslim invasion of the country in the early eight century. The epoch saw a succession of national church councils at Toledo, the emergence of the Mosarabic liturgical rite, and the development of canon law through the so-called *Hispana* collection. Monasticism also flourished. The most notable scholar was Isidore of Seville (560–636), who did much to hand on to medieval Christians the earlier learning and traditions of the Church.

Britain – or England, the land of the Angles, as it began to be called – is the country whose re-conversion is best documented, thanks largely to Bede's *Church History*. The work records the mission of Augustine and companions, who were sent from Rome by pope Gregory to evangelize the country. On the way 'they began to contemplate returning home rather than going to a barbarous, fierce and unbelieving nation whose language they did not even understand' (1.23). But they persevered and reached their destination in 597. The work of evangelization began in Kent, one of the seven kingdoms ('heptarchy') into which England was then divided, and by the end of the seventh century the whole country had received Christianity. Bede emphasizes the role of missionaries from Rome – Augustine and companions, and others, notably Theodore of Tarsus, who was originally from the Greek-speaking city of Tarsus in southern Turkey and became a monk in Rome, where he was ordained archbishop of Canterbury by pope Vitalian in 668. Theodore held the see until his death in 690, presiding over an important period of development for the English church. In Bede there is the underlying thesis that Britain was returning to the Roman Empire, indeed helping to revive this Empire, by its acceptance of the religion of Rome. We are given little information about the survival of Christianity among the native Britons, or about the attractiveness of paganism, though other evidence suggests that both factors were more important than Bede allows. Two other missionary groups are recounted by Bede: those from France and those from the Celtic world, principally Ireland.

Bede's sophisticated and brilliantly written account, with its graphic portrayals of events and personalities, was ideally suited to a lector reading aloud to a group of people – whether at a royal court (Bede probably had the court of the king of Northumbria particularly in mind), or in monasteries, or at social gatherings, during meals or at other times – as was normal practice at the time. The book was intended to be a work of evangelization and edification; it influenced Christian attitudes in Britain and beyond throughout the Middle Ages. Bede is attentive to the role of women. Several kings, notably Ethelbert of Kent in 597, and Edwin of Northumbria in 627, were converted to Christianity partly through their Christian wives; Abbess Hilda of Whitby governed a double-monastery of men and women, which was famous for its learning and for hosting the synod of Whitby in 664. We are given various glimpses of the religious roles of women both within and beyond the family. Bede is appreciative of the zeal and learning of the Irish missionaries, even more so of the good order and links with the papacy of the Roman missionaries. He had his concerns, even prejudices, yet his work is remarkably informative history. The country was not troubled by Arianism, it appears. The synod of Whitby settled the contentious issue of the date of Easter and thus furthered harmony between the various missionary groups. Soon Britain became an exporter of Christianity, a powerhouse for missionary endeavour abroad.

Long before Augustine's arrival in Britain, Christianity had reached Ireland and Scotland. Both countries had remained outside the Roman Empire. The great missionary in Ireland was Patrick (*c.* 400–460), though there is evidence of earlier Christian presence in the country: Prosper of Aquitaine speaks of pope Celestine (422–32) sending Palladius to be the 'first bishop of the Irish believing in Christ'. Patrick outlined his own life mainly in his autobiographical *Confession*. The son of a local official in the north-west of Britain who was also a deacon, he was captured by Irish pirates at the age of sixteen and spent six years as a herdsman in Ireland. Eventually he escaped back to Britain, underwent training for the Christian ministry and was ordained 'bishop in Ireland'. Patrick spent the remainder of his life in Ireland, outstanding as both evangelical preacher and organizer of the Church.

Christianity remained vibrant in Ireland during the sixth century. Monastic life was a notable feature and many monks were also missionaries. Columba (521–97) sailed from Ireland 'as a pilgrim of Christ', according to his biographer Adomnan, and founded a monastery on the Scottish island of Iona. Later he founded other monasteries and churches in both Scotland and Ireland. Of royal Irish lineage himself, he kept good contacts with kings and other civil authorities. According to Bede, he converted king Bridei of the northern Picts to Christianity. Columbanus (+615) was an Irish monk who travelled even further. He cultivated the idea of Christian life as a perpetual pilgrimage. First he was a monk at Bangor in Wales, then he founded various monasteries of strict observance in France, finally he settled with his companions at

Bobbio in northern Italy. Among women, saint Brigid was specially venerated. Two early Lives of Brigid survive in Latin and one in Old Irish, though the details of her life remain difficult to unravel.

Irish monks developed the Penitential as a code for monastic discipline, in which penances were assigned for particular faults. Use of the various written codes was soon extended to the laity. Many of the penances were fierce. The Penitential became an important intermediary stage in the development of Christian penance, replacing the public penance of the early centuries and then, in turn, giving way to the sacrament of Confession.

In Scotland, Columba's activity focused on the northern Picts. Earlier, within dates that are disputed but probably sometime in the fifth century, Ninian, who was a native of Britain, evange-lized among the southern Picts. Bede described him as a bishop 'who had received orthodox instruction in Rome' and who built a stone church at a place called 'Ad Candidam Casam' – which may be identified with Whithorn – and was buried there. His tomb became a place of pilgrimage in the Middle Ages. At least parts of Scotland, therefore, were Christian well before the arrival of Augustine in England.

The Celtic world of Ireland, Scotland, Wales and parts of western Britain went much together in terms of both ethnicity and Christianity. There was plenty of exchange by way of both personnel and ideas. The Irish Sea provided the central means of transport and communication; it has been aptly called the 'Celtic Mediterranean'.

From the late seventh century onwards, England and France became major sources of missionary activity into those parts of Europe that lay beyond the frontiers of the former Roman Empire. The most notable missionary was Boniface (675–754), who remains today the patron saint of Germany. Born in Devon, his early life passed as monk, priest and noted scholar at the monastery of Nursling near Southampton. At the age of about forty, he embarked upon his remarkable missionary career. He went first to Frisia in the Netherlands, but finding the situation there inauspicious, he turned to Germany. There he quickly became famous as missionary preacher and teacher. In 722 he went to Rome, where pope Gregory II consecrated him as bishop for all Germany. Boniface had an exceptional capacity for organization as well as for friendship and loyalty. The framework of dioceses that he established in Germany remains largely intact today. Directly or through his disciples, he was responsible for the foundation of numerous monasteries. In a famous letter to the English people, he appealed for their prayers and help in the conversion of those who 'are of one blood and bone with you'. Indeed, they supported his work with men and women – many of them becoming monks or nuns, and some bishops, in Germany – as well as with books and liturgical and other gifts.

Boniface could be ruthless. At an early stage of his missionary work in Germany, his courage in felling an oak tree at Geismar, which was sacred to the god Thor, and the resulting sense of liberation for the local people, gained many converts to Christianity. He maintained close links with the popes of his time, who supported his efforts. Pope Gregory III made him archbishop in 732 with power to consecrate bishops throughout Germany. He visited Rome again in 738, where he was joined by new companions for the mission in Germany: Romans, Franks and Bavarians as well as the English brothers Winnebald and Willibald. He paid attention to relations with secular rulers, considering their support to be crucial for the work of evangelization. For a while, with the encouragement of king Charles Martel and his successors Carloman and Pepin, he turned his attention to France, where he presided over a succession of reforming councils in the 740s. Boniface had the wisdom and humility to hand over his responsibilities to others as he grew old. He returned as a missionary to Frisia, where he was martyred by pagans on the banks of the river Borne near Dokkum. His body was recovered and buried at the monastery of Fulda, where his tomb is still venerated today. Boniface has exerted, perhaps, a deeper influence on the history of Europe than any other Englishman.

Willibrord (658–730) was a native of Northumbria in northern England. In 690 he and twelve companions went as missionaries to the Netherlands. He worked there, as well as in Luxembourg and Denmark, for the rest of his life. He was consecrated archbishop by pope Sergius and established his see at Utrecht, which remains today the primatial see of the Netherlands. Willibrord kept close links with successive popes. Indeed, he and Boniface, together with Augustine and his companions in England, were key instruments in the spread of papal authority north of the Alps during the early Middle Ages. He also maintained close relations with Pepin, the Frankish king who had extended his rule into Frisia. He died and was buried at the monastery of Echternacht in Luxembourg, which he had founded. Willibrord is the patron saint of both the Netherlands and Luxembourg, in recognition of his crucial contribution to the evangelization of both countries.

Anskar (801–65), the 'Apostle of the North', was born in Picardy in northern France and became a monk at Corbie nearby. Like Boniface, he left his monastery to work as a missionary. First he went to Westphalia in Germany. Then king Harold of Denmark, who had converted to Christianity while in exile in Picardy, brought Anskar to Denmark to evangelize the country. However, he met much opposition there and moved to Sweden, where he built the first Christian church. He was appointed bishop of Hamburg by pope Gregory IV in about 832. After the sack of the city by Vikings in 845, pope Nicholas I made him archbishop of both Hamburg and Bremen and gave him wide authority over Denmark, Norway and Sweden. Anskar returned to Denmark in 854 and was instrumental in the conversion of king Erik of Jutland. Austere and a man of prayer, Anskar encouraged education by founding schools, and was noted as a preacher. He was outstanding in his charity to the poor and he tried hard to mitigate the evils of the slave trade, which was prevalent among the Vikings.

Much of Anskar's work was reversed after his death when paganism reasserted itself. However, a second evangelization, with enduring results, took place between the late tenth and mid-eleventh centuries. The conversion of Norway took root during the reign of king Olaf (1016–28). He was baptized in France and subsequently obtained the kingdom of Norway. He did much to promote Christianity during his reign, though he was eventually expelled from the country on account of his harsh ways and was killed in battle in 1030. Soon afterwards, however, he was proclaimed a saint and Norway remained Christian. Christianity reached Iceland and Greenland in the ninth and tenth centuries and the Althing (ruling council) of Iceland formally accepted Christianity in the year 999/1000.

Poland received Christianity in the tenth century. Prince Mieczyslaw, ruler of the country, was baptized in 966 and Gniezno was established as the archiepiscopal see in 1000. However, the confirmation of Christianity in Poland took time: there were strong anti-Christian outbreaks in the early eleventh century when many Christians were martyred.

Much of Hungary had formed part of the Roman Empire, as the province of Pannonia, and so had received Christianity at an early date though apparently without lasting results. Some missionaries arrived in Hungary in the ninth and tenth centuries, but the crucial events awaited the reign of king Stephen. He became a Christian in 985 and on his accession to the Hungarian throne in 997 he set out to Christianize the country. A strong supporter of the papacy, he obtained the royal crown from pope Sylvester II in 1001. He organized the Church into ten dioceses and the archdiocese of Esztergom, which remains today the primatial see of the country.

Further south, on the borders of the churches of Rome and Constantinople, laboured the brothers Cyril (826–69) and Methodius (815–85), 'Apostles of the Slavs'. They had to struggle with the claims of both Rome and Constantinople to have jurisdiction over missionary work in the region, but they came to be greatly respected in their lifetime, and subsequently honoured as saints, in both churches. Cyril's most remarkable contribution was the invention of the 'Glagolithic' script, whereby the Slavonic language passed from an oral to a written language. Cyril went on to use this new script in publishing Scriptural works and liturgical texts. After his brother's death, Methodius was consecrated by the pope as archbishop of Sirmium in Bosnia.

Bulgaria had formed part of the Roman Empire and so had received Christianity at an early date. The re-Christianization of the country began under prince Boris, who was baptized in 864/5. Both Byzantine and German missionaries worked in the country but Boris finally opted in favour of Constantinople. Clement of Ochrid (+916) was a noted evangelist. Christianity flourished during the reign of Tsar Simeon (893–927) and the Bulgarian church was declared a patriarchate. Like Bulgaria, Russia would also side with Constantinople when the schism between East and West began in 1054. Christian missionaries first preached extensively in Russia in the ninth and tenth centuries. About 988 prince Vladimir was baptized and established Christianity as the official religion of his dominions. Institutional ties were principally with Constantinople, and the influence of Mount Athos was seminal regarding monasticism. Even so, the Russian church quickly acquired its own distinctiveness and energy.

In Africa, Nubia lay between Ethiopia, which had been evangelized by Frumentius in the fourth century, and Egypt. Missionaries came to Nubia in the sixth century from both Constantinople and Alexandria. The ties with Alexandria prevailed and Nubia followed the Egyptian church into schism with both Rome and Constantinople. Beginning with the reign of king Mercurios (697–710), Christianity enjoyed in Nubia a golden age that lasted into the early thirteenth century, when Muslim influence took over.

Here we conclude this brief survey of the expansion of Christianity. The surviving evidence tells us principally about institutional developments and the great saints and missionaries of the period. Even so, we are quite well informed about Christianity at the more popular level, about motivation and the practice or religion among the large majority of Christians. This information comes to us both through some of the written histories of the period, most notably those of Bede and Gregory of Tours, and from a variety of hints and insights that are to be found in other records. Altogether it is a remarkable story of success. Almost all the lands of western and central Europe were retained or brought within the orbit of Christianity. A good balance seems to have been achieved, on the whole, between presenting the challenges of the gospel and respecting the personalities and circumstances of individuals and peoples. Evangelization and inculturation were combined well. It is remarkable how few missionaries were martyred, a sign that they and their endeavours were appreciated. Certainly the results were deep and long lasting.

ii. Contraction

Alongside the expansion of Christianity was an even greater contraction, which continued into the fifteenth century. In western Europe, the principal theatre for contraction was Spain. Muslim armies crossed from north Africa into southern Spain in the early eighth century and quickly conquered almost the entire peninsula (including Portugal). For a while only parts of the northern coastlands remained unconquered. Christianity was generally tolerated in the occupied territories, though there were some episodes of persecution, as at Cordoba in the mid-ninth century. The Muslim advance continued briefly into southern France, but the victory of the Christian army, led by Charles Martel, at the battle of Tours/ Poitiers (the battle was fought somewhere between the two towns, the precise location is unclear) in 732 proved decisive. The advance was halted and never again was France seriously threatened. By the mid-eleventh century the Christian *Riconquista* (Reconquest) of Spain was well under way in the north, though more than half the country still remained under Muslim control. The experiences of Muslim occupation and *Riconquista* are fundamental to understanding the history of Christianity in the Iberian peninsula. However, the *convivencia* (living together), and mutual enrichment in art, intellectual life and much else, should also be remembered alongside the tensions and conflict.

In north Africa, the Muslim advance was rapid. Within a decade of Muhammad's death in 632, the capital city of Alexandria had been taken and the entire coastal strip of north Africa was under Muslim control by the end of the seventh century. For some time Christians remained in the majority. Gradually the numerical balance changed, so that by the end of the Middle Ages the overwhelming majority of the population was Muslim. A significant Christian population belonging to the Coptic church, which was independent of both Rome and Constantinople, remained in Egypt and in Nubia. The Coptic church further south, in Ethiopia, remained vigorous throughout the Middle Ages. It was helped by the special protection which Muhammad had insisted should be always granted to Christians there, on account of the protection he had once received in Ethiopia during a period of exile.

In view of the vigour of Christianity in north Africa during the first five centuries, the subsequent conversion to Islam is remarkable. The conversion proved enduring and constitutes one of the major shifts in the history of the Church, indeed in world history. Several factors go some way towards explaining the change. The high point of Christianity in north Africa appears to have been reached in the fourth and early fifth centuries. Thereafter there were serious problems which weakened the Church well before the beginning of the Muslim invasion. The success of the Alexandrian church at the councils of Nicea (325) and Ephesus (431) was followed by the humiliation of this church at the council of Chalcedon (451), when Dioscorus, bishop of Alexandria, was condemned for heresy and irregular procedures and deposed from his see. Further west, Vandal invaders were at the gates of Hippo as Augustine lay dying and soon afterwards they completed their conquest of north-western Africa. Vandals converted to Christianity, but in an Arian form and the lands they conquered never regained their earlier Christian energy and splendour. There were many divisions, too, within the north African churches. Arians, Meletians, Donatists, Monophysites, Montanists, Gnostics and many other smaller dissenting groups, were all present. The north African church was very energetic, but this dynamism was accompanied by some lack of attention to church unity, so that the Muslim invaders confronted divided rather than united Christian communities.

Another crucial factor was that the inhabitants of the Arabian peninsula, who first converted to Islam, were neigbhours of the Egyptians. Byzantine rule in Egypt, especially from the time of the energetic emperor Justinian (527–65) onwards, was perceived to be somewhat foreign and heavy-handed. These factors helped to present the Arab invaders as friendly liberators more than as conquerors. Islam, too, was close to Christianity in many respects. Muslims accepted the Old Testament, Christ was respected as a great prophet, and Mary was honoured as the mother of Jesus. Islam appeared to many Christians as a form of Christianity rather than a new religion. The new Muslim rulers were normally tolerant and quite respectful towards Christianity. However, conversion to Islam was encouraged by exemption from taxes, which Christians and other non-Muslims were obliged to pay, and by better possibilities of advancement in social and political life. As Christians were reduced to a minority, life became more difficult for them.

Sometimes it is suggested that Christianity was insufficiently inculturated into north African culture, and its theology was too elevated and abstract, in contrast to the better inculturation and the simpler and more direct theology of Islam. In terms of theology, we have met the remarks of Gregory of Nyssa regarding popular interest in debates about the Trinity and the Incarnation, in the context of Constantinople in the late fourth century (see p. 39). Plenty of evidence suggests there was similar interest in theological debate among the Christian people of north Africa, certainly in Alexandria and Carthage and in Augustine's Hippo. In terms of inculturation, the argument may be at least half true. While Christianity appears to have been well rooted in north Africa until around 450, thereafter there was a measure of cultural and religious alienation. The Egyptian church gradually moved into schism with the rest of the Church following the council of Chalcedon in 451. The reassertion of Byzantine control over north Africa during the reign of emperor Justinian, which was accomplished principally through the military campaigns of Belisarius, gave Christianity a more colonial, less indigenous, character. Greek and Latin, the main official languages of the church in north Africa, originated from outside the continent. But there do not appear to have been objections to the use of these languages either before or after 450. The two languages had established themselves as the principle languages of communication for the entire Christian world, so it was reasonable for north Africa to use them too. Most local languages, including Berber, were not written languages, so their wider use would have been difficult: though we still need to know more about the use of local languages in the oral communication and practice of Christianity. Also, while the new Arab rulers were attentive to inculturation in some ways, this was not notably the case regarding language: Arabic, a foreign tongue, became the official language of the conquered countries in north Africa as well as remaining the irreplaceable language of the Koran.

In Asia the contraction of Christianity covered an even larger geographical area, yet there were many parallels with north Africa regarding the reasons for this decline. In both continents Christianity faced in Islam a coherent and comprehensive message, formulated in the Koran and other written texts, which was proclaimed by fervent and well organized followers. Muslims were dedicated to proclaiming their faith and military success bred further assurance. In Asia, as in north Africa, Christianity was disturbed by schisms – Nestorian, Monophysite and others – and rule from Constantinople was felt by many as alien and heavy-handed. The expansion of Islam was very rapid. Muslim armies captured Jerusalem and Antioch in 638 and Constantinople was threatened several times at an early date. Subsequently the Byzantine empire recovered and its authority remained quite extensive, reaching eastwards through modern Turkey and even beyond, until the eleventh century. In areas conquered by Muslim armies, Christians were accorded a measure of liberty and they remained numerous, even a majority of the population in some areas, for several centuries. As the number of Muslims grew, life for Christians became more difficult and the attractions of converting to Islam more evident.

While eastern Christendom remained important throughout the period of this chapter, the balance in the number of Christians and in influence was moving towards the West after about 600.

iii. Ecumenical councils

Five ecumenical councils were held between the fifth and eighth centuries: Ephesus in 431, Chalcedon in 451, Constantinople II in 553, Constantinople III in 680–1 and Nicea II in 787. Together they had a profound influence upon the clarification and development of Christian doctrine. Whereas Nicea I and Constantinople I had taught about the Trinity, the next four councils, Ephesus to Constantinople III, focused on Jesus Christ and the relationship between his divinity and humanity – 'Christology' in the technical language of theology. Nicea II condemned iconcoclasm: its teaching may be seen as an application of the teaching of the first six councils to the realm of religious art.

Ephesus

The immediate concern of the council of Ephesus was Mary's title *Theotokos*. The title signifies 'Mother of God' or 'God-bearer' and derives from the two Greek words *Theos* meaning God and *tokos* meaning 'birth-giver'. Immediately, therefore, the controversy was about Mary, but underlying it were Christological issues.

Theotokos was a popular title for Mary within the Egyptian church, particularly in Alexandria. Nestorius, a disciple of Theodore of Mopsuestia, the acclaimed theologian of Antioch, was appointed bishop of Constantinople in 428 and almost immediately began to criticize this title of Mary. It might suggest, he argued, that Mary was a goddess; much better therefore the title *Christotokos*, mother of Christ. The controversy bypassed 'Mother of Christ', which is indeed a fully orthodox title for Mary, and focused on Nestorius's objections to *Theotokos*. Cyril, the

energetic bishop of Alexandria, responded to Nestorius's criticisms with a vigorous defence of the title. Obviously, he argued,
it did not mean that Mary was a goddess – an implied criticism
of Nestorius was that Egyptian Christianity remained too close to
earlier pagan religion in Egypt, where feminine cults and worship
of goddesses abounded – but rather that the child born of Mary
was truly Son of God, the second person of the Trinity become
incarnate, as well as son of Mary.

We can see in the controversy the rivalry between the two great
cities of the eastern empire. Alexandria had the longer tradition as
a major city and intellectual centre, but the emperor Constantine
had preferred to establish his eastern capital at Constantinople. Even
more importantly, the dispute pitted the two theological schools of
Antioch and Alexandria against each other. It was a dispute that
had profound implications for Christian devotion and the practice
of Christianity. The Alexandrian school – following the tradition
especially of Athanasius – emphasized Christ's divinity, that 'the Word
of God became flesh' (John 1.14). It has been described as Christology
'from above' both in the sense that Christ 'descended' from the Trinity
to this earth and because our role is to accept this salvation offered
'from above'. Theologians of the Antiochian school, led by Theodore
and Nestorius, criticized the Alexandrian theologians for diminishing
Christ's humanity. They argued that Christ became man, not just took
flesh. There is a duality of human and divine in Christ, rather than
divinity dominating the humanity. Our salvation, accordingly, comes
more 'from below', in our following of Christ in his obedience to the
Father's will and in his acceptance of the trials and sufferings of this life
alongside its joys.

The controversy between Nestorius and Cyril became heated,
with an exchange of letters between them. Both parties appealed
to Celestine, the bishop of Rome – a good example of the primacy
accorded to the see of Rome at this date. Celestine soon pronounced
in favour of Cyril, stating that *Theotokos* was a legitimate title for
Mary provided it was understood correctly. We may note, too,
Cyril's greater discretion. Whereas Nestorius wrote his letter of
explanation in Greek, which few in Rome then understood, Cyril
provided a Latin translation to accompany his letter in Greek and
also sent a translator to help with any queries.

Pope Celestine commissioned Cyril to call a council in the East in
order to pronounce finally on the issue, following his own decision

in favour of *Theotokos*. In the event, the council was convoked by the eastern emperor, Theodosius II, to meet in Ephesus: an appropriate choice in view of the tradition that Mary lived there towards the end of her life in the house of the apostle John. Cyril and his supporters – bishops and many monks from Egypt – arrived by the date fixed for the council's opening, the feast of Pentecost, and indeed Nestorius was also present. However, Nestorius's supporters, led by bishop John of Antioch, were delayed along the land route through Turkey. Cyril waited for a while but then opened the council before the arrival of the party from Antioch. On the first day, 22 June 431, the council condemned Nestorius for his refusal to attend and deposed him from his see. Then, four days later, the party from Antioch arrived. Since Cyril refused to go back on the condemnation of Nestorius, the Antiochenes declined to join the council and established their own assembly in the same city. Two legates sent by pope Celestine arrived a few days later and they joined the council led by Cyril. Each council condemned the other and deadlock ensued for over a month. Finally the imperial official presiding over the proceedings, acting on the instructions of the emperor, dissolved both councils and ordered the detention of both Cyril and Nestorius. Nestorius accepted his confinement but Cyril escaped back to Alexandria, where he was received in triumph.

The council, therefore, ended in disarray. Technically an outlaw, Cyril assuaged the courtiers of Constantinople with an expensive array of gifts in money, furniture and – prized gifts – sixteen ostriches. He was left at liberty in Alexandria. Two years later John of Antioch wrote a letter to Cyril, known as the 'Formula of Union', in which he tacitly accepted Nestorius's deposition from the see of Constantinople and explicitly acknowledged the title of *Theotokos*, while interpreting it in an Antiochene sense. Cyril wrote back to John gladly accepting the Formula and adding some qualifications of his own. Nevertheless the results remained somewhat inconclusive. Definitive approval of Ephesus would come only with the council of Chalcedon.

Chalcedon

Twenty years elapsed between Ephesus and the next ecumenical council, Chalcedon in 451. In between, providing the immediate background to Chalcedon, occurred the so-called 'Robber' council of Ephesus, or Ephesus II. Cyril had died in 444. He was succeeded as bishop of Alexandria by Dioscorus, who exceeded Cyril's devotion to the 'high Christology' of Alexandria while lacking his diplomatic skill. The eastern emperor Theodosius II convoked a council at Ephesus in 449, which was dominated by Dioscorus and his friend Eutyches, abbot of a monastery in Constantinople. The council taught that Christ's divinity was so dominant that the one person of Christ was accompanied by only one 'nature' (Greek *phusis*, hence 'monophysite'). Bishop Flavian of Constantinople, who had earlier condemned the teaching of Eutyches, was ignored at the council, assaulted, and died shortly afterwards. Pope Leo had written a long letter, or 'Tome', in support of Flavian's condemnation of Eutyches, but the letter was ignored and his representatives (legates) at the council were spurned. On the legates' return to Rome, Leo famously declared the council to be a robbery (Latin, *Latrocinium*) and urged a new council to right the situation. Emperor Theodosius, on the other hand, regarded it as a valid ecumenical council and refused to convoke another.

Providence then intervened. Theodosius was killed in a hunting accident in 450 and was succeeded on the imperial throne by his sister Pulcheria. In order to obtain the throne she was obliged to marry and took for her husband the military general Marcian. More resolute than her brother and unhappy with Ephesus II, Pulcheria, acting alongside her husband, quickly convoked the new council. They summoned it to meet in the imperial palace in Chalcedon, which lies close to Constantinople on the eastern, or Asian, side of the Bosphorus sea. Pope Leo, meanwhile, had cooled to the prospect of a new council on the grounds that it might reopen wounds and that his 'Tome' was sufficient to resolve the crisis. He eventually complied, at Pulcheria's urging, on strict condition that his legates would preside and that the 'Tome' would provide the basis of the council's decree.

Some five hundred to six hundred bishops attended, making Chalcedon the largest council until then. The large majority of them came from the East, though the western Church was represented by the legates of pope Leo – altogether five were sent, three bishops and two priests – who duly presided during the sessions. The first business was to put right the 'Robber' council. Dioscorus, who was present in person, was condemned for his irregular conduct of this council and its monophysite teaching and was deposed from his see. This painful action left lasting bitterness within Egypt and contributed to the Coptic church, as the Egyptian church came to be called ('Copt' derives from the Greek word for Egypt, *Aigyptos*), moving into schism with both Rome and Constantinople.

Having dealt with Dioscorus and the monophysite teaching, the council moved to its own declaration. With remarkable speed – the council lasted about a month, beginning on 8 October – a committee of the bishops drew up a 'Definition of Faith' which was approved by the whole council. It reaffirmed the creeds of the earlier councils of Nicea and Constantinople, speaking of them as a single creed. It confirmed the controversial (first) council of Ephesus together with its defence of *Theotokos* and the deposition of Nestorius. Finally, it stated the teaching of Christ's one 'person' in two 'natures', human and divine, which has remained fundamental to Christian orthodoxy ever since. In this teaching, the Definition drew upon and praised Leo's Tome and then added a core paragraph which followed closely the 'Formula of Union' that John of Antioch had sent to Cyril of Alexandria in 433. This paragraph reads as follows:

> *Following the saintly fathers, we all with one voice teach the confession of one and the same Son, our Lord Jesus Christ: the same perfect in divinity and perfect in humanity, the same truly God and truly man, of a rational soul and a body; consubstantial with the Father as regards his divinity, and the same consubstantial with us as regards his humanity; like us in all respects except for sin; begotten before the ages from the Father as regards his divinity, and in the last days the same for us and for our salvation from Mary, the virgin mother of God, as regards his humanity; one and the same Christ, Son, Lord, only-begotten, acknowledged in two natures which undergo no confusion, no change, no division, no separation. At no point was the difference between the natures taken away through the union, but rather the property of both natures is preserved and comes together into a single person and a single subsistent being. He is not parted or divided into two persons, but is one and the same only-begotten Son, God, Word, Lord Jesus Christ, just as the prophets taught from the beginning, and as the Lord Jesus*

> *Christ himself instructed us, and as the creed of the fathers handed it down to us. (Decrees*, pp. 86–7)

We may note the strong and beautiful emphasis upon Christ's solidarity with us, through the phrase 'consubstantial with us as regards his humanity'. Thus the same word 'consubstantial' (Greek, *homoousios*), which had been introduced into the creed of Nicea to underline the Son's intimate relationship with the Father, is now used to express Christ's close relationship and solidarity with us. Mary's virginity, proclaimed in the creed of Constantinople I, is restated alongside her title *Theotokos* (Mother of God).

A few words about language are in order here. Human language, especially about the divine, is always imperfect. Credit may be given to the early Christians for being ready, in their passion to proclaim the gospel to all people, to move out of Aramaic and Hebrew, used by Jesus and the first disciples, into the more widespread Greek language. But how could Greek – the dominant language of the eastern empire and already complicated from the Christian point of view by being the medium of the sophisticated philosophy of Plato and Aristotle – be harnessed to express the relatively new concepts of Christian theology? Some idea of the difficulties may be gained by looking up in a dictionary of classical Greek three words that were eventually accepted as keys and which appear in the passage from Chalcedon just quoted: *prosopon*, which is translated in the passage as 'person', *hupostasis* which is rendered as 'subsistent being' but may also be translated as '(inner) person', and *phusis* which is translated as 'nature'. The dictionary will show a welter of meanings for each of the three words, yet gradually the Church settled upon them as best expressing the mystery of Christ's incarnation. To some extent the debates of the early Church were exercises in linguistic analysis.

Constantinople II and III

The second and third councils of Constantinople, held in 553 and 680–1, sought to explain further the relationship between Christ's divinity and his humanity.

Constantinople II may be seen as an unfortunate adventure on the part of the eastern emperor Justinian I. The emperor, whose dominions included Egypt and most of north Africa, sought to placate the Egyptian church, and to halt its drift into schism, by condemning three men associated with Nestorius: Theodore of Mopsuestia (+428), Theodoret (+460) and Ibas (+457). Few favoured the proposal. It was considered particularly objectionable to condemn three men who were long deceased. Theodore, moreover, had died before the controversial council of Ephesus and both Theodoret and Ibas had been reconciled at Chalcedon. Justinian was a powerful ruler and eventually his will prevailed. The three men and/or their writings were condemned in 'The Three Chapters', the key decree of the council. Pope Vigilius (537–55) reluctantly came round to accepting it. While it may be regarded as distasteful, the decree is doctrinally orthodox and therefore does not jeopardize the theological status of ecumenical councils.

The 'Three Chapters' decree of this pressurized council begins, paradoxically, with a fine statement on the importance of proper discussion within the Church:

> *The holy fathers, who have gathered at intervals in the four holy councils (Nicea to Chalcedon), have followed the example of antiquity. They dealt with heresies and current problems by debate in common, since it was established as certain that when the disputed question is set out by each side in communal discussion, the light drives out the shadow of lying. The truth cannot be made clear in any other way when there are debates about questions of faith, since everyone requires the assistance of his neighbour ... and as the Lord says, 'Where two or three are gathered in my name, there am I in the midst of them'.* (*Decrees*, p. 108)

Constantinople III, meeting a century later, expanded on Chalcedon's teaching on the two natures in the one 'person' of Christ, by declaring that Christ had both a human will, accompanying his human nature, and a divine will, accompanying the divine nature, while 'the two wills are not in opposition, but rather Christ's human will follows, without resisting or struggling, and is subject to his divine and all powerful will.' Thus the fullness of Christ's humanity is underlined as well as his solidarity with people in the trials and perplexities of life. Jesus's prayer in the garden of Gethsemane before his passion, 'Father, if you are willing, remove this cup from me; yet not my will but yours be done', would be interpreted as revealing the conformity of Christ's human will with his divine will – rather than conflict between the two wills – as well as the fullness of his humanity which was fearful of impending suffering.

Among those condemned in Constantinople's decree for teaching 'monothelitism' – the doctrine that Christ possessed only one will (*monos* is 'one', and *thelos* is 'will', in Greek), such that his divine will controlled his humanity – was pope Honorius (625–38). In two letters to Sergius, patriarch of Constantinople, the pope supported the patriarch's teaching of monothelitism. His error would be cited during the debate on papal infallibility at the first Vatican council in 1870. The two letters are of an official nature, yet Honorius is stating his own opinion, it seems clear, rather than seeking to provide definitive teaching such as would come within the terms of Vatican I's declaration on infallibility. In the list of monothelites condemned by Constantinople III, Honorius is accompanied by Sergius and three other bishops of Constantinople as well as by bishops Cyrus of Alexandria and Macarius of Antioch. We have already noted the censures of Nestorius of Constantinople and Dioscorus of Alexandria. Other bishops of both sees fell into error. Regarding the see of Rome, however, the condemnation of Honorius is exceptional. Almost always the bishop of Rome eventually reached the correct teaching on delicate theological issues during the first millennium AD. Special guidance of the Holy Spirit seems necessary to explain this remarkable achievement.

Nicea II

The second council of Nicea in 787, the last of the seven councils recognized as ecumenical by both Catholic and Orthodox churches, defended religious art against the criticisms of iconoclasts. The convoker and astute organizer of the council was the empress Irene, who had succeeded to the Byzantine throne on the death of her husband in 780. She was supported by pope Hadrian I, who sent two legates to preside at the council. We notice, indeed, close cooperation between Rome and Constantinople. The council made a succinct 'Definition' which has remained fundamental for Catholic art and devotion ever since:

*Representational art ... is quite in harmony with the history
of the spread of the gospel as it provides confirmation that the
becoming man of the Word of God was real, not just imaginary,
and brings us a similar benefit. For, things that mutually illustrate one another undoubtedly possess one another's message
... Therefore we decree with precision and care that, like the
figure of the honoured and life-giving cross, the revered and holy
images, whether painted or made of mosaic or of other suitable
material, are to be exposed in the holy churches of God, on
sacred instruments and vestments, on walls and panels, in houses
and by public ways. These are the images of our Lord God and
saviour, Jesus Christ, and of our Lady without blemish, the holy
mother of God, and of the revered angels and of the holy saints.
The more frequently they are seen in representational art, the
more are those who see them drawn to remember and long for
those who serve as models, and to pay these images the tribute
of salutation and respectful veneration. Certainly this is not the
full adoration in accordance with our faith, which is properly
paid only to the divine nature. But it resembles that given to the
figure of the honoured and life-giving cross, and also to the holy
books of the gospels and to other sacred cult objects. Further,
people are drawn to honour these images with the offering of
incense and lights, as was piously established by ancient custom.
Indeed the honour paid to an image traverses it, reaching the
model; and whoever venerates the image, venerates the person
represented in that image. (Decrees, pp. 135–6)*

The introductory paragraph of the Definition of Nicea II
provides a fitting conclusion to this section on the ecumenical
councils. It begins by quoting the creed of Constantinople I (381),
thus recognizing this text as the official version of the Nicene creed.
It then summarizes the decisions of the previous six ecumenical
councils, revealing well the Church's sense of the importance of
history and tradition. Some of the language is strong: correct
doctrine was seen as vital for salvation, so heresies were very
dangerous. The only significant change from the story we have
outlined is the account of Constantinople II. Instead of the
'Three Chapters' we find the condemnation of various individuals
including Origen. Their teachings were probably condemned
towards the beginning of the council, without the censures finding

their way into the council's only surviving doctrinal decree, the 'Three Chapters'. The 'mythical speculations' of Origen probably included his teaching on the transmigration of souls: an interesting indication of the influence of eastern – including Hindu – thought upon Christian theologians. Thus, after quoting in full the Constantinople version of the Nicene creed, the paragraph continues as follows:

> *We abominate and anathematize Arius and those who think like him and share in his mad error; also Macedonius and those with him, properly called the Pneumatomachi. We confess our Lady, the holy Mary, to be really and truly mother of God, because she gave birth in the flesh to Christ, one of the Trinity, our God, just as the first synod at Ephesus decreed. It expelled from the church Nestorius and those with him, because they were introducing a duality of persons. Along with these synods, we confess the two natures of the one who became incarnate for our sake from the God-bearer without blemish, Mary the ever virgin, recognizing that he is perfect God and perfect man, as the synod at Chalcedon proclaimed when it drove from the divine precinct the foul-mouthed Eutyches and Dioscorus. We reject along with them Severus, Peter and their interconnected band with their many blasphemies, in whose company we anathematize the mythical speculations of Origen, Evagrius and Didymus, as did the fifth synod assembled at Constantinople. Further we declare there are two wills and principles of action, in accordance with what is proper to each of the natures in Christ, in the way that the sixth synod, that at Constantinople, proclaimed when it publicly rejected Sergius, Honorius, Cyrus, Pyrrhus and Macarius, those uninterested in true holiness, and their like-minded followers. To summarize, we declare that we defend free from any innovations all the written and unwritten ecclesiastical traditions that have been entrusted to us.* (Decrees, pp. 134–5)

iv. Theologians

Theology stood at the core of the last section on ecumenical councils. Theological statements of the highest quality, and of lasting significance, were forged through collective debate. This collectivity proved to be a great strength, to be repeated in theology on a similar scale only at the councils of Trent and Vatican II. Creeds and definitions emerged that were beyond the capacity of any individual theologian or bishop. They possessed great authority inasmuch as they were the considered statements of bishops representing the whole Church. We have glimpsed, too, the importance of local councils: the third council of Toledo in 589, the synod of Whitby in 664, councils in France convoked by Boniface in the eight century. The statements issued by these councils, principally the ecumenical councils, may be considered the high peaks of a mountain range. The foothills, as well as other high peaks, were provided by the reflections and writings of individual theologians.

In the East, including Egypt, a number of individuals had high profiles at the councils of Ephesus and Chalcedon – some were approved, others were condemned. The two most esteemed as theologians were Cyril of Alexandria and Theodore of Mopsuestia. Maximus the Confessor (580–662) influenced the third council of Constantinople in 680–1 through his writings against Monothelitism. A prolific writer on doctrinal, liturgical and biblical topics, he is considered a martyr on account of the sufferings he bore.

Between the eighth and tenth centuries, the most important theologian in the East was John of Damascus (660–750, also called John Damascene). A strong defender of religious art, he influenced Nicea II's decree against iconoclasm. His major work 'Fountain Head of Knowledge' was divided into three parts: a textbook of logic, a list of heresies, and an exposition of the orthodox faith. It reveals extensive knowledge of Christian writers and treats of ancient philosophers such as Aristotle and Porphyry as well as the new challenge of Islam. The work, written in Greek, was early translated into Arabic, Old Slavonic, Georgian and Armenian, and later into Latin. It exercised wide influence. John was a famous preacher, though only a few of his sermons survive. He was noted, too, for his liturgical hymns, especially those for Easter, Christmas, the Transfiguration and Mary's Dormition (Assumption).

On the borders of East and West, the remarkable work of Cyril and Methodius has been mentioned. In western Europe, the two most important papal authors were Leo I, whose 'Tome' was important for the council of Chalcedon, and Gregory I, who sent Augustine to England and was besides a prolific writer of books and letters which contained much that may be described as pastoral theology. Bede is best known today as an historian but he also wrote works of theology, passing on the theological knowledge of the early Church to his own generation. Similarly in Spain, Isidore of Seville did much to preserve the learning of the early Church for his own and future ages.

Augustine of Hippo merits special attention. We know about his life principally through his autobiography, *Confessions*. He was born at Thagaste in modern Algeria, offspring of a pagan father and a Christian mother, Monica, through whom he was made a catechumen in infancy. He received a classical education in Latin literature and rhetoric and he acquired some knowledge of Greek. In adolescence Augustine lost his Christian faith and lived for some fifteen years with a concubine. He was a Manichee for almost a decade, during which time he held teaching posts at Carthage, Rome and Milan. In Milan he fell under the influence of bishop Ambrose and was baptized by him at the Easter vigil in 387. Soon he returned to Africa. There, while visiting the city of Hippo, he was seized by the people and ordained priest. He became bishop of the city in 396 and remained in this post until his death in 430.

Augustine's prolific writings (in Latin) make him probably the most penetrating and influential of all theologians of the western Church – he is claimed by the western Church inasmuch as Hippo in Latin-speaking north Africa lay within the patriarchate of Rome. In his *Confessions*, he refuted at length the Manichean dualist doctrines to which he had once adhered. Against the Donatists, he upheld the validity of baptism and ordination even when these sacraments are conferred by sinful ministers: teaching that had profound implications for the practice of Christian life and ministry. In his writings against Pelagius, who came originally from Britain, he developed the doctrines of original sin and our absolute need of God's grace: we cannot earn eternal life through our own efforts alone, or in any way put God in our debt. Augustine took a gloomy view regarding the number of the saved, though whether he taught a strict doctrine of predestination, holding that the vast majority of people are condemned to hell regardless of what they do or believe, is disputed. His views on sex and marriage were also rather pessimistic, reflecting his own inner struggles. He was the foremost western theologian to whom Protestants appealed at the time of the Reformation, principally regarding his teachings on predestination and justification by faith. But the Counter-Reformation claimed Augustine for Catholics too. His treatise *De Trinitate*, which placed love at the centre of the Trinity, has remained the principal classic of the western Church on this sublime mystery. *The City of God* profoundly influenced political theory in the West. It urged Christians to respect civil authorities but to struggle principally for the kingdom of God, which would be realized fully only in the next life. He wrote extensive commentaries on various books of Scripture, most notably a treatise on John's gospel, and he kept written copies of many of his lively sermons to the people of Hippo. Augustine was regarded as a theological giant in his own lifetime in the West; less so in the East both then and later. He was invited to attend the council of Ephesus (431), but died before the invitation reached him.

v. Rome and Constantinople

This section traces relations between the churches of Rome and Constantinople from 400 to the beginning of the schism in 1054. Already in the fourth century the emperor Constantine had selected the city of Byzantium as the new capital of the Roman Empire. He renamed the city after himself, 'Constantinople' meaning the city (Greek *polis*) of Constantine. Initially it was the sole capital of the empire. However, soon after his death in 337 it became clear that the Empire was too vast, and Constantinople too far to the East, for this city to be the only capital. Rome was restored at a capital city, for the western half of the empire, while Constantinople remained the capital of the eastern half. The division followed the linguistic divide within the empire, between the Greek-speaking eastern half and the Latin-speaking western half. The situation received a new twist in the fifth century, when the barbarian invasions destroyed the Roman Empire in the west but Constantinople and the eastern half of the empire survived the onslaughts. Then the balance shifted again. The barbarian tribes converted to Christianity and injected new life into western Christendom, while eastern Christendom was threatened by the emerging power of Islam. Muslim armies in the seventh century captured the cities of Alexandria, Antioch and Jerusalem. As a result, only two of the five patriarchal sees retained effective freedom for governing the Church: Rome and Constantinople.

It would be quite wrong, in my opinion, to view the schism that eventually occurred as inevitable. Even among historians there is a tendency to write history backwards: the final schism is known and the story of the first millennium is written as if it inevitably led up to the breach. The outcome at the time was less predictable. There were the differences between Rome and Constantinople that have been mentioned. On the other hand, there was close unity between the two churches at the crucial council of Chalcedon in 451. The Acacian schism began in the late fifth century and endured intermittently for almost forty years, from 482 to 519. Acacius, patriarch of Constantinople, sought to placate the Egyptian church, which remained opposed to the council of Chalcedon, by minimizing the council's teaching. A succession of popes refused to go along with this conciliatory approach, insisting on the integrity of Chalcedon, and excommunicated Acacius and several of his successors when they refused to back down. Eventually communion between the two sees was restored and in the following two centuries there was close cooperation between Rome and Constantinople at the councils of Constantinople III and Nicea II.

The introduction of the *Filioque* clause – adding the Son to the Father in the procession of the Holy Spirit – into the Nicene creed by the council of Toledo in 589 has been mentioned. The clause received wider acceptance in the West through its adoption in 794 by the council of Frankfurt, which was convoked by the emperor Charlemagne. As at Toledo, the addition at Frankfurt was intended only for the West, in order to counter residual Arianism. Nevertheless its introduction offended the East. As well as various theological objections, there was the procedural point that the West was unilaterally tampering with a text approved by an ecumenical council. The papacy was initially reluctant to countenance the *Filioque* clause, but gradually became an advocate of the change. As a result, the issue of papal authority entered the debate. Was the pope superior to an ecumenical council, with authority to alter its doctrinal decrees? Papal authority of this kind was quite unacceptable to the church of Constantinople. Here we may note the recent discovery that the earliest known introduction of the *Filioque* clause may have come at an eastern council, that held in

Seleucia-Ctesiphon in Persia around 410 (*Annuarium Historiae Conciliorum*, xxxii, 2000, p. 10).

The crowning of Charlemagne as emperor by pope Leo III, on Christmas day 800 in Rome, also irritated Byzantium (as Constantinople and the eastern empire continued sometimes to be called). There it was felt that with the collapse of the western empire in the fifth century, through the barbarian invasions, only the ruler of the eastern empire could truly claim the title of emperor. Charlemagne might be considered a king but not an emperor. That the pope had been responsible for this unwelcome act led to some distancing from Rome on the part of eastern Christians, to their looking more to the patriarch of Constantinople as the one and only head of their Church. But the scale of the affront should not be exaggerated; communion between the two churches remained.

Tension flared again in the ninth century during the Photian schism. There were two claimants to the see of Constantinople, Ignatius and Photius. Initially the papacy was reluctant to enter the dispute, on the grounds that it was an internal affair of the eastern Church. Gradually the pope was drawn in and pronounced in favour of Ignatius, the original occupant of the see. The eastern emperor, Basil, also supported Ignatius. The result was the fourth council of Constantinople in 869–70, which ratified the choice of Ignatius and the deposition of Photius. Pope Hadrian II sent legates to preside at the council and approved its decision, but the convocation and ratification of the council belonged primarily to the eastern emperor. On the death of Ignatius in 877, Photius regained the see of Constantinople and indeed enjoyed good relations with pope John VIII. Photius was a profound theologian and a brilliant writer – polemical too in his criticisms of the western Church – and he is regarded as a saint by the Orthodox church. His deposition is a painful episode in Orthodox memory. But it should be remembered that much of the responsibility for the deposition lies with the eastern authorities, and the friendship between Photius and John VIII shows the restoration of better relations.

Almost two centuries elapsed before the definitive breach in 1054. Cerularius was the determined patriarch of Constantinople. He was critical of the western Church on a wide range of issues: use of unleavened instead of leavened bread in the Eucharist was reproved; the introduction into the creed of the *Filioque* clause was condemned; papal claims to authority were judged to be unfounded in Scripture or early Tradition; Lent was considered to be a week short in the West. Even beards became a contentious issue. The western practice of clean-shaven clergy was criticized as effeminate and suitable for men constantly on the move, such as soldiers; clergy rather should be contemplatives and therefore bearded, following the example of Christ and the apostles as well as that of Plato and Aristotle and the philosophers of Antiquity. Some Catholic churches in Constantinople were closed on the patriarch's orders. Pope Leo IX sent Cardinal Humbert to Constantinople as his legate to seek a solution, but also entrusted to him a bull excommunicating Cerularius, which was to be promulgated if no solution to the crisis was forthcoming. Humbert proved as contentious as Cerularius. Unable to persuade Cerularius to change his mind, he promulgated the bull of excommunication by leaving it in Hagia Sophia, the cathedral church of Constantinople, and hastily returned to Rome. Cerularius, in turn, excommunicated Humbert and the members of his entourage.

In fact, unknown to Humbert, pope Leo had died before the bull excommunicating Cerularius was promulgated. It is widely reckoned that papal legates lose their authority when a pope dies, so it may well be that, according to western canon law, Cerularius was never excommunicated. At the time the crisis was expected to be a passing one, less serious than the Photian schism, but it soon passed from personal excommunications to schism between the two churches. Sadly the schism was never satisfactorily resolved and remains today the most fundamental divide within the Christian community.

We have traced relations between Rome and Constantinople largely at the institutional level. But the underlying cultural and religious differences should be kept in mind: language and geography and many other factors made the two churches rather distant from each other. Neither church had obvious or immediate need of the other. It was only after the split that the resulting mutual impoverishment gradually became apparent.

vi. Institutional developments

Various institutional developments have already been treated, particularly in the sections headed 'Ecumenical councils' and 'Rome and Constantinople'. Institutions were an essential dimension of popular religion, the topic of the next section. The present section seeks to bring together the main institutional developments that are not covered in these other sections and to survey more generally the institutional dimension of the Church during this long period of six and a half centuries.

One Church

There were plenty of schisms during this time and some of them were serious and long-lasting, most notably those associated with Arian, Nestorian and Monophysite teachings.

The Arian schism was largely resolved in Egypt and Asia by the end of the fourth century. In the West, as we have seen, many of the barbarian tribes first converted to an Arian form of Christianity before they embraced the orthodox faith; as late as 794 the council of Frankfurt inserted the *Filioque* clause into the creed in order to counter residual Arianism in parts of Europe. But Arianism does not appear to have continued as a serious threat to orthodox Christianity and it ceased to exist as an extensive and organized church.

The Nestorian church expanded in the East as far as India and China and has influenced Christianity in parts of Asia until today. However, the rise of Islam cut off this church from its roots in the Mediterranean world and it became somewhat peripheral to the mainstream of Christianity.

Three significant communities rejected the Definition of the council of Chalcedon and retained Monophysite doctrine. The Armenian church was never represented at the council and, largely as a result, formally rejected Chalcedon's teaching in the sixth century. Jacob Baradeus (500–578), bishop of Edessa in Syria, was the energetic organizer of the second community, which is sometimes called the Jacobite church but more properly the Syrian Orthodox Church. This church spread to various parts of Asia, including India, and survives today as a significant presence in many parts of the world. Thirdly, the Coptic church based in Egypt ('Copt' derives from the Greek word for Egypt *Aiguptos*), which provided the core opposition to Chalcedon. This church was much reduced by conversions to Islam, but it remains today the principal Christian church in Egypt and a diaspora of Coptic communities flourish in other countries. Linked to the Copts as daughter churches, and following their rejection of Chalcedon, were the churches of Ethiopia and Nubia.

Despite these significant splits, the preservation of basic unity within the Christian church during the first millennium is very remarkable. There were tensions and times of mutual excommunication between the churches of Rome and Constantinople, as we have seen. Even so, the two churches, which together counted the large majority of Christians, remained fundamentally in communion with each other, and thereby formed a single Church, for over a thousand years.

Hierarchy and ministry

Already in the fourth century, through the conversion of Constantine and the establishment of Christianity as the official religion of the empire, papal authority became acknowledged quite widely and openly. Popes played an important role in most of the five ecumenical councils from Ephesus to Nicea II. The support of pope Leo I was crucial to the success of the council of Chalcedon. Pope Gregory I was highly respected on account of his writings and saintly life. He is considered the founder of the Papal States on account of the gift of his extensive property to the papacy. The mission he entrusted to Augustine proved crucial for the evangelization of northern Europe as well as for the extension of papal authority north of the Alps. Leo I and Gregory I are the only two popes in the history of the Church to be commonly accorded the title 'Great'.

The ninth and tenth centuries proved difficult times for the papacy. Some forty-four popes are counted during this time; therefore an average reign of less than five years each. There were many anti-popes and disputed elections. A few powerful families in Rome dominated the papacy, which they regarded almost as their personal property. To this period belongs the legendary Pope Joan. The legend – clearly a fabrication – first appeared in the thirteenth century. Her reign was assigned to the mid-ninth century because the confusion of this period allowed it to be inserted without obviously contradicting the known chronology. According to the legend, Joan had a short and successful reign as pope, disguised as a man, but when her true sex was discovered through her giving birth to a child, she was stoned to death.

The revival of the papacy in the eleventh century, which is often called the Gregorian Reform after it's most notable pope, Gregory

VII (1073–85), will be treated in the next chapter. Leo IX (1048–54), the first pope associated with the reform, has already appeared in the context of the beginning of the East–West schism in 1054.

The title 'cardinal' derives from the Latin word meaning a hinge, *cardo*. In the early Church the principal priests and bishops within Rome and its suburbs were sometimes referred to as 'cardinals' and they participated in the election of the pope. Their number is mentioned as twenty-four or twenty-five in some sources. *Liber Pontificalis*, the early collection of papal biographies, states that a synod in Rome in 769 decided the pope should be elected from among the deacons and 'cardinal priests'. The same work, for approximately the same date, mentions 'cardinal bishops' who conducted the liturgy in the cathedral church of the diocese, St John Lateran. The principal deacons in the city were sometimes referred to as 'cardinal deacons'. However, the decisive developments in the college of cardinals occurred during the Gregorian Reform and afterwards, so they will be treated in the next chapter.

We have already noted the three tiers in the episcopate of the early Church. This basic framework remained throughout the first millennium. The senior tier of five patriarchates was affected by the Muslim conquests of Alexandria, Antioch and Jerusalem, which severely restricted the freedom and activity of their three patriarchs. The middle tier, usually called metropolitan sees in the East and archbishoprics in the West, remained essentially the same. Bishops below the rank of patriarch or metropolitan formed the third tier: they remained fundamental to the organization of the church. Following the barbarian invasions in the West and the conversions of these peoples to Christianity, some bishops were appointed to a particular tribe rather than to a town or city. Bede's *Ecclesiastical History* is informative about this arrangement in seventh-century England. But gradually the system of more fixed sees, based on particular towns or cities, reasserted itself.

Priests, too, retained the essential features that had developed in the early Church. They remained crucial to the organization and practice of Christian life. Deacons were better appreciated in the East than in the West, where many of their functions were taken over by priests. The subordinate ministries of subdeacons, acolytes, exorcists, cantors, lectors/readers and door-keepers remained at least vestigially in both East and West, though many of their duties were taken over by priests or deacons, or were undertaken by the laity without their having an official title for their ministry.

We have encountered deaconesses in canon 19 of the council of Nicea and the ordination of women as deacons in canon 15 of the council of Chalcedon (above, p. 32). Both councils permitted women in these roles rather than showing enthusiasm for the offices. Subsequently, adult baptism largely gave way to the baptism of infants, so a key function of female deacons almost disappeared: namely, as attendants while women, divested of their clothes, were baptized by full immersion. Even so, women deacons remained quite numerous in the eastern Church. In the West they were much less numerous, though some continued to adorn the Church throughout the Middle Ages. Whether the western Church can be accused of suppressing female deacons, or rather women preferred the many other opportunities for Christian life and ministry, outside the diaconate, is difficult to say.

Councils

Ecumenical councils of the time have been discussed at some length. We have encountered, too, various church councils at the diocesan, provincial and national levels. Canon 5 of Nicea I legislated for provincial councils to be held twice a year. The recommendation of Constantinople II, regarding the importance of 'debate in common', applied immediately to ecumenical councils but it would seem to have local councils also in mind. Altogether we can say that the Church of the first millennium was fundamentally conciliar.

Mansi, *Conciliorum*, reveals a remarkable number of regional councils during this first millennium and gives some idea of the topics debated and the lively discussions. Just in the city of Carthage, *Concilia Africae*, ed. C. Munier (Corpus Christianorum, vol. 149) provides evidence of eighteen regional councils between 393 and 419. Surely, too, many local councils were held for which no evidence survives.

Parishes

Perhaps the institutional change of most significance during this period was the development of the parochial system in western

Christendom. Many churches were built in the fourth century but their construction occurred principally in the towns and cities. In the countryside, house chapels were often used, as at Lullingstone and Hinton St Mary in Britain. Following the new conversions to Christianity in the West from the fifth century onwards, much of pastoral care was based upon the tribe. The Eucharist and other church services were often celebrated in existing buildings, such as halls. In some regions they were regularly celebrated in the open air – the beautiful ornamental crosses that survive in the Celtic world were used to mark and sanctify such spaces.

Gradually, however, a network of parish churches was constructed, eventually covering most of the territory of western and central Europe. Each parish normally had recognized boundaries. The parish priest was responsible for the pastoral care of the parishioners. Maintenance of the building belonged to the laity, resulting in a real sense of their ownership of the parish and its church. Altogether there was genius in the arrangement, which combined efficiency, responsibility and a sense of belonging. In the parish church were celebrated the Mass, principally on Sundays but also on weekdays, as well as baptism, sometimes marriage, and various other services. In the adjoining churchyard parishioners were normally buried. In these and other ways there was association throughout life and after death. The parish and its church may be considered principal reasons for the deep rooting of Christianity in western Christendom.

Parish churches began to be constructed in France at an early date. Gregory of Tours, *Historia Francorum*, provides fine evidence of the initiative of Martin of Tours in the construction of parish churches in the countryside as early as the late fourth century. In England, the development was largely after the period described in Bede's *Ecclesiastical History*. Yet by the time of the Domesday Survey in 1086 some 9,000 parishes, each with its parish church (sometimes with more than one church), covered the whole country, a network of parishes that survived basically unchanged until the nineteenth century. Some of the parish churches of Anglo-Saxon England can still be appreciated today, such as St Laurence church at Bradford-on-Avon in Wiltshire and All Saints at Brixworth in Northamptonshire.

vii. Popular religion

Popular religion – a topic that is essential to cover though difficult to define, perhaps best described for the present book simply as the religion of the people of God – was both traditional and innovative during this period. The experiences of the early Church remained very influential. Initially, continuity with this earlier period remained particularly strong in eastern Christendom, which managed to ward off the various barbarian incursions and to preserve well the earlier traditions. Some of this continuity came to an end through the Muslim conquests, which obliged many eastern Christians to practice their religion under radically different conditions. Though, as often happens with people suffering from discrimination or persecution, respect for the past became in many ways all the stronger.

In the West, the conversions of barbarian tribes brought new energy and creativity to Christianity both within and beyond the boundaries of the former Roman Empire. At the same time, the new converts were notably respectful towards many Christian traditions. The result, in terms of popular religion, was a remarkable blending of old and new, of continuity and innovation.

Theology and institutional developments, which were treated in sections iv and vi of this chapter, had many implications for popular religion. The three facets of church life influenced one another. Regarding popular religion and theology, we noted earlier Gregory of Nyssa's comments about interest in theology among the money-changers, bath attendants and shop assistants of Constantinople towards the end of the fourth century. Similarly, not long afterwards, fascination with the doctrines of Trinity and Incarnation, and other mysteries of the Christian faith, was characteristic of the tribes who converted to Christianity in the West. Links between popular religion and institutional developments are particularly evident in the establishment of parish churches, as outlined in section vi. They are evident, too, in the development of religious orders.

Religious orders

We have seen that inspiration for the early growth of consecrated life in the Church, which centred on Egypt in the third and fourth centuries, came partly from a reaction against the institutional Church of the time: a flight to the desert, away from church life in the cities. However, following the development from hermits to religious communities, consecrated life soon became an integral part of the institutional church, even while it retained a critical perspective. In Egypt, monastic life continued to flourish until the widespread conversion of the country to Islam beginning in the seventh century. Further south, monasticism was particularly strong in Ethiopia, but the country followed Egypt out of communion with Rome and Constantinople.

Towards the East, in the church loyal to Constantinople and therefore in communion with Rome, we have noted the founder-figure of monasticism in the fourth century, Basil of Caesarea, and the importance of his *Rule*, as well as the role of his sister Macrina in the establishment of religious life for women. Also important were the lavras (colonies of hermits) established in Palestine between the fourth and early sixth centuries, notably those founded by St Euthymius (+473) and his disciple St Sabas (+532). Muslim conquests affected monasticism adversely in various regions. But there were positive developments too. The beginning of monasticism on Mount Athos in Greece is dated to the lavra founded by St Athanasius the Athonite in 961. Mount Athos proved seminal for the introduction of monasticism into the Russian church and it gradually became the heart of monastic life for much of the Orthodox church.

For western Christendom, we have already encountered many monks and some nuns: Augustine and companions who left their monastery in Rome to begin the reconversion of England; Celtic monks who had an important role in the evangelization of Britain and various other countries; Theodore of Tarsus, monk in Rome and then archbishop of Canterbury; Hilda and the double-monastery at Whitby; the communities of men and women established in Germany by Boniface, himself a monk of Nursling; Anskar, monk at Corbie in France and evangelist in Scandinavia; Cyril and Methodias, 'apostles of the Slavs', who lived as monks for some time.

Benedict of Nursia (480–550) is regarded as the father, or patriarch, of western monasticism. Most of our information about his life comes from the *Dialogues* of pope Gregory I. Born and educated in

Rome, he withdrew from the worldly life there to become a hermit at Subiaco. Disciples joined him and communities were established in the neighbourhood but they did not prosper. Benedict then moved south to Monte Cassino, where he established a monastery which endured. His most important contribution was the *Rule* which he composed for this community. A masterly balance of high ideals and understanding of the human condition, it has exercised a profound influence upon western monasticism and, indirectly, upon other styles of religious life. Pope Paul VI acknowledged this contribution when he named Benedict 'Patron of Europe'.

There is debate among historians as to how much dependence and linear continuity there was between Monte Cassino and the monasteries established in Europe between the sixth and eighth centuries, and to what extent Benedict's *Rule* was known during this time. Benedict of Aniane (751–821) was the key figure of his time in the propagation of the Benedictine way of life in Germany and France. Certainly by the end of the tenth century Benedict's *Rule* had become normative for monasticism throughout most of western Christendom.

Pope Gregory's *Dialogues* relates that Benedict's sister, Scholastica, established a monastery for women at Plombariola, some five miles from Monte Cassino. She is regarded as the founder of the Benedictine way of life for women.

Liturgy

Christian liturgy (the word derives from the Greek *laos* and *ergon* meaning 'people' and 'work') was shaped by both monks and the parish community. Monasticism was particularly important for the development of the Divine Office (Latin *Officium divinum*). Gradually this liturgical prayer – principally singing the Psalms of the Old Testament – came to be formalized in the West as the seven 'hours' of Matins (morning prayer), Lauds (praise), Terce (third hour after sunrise), Sext (sixth hour), None (ninth hour), Vespers (evening prayer) and Compline (final prayer). Prime (first hour) was added in some places. This prayer stood at the heart of the Benedictine monk's daily life.

Monasticism was also crucial – in both East and West – for the development of the liturgical calendar: the year-long cycle of 'feasts' commemorating, principally, events in Christ's life on earth and

Christian saints. We have noted the liturgical season of Lent, from its mention in canon 5 of the council of Nicea. The peace brought to the church in the fourth century allowed further additions to the liturgical calendar. Subsequently monasticism led the way in developments, so that the entire year was mapped out. There were two main 'seasons' commemorating the life of Christ: Advent followed by Christmas, and Lent followed by Eastertide. Interspersed were days commemorating individual saints and martyrs, or groups of them, and some further 'divine mysteries' such as the Ascension and Pentecost. Texts appropriate to the feasts were incorporated into the Divine Office and the Mass, so there was both stability and appropriate variety in the daily liturgy.

Parish churches enabled this liturgical calendar to be celebrated by the wider Christian community: through the Mass on Sundays and weekdays, and participation in at least parts of the Divine Office, principally Matins and Vespers. Various other liturgical services, such as baptisms and funerals, normally took place within the context of the parish. Greek was the main liturgical language for the eastern Church, though Syriac and other languages were used in some regions. Latin was the principal written language throughout western Christendom, therefore reasonably it was the prevalent language in the liturgy. Local languages, such as old French or Anglo-Saxon English, were used in sermons and various prayers, as appropriate, but there seems to have been general acceptance that the core texts should normally be said or sung in Latin. It was a language that most people understood at least to some extent. In the liturgy, therefore, there remained the basic linguistic distinction that had been with the Church almost from the beginning, between the Greek-speaking East and the Latin-speaking West. There were many rites and variations within each of the two areas: diversity that may be explained partly by geography and partly by the need to accommodate distinctions between monastic and lay communities. This variety was both inevitable – granted that we are well before the advent of printing – and, it seems, appreciated. Unity, moreover, was much more fundamental than the differences: a shared belief in the central mysteries of Christianity and respect for the traditions which had handed down this faith through the centuries.

Chapter 3
Central and Late Middle Ages

This chapter covers the western Church – hereafter also called the Catholic church – during the second part of the Middle Ages: from the late eleventh to the end of the fifteenth century. The period is bracketed by the two most serious schisms in the history of Christianity: at the start, the schism with the Orthodox church; at the end, the eve of the Protestant Reformation. It represents a crucial and very fruitful stage in the Church's pilgrimage. Many of the distinctive features of the Catholic church today were determined during this time. On account of this central importance, it is the longest chapter in the book. The first half of the period, to around 1300, is often called the high Middle Ages: 'high' in the sense that it comes between the early and the late Middle Ages, and because it was a period of high achievement. The second half is usually called the late (or later) Middle Ages since it comes at the end of the period and, implicitly, because many historians regard it as a period of decline from the remarkable achievements of the preceding centuries. For the first half, however, the more neutral term 'central' Middle Ages has been preferred mainly because this writer views the late Middle Ages as a period of notable achievement as well as of difficulties.

The chapter begins with a brief survey of the extent of the Catholic church during the period, of contraction and expansion within western Christendom. In Chapter 2, popular religion was the focus of the final section even though it pervaded much of the earlier material. In this chapter it will be considered early on, as section ii, and at length, in order to underline the centrality of the topic: that at the centre of the Church, and therefore of its history, comes the people of God. Thereafter the chapter moves between more institutional aspects of the Church, those that are closer to popular religion, and those that are a mixture of both. Section iii focuses on the papacy, general councils and lay rulers. They were inextricably linked throughout the period and there was both cooperation and tension. Religious orders were prominent features of the Church throughout the period, both the older monastic orders and new foundations, principally the four orders of friars. They, and some parallel movements, principally beguines, are considered in section iv. Other major and partly innovative features of the medieval Church, which had long-lasting effects, are treated in the next three sections as follows: 'Intellectual developments', which focuses on universities, theologians and canon law; 'Liturgy, prayer and mysticism'; and 'Art, architecture and music'. The final section 'Challenges to western Christendom' concerns dissident movements within the western Church, attempts at reunion with the Orthodox and other separated churches, and attitudes towards other beliefs.

i. Contraction and expansion

The principal *contraction* for the Catholic church in this period came about through the schism between Rome and Constantinople. This schism, beginning in 1054, was never healed satisfactorily. The church of Constantinople, better known as the Orthodox church, became increasingly threatened by the expansion of Islam, culminating in the capture of Constantinople by Muslim forces in 1453. There were, however, important areas of expansion for the Orthodox church, principally in Russia. The churches which had earlier become separated from both Rome and Constantinople, principally those of Nestorian and Monophysite teachings, also remained largely separate from the Catholic church in this period. There were attempts at reunion with groups within these churches, and with the Orthodox church, at the council of Florence in 1453.

Muslim expansion menaced the lands of the Catholic church, though much less so than those of the Orthodox and other separated churches. Christian control of Jerusalem and the Holy Land, and some adjacent regions, was established for the western Church through the first crusade of 1098/99 and subsequent campaigns. But the gains proved short lived. Jerusalem was recaptured by the Seljuk Turks in 1177 and the city of Acre, the final Christian outpost in the Holy Land, was lost in 1291. Muslim forces came to threaten as far west as Italy. As late as 1480, Turkish forces captured Otranto in southern Italy and held the city for a year.

Equally threatening for western Christendom for some time were the incursions of the Tartars. Coming from the steppes of Russia, they penetrated deep into central Europe. Their armies of horse-born warriors for long seemed invincible. In 1242 they captured and sacked the city of Budapest in Hungary. Three years later the general council of Lyons issued this solemn warning:

> *The wicked race of the Tartars, seeking to subdue, or rather utterly destroy the Christian people, having gathered for a long time past the strength of all their tribes, have entered Poland, Russia, Hungary and other Christian countries. So savage has been their devastation that their sword spared neither sex nor age, but raged with fearful brutality upon all alike ... As time went on, they attacked Christian armies and exercised their savagery more fully upon them. Thus when, God forbid, the world is bereaved of the faithful, faith may turn aside from the world to lament its followers destroyed by the barbarity of this people.* (*Decrees*, p. 297)

The extinction of Christianity almost seemed a possibility. Hungary was the furthest west the Tartars came, but at the time few expected this to be the case. Tartars continued for long to hold sway over much of Russia and to threaten eastern lands of the Catholic church. The threat became identified with Islam in the fourteenth century when the Tartar people embraced the Muslim faith.

Despite this contraction, there were two significant areas of *expansion* for the Catholic church. First, there was Christian recovery of Muslim-held territory, principally in Sicily and Spain. Sicily, whose ecclesiastical loyalty had been contested between Rome and Constantinople, was conquered by Muslim Arabs in the ninth century. The island was regained for Christendom, and decisively incorporated into the western Church, by armies led by Normans (from Normandy in France) in a series of campaigns between 1061 and 1091. In Spain, the *Reconquista* (Reconquest) of the country was completed in 1492, when Granada, the last

Muslim stronghold, was captured by the Catholic army of king Ferdinand and queen Isabella.

The second area of expansion was in the North. Finland converted to Christianity in the twelfth century, with missionaries coming from both Sweden and Russia. In Lithuania, grand-duke Mindaugas and his family were baptized Christians in 1251 and many Lithuanians followed his example. After his reign, however, the return to paganism was widespread. The next, decisive step occurred in 1386 through the marriage of grand-duke Jagiello of Lithuania with Jadwiga, heiress of the Polish throne. As a condition of the marriage, Jagiello was baptized along with a number of his nobility, and thereafter Christianity took firm roots in the country.

To this expansion might be added various Catholic missionary endeavours eastwards. Francis of Assisi and companions journeyed to Egypt in 1219. They were received with respect and Francis preached before Sultan al-Kamil, but no widespread conversions resulted. Marco Polo, the Venetian traveller, reported on the existence of Nestorian communities in China in the mid-thirteenth century and hoped Catholic missionaries would arrive there. Soon afterwards, Franciscan friars led by John of Montecorvino established a flourishing Catholic community in the region of Khanbaliq (later Beijing), which was said to number some 30,000 Christians when John died in 1328. Afterwards the community declined, due in part to the advent of the hostile Ming dynasty in 1368. John of Montecorvino also visited Persia and India, and the Dominican friar Jourdan Catalani travelled to India in the early fourteenth century, but they made little impression in changing the Nestorian loyalties of Christians in these regions. Franciscans travelling to China also visited parts of Indonesia, but the small Christian communities established there – the oldest at Baros on the west coast of Sumatra may have dated back to the seventh century – appear to have died out before the close of the Middle Ages.

The evangelization of the 'New World' began at the very end of the period. Portugese discoverers ventured south along the west coast of Africa, Christopher Columbus reached America in 1492. This eventually momentous expansion of Christianity will be treated in the next chapter.

The population of western Christendom reached a peak around 1300. The Black Death plague in 1347–50 and its recurrences severely reduced the population, perhaps by as much as a third. While there was some recovery in the fifteenth century, the 1300 figure had probably not been reached again by 1500. For the year of 1300 it may be estimated – very approximately since precise figures do not exist – that the total population of the Catholic church was around sixty million, with some twenty million more Christians belonging to the Orthodox and other churches separated from Rome. In terms of creativity, too, both theological and devotional, the centre had shifted away from the East and north Africa. For all its faults, and they were many, western Christendom may be said to represent the mainstream of Christianity during the central and late Middle Ages.

ii. Popular religion

Perhaps the best way into the vast and complex topic of the religion of the laity is through their minimal religious obligations. Thereafter optional devotions will be treated and, finally, the role of relaxation and enjoyment. Clergy and religious orders are covered in other parts of the chapter, so the primary focus here will be on the laity. Footnote references for the quotations are to be found in full in Tanner (1996) and (2006).

Minimal requirements: knowledge

What the laity should know, and how this knowledge related to belief, came under wide scrutiny in the twelfth and thirteenth centuries. The tolerant attitude of most writers was based upon the distinction between implicit and explicit knowledge. Pope Innocent IV (1243–54) gave clarity and authority to this distinction, stating that 'the measure of faith to which the laity were bound' was to believe explicitly that God exists and rewards the good, and implicitly the articles of the faith. He argued that lay people might seek to learn more, but there was no sin if they did not since it was sufficient for them to devote themselves to good works. In a similar vein, Thomas Aquinas stated that intellectual study was not necessary for salvation, that the implicit faith of most people was held in trust and guaranteed by the faith of the Church. Duns Scotus was somewhat more exigent, arguing that those endowed with reason ought to know 'the more easily intelligible articles' of the faith. Of lay people who addressed the issue, king Louis IX of France urged his courtiers that 'the Christian religion as defined in the creed is something in which we ought to believe implicitly, even though our belief in it might be founded on hearsay'. The devout king was exhorting rather than legislating, and relying on his courtiers' implicit belief in even so fundamental an aspect of faith as the Creed. Such unshakeable belief, Louis argued, would guard against the devil who 'tries all he can to make people die with some doubt in their minds on certain points of our religion'.

Most ecclesiastical legislation took a similarly tolerant approach. At the highest level, the decrees of the general councils of the western Church during this period, from Lateran I (1123) to Basel-Florence (1431–45), contain no legislation enforcing inquiry into the religious knowledge of the laity, unless their orthodoxy was suspect. Neither are regulations of this kind to be found in *Corpus Iuris Canonici*, the other great source of medieval canon law. Canon lawyers generally concurred with this tolerant approach. Some recommendations were expressed locally, through legislation exhorting parish priests to instruct their parishioners. Robert Grosseteste, bishop of Lincoln in the mid-thirteenth century, directed that the laity should know the ten commandments and the seven deadly sins and possess a 'rudimentary understanding' of the seven sacraments. Peter Quinel, bishop of Exeter, required that lay people have knowledge of the seven sacraments and their effects, the Our Father prayer, the articles of the Creed, and the Hail Mary. In the fourteenth century, Spanish clerics were instructed by the council of Valladolid in 1322 to convey basic aspects of the faith to the laity. While there was plenty of ecclesiastical legislation obliging the clergy to know the basics of the faith and to teach them, for the most part it refrained from inquiring into the laity's response.

Various historians have focused on scepticism and unbelief. Alexander Murray (1984) suggested that both unbelief and lack of knowledge were present in some thirteenth-century northern Italian cities. Unbelief and bizarre beliefs, in some cases coinciding with considerable knowledge, have been brought to light by Emmanuel Le Roy Ladurie (1978, pp. 306–26) in his study of the late thirteenth and early fourteenth-century village of Montaillou in the Pyrenees; and by John Edwards (1990) for the late fifteenth-century diocese of Soria and Osma in northern Spain. Susan Reynolds (1991) went further in suggesting more widespread scepticism in medieval Europe. Cases of this kind may have been exceptional rather than the norm, yet they suggest that the lower end of religious knowledge could be frail, and that ecclesiastical authorities usually preferred not to pry into the situation too closely. The authorities' reluctance seems to have stemmed from practical considerations in administering such a large body as western Christendom as well as the desire to protect the laity from both easy charges of heresy and impossibly high prerequisites for salvation.

Minimal requirements: sacraments

At the second council of Lyons in 1274 the Church had declared in a definitive manner, for the first time, that the sacraments numbered seven and listed them: baptism, confirmation, confession, Eucharist, marriage, orders and last anointing. Apart from the sacrament of orders, which concerned the ordination of deacons, priests and bishops, these sacraments provided a framework for many of the basic religious obligations of the laity.

Regarding *baptism*, historians have generally assumed that baptism of infants was widely practiced during the Middle Ages. Without baptismal registers, which survive in quantity only from the sixteenth century, it is impossible to verify the assumption with any conclusiveness. There is, nevertheless, considerable indirect evidence in favour of the assumption, notably a sense that parents understood and desired the rite for their child's salvation. In the early Middle Ages, there had been some fierce legislation compelling baptism. The notorious laws of Charlemagne threatened with death anyone actively avoiding baptism, and required all children to be baptized within a year of birth. Anglo-Saxon penitentials and law-codes imposed penances and fines upon parents who failed to have their children baptized. Such concern, and its implications that the rite was not universally observed, was mainly confined to this earlier, missionary period. By the twelfth century there is little evidence to suggest people needed such compulsion; observance of the duty to baptize was almost taken for granted. In the later Middle Ages, when failure to baptize appears as an infrequent charge at visitations of parishes, it usually concerned carelessness or a dispute about who was responsible for the baptism of a particular child, rather than any resistance to the rite. At the extensive visitations of parishes in Lincoln and Hereford dioceses in England, for example, the only complaints of failure were made by the laity against the clergy: that the baptistery was not kept locked or properly cared for or that the rector failed to baptize infants. Church writers were less concerned to exhort or explain the need for baptism than to ensure that the laity understood that anyone – including a Muslim midwife – could baptize an infant at risk of death and therefore it was important to know the words that would effect the rite. Baptism, the most fundamental of the sacraments, seems to have enjoyed widespread support and observance.

Confirmation remained an enigmatic sacrament throughout the Middle Ages. With no clear precedent in the New Testament, it was not generally separated from baptism until the eighth century, and remained for long afterwards a subject of debate both as to whether it was a sacrament and regarding the proper age of its reception. It seems likely that the majority of people never received the rite even in the later Middle Ages, though by then reception was becoming more common. Most theologians did not regard it as necessary for salvation, nor thus compulsory. In the thirteenth century, Aquinas wrote that confirmation contributes to the perfection of salvation but is not indispensable, provided it is not refused out of contempt. Since the sacrament, in western Christendom, was normally administered by the diocesan bishop or his suffragan, its conferral was logistically difficult, particularly in the large dioceses that were common north of the Alps. Few records suggest that confirmations took place regularly. Bishop Grosseteste of Lincoln made it his practice to confirm all the children in his diocese, deanery by deanery, but he admitted this practice was unusual. There was a growing amount of legislation from the thirteenth century onwards insisting on the importance of confirmation, but it was local or directed at specific groups. The decree of the second council of Lyons, while declaring confirmation to be a sacrament, said nothing about its conferral. Soon after, a synod of Cologne ruled that confirmation was a prerequisite for becoming a cleric. Though encouraged more, confirmation still appears to have been far from widespread in the fourteenth and fifteenth centuries, nor was it declared by the ecclesiastical authorities to be obligatory in any full sense. There is little evidence, too, of pressure from the laity to make the sacrament more widely available.

For the sacrament of *confession* (penance), the crucial legislation was canon 21 of the fourth Lateran council in 1215. The canon mandated all Christians – the text reads 'everyone of both sexes' (*omnis utriusque sexus*) but Richard Helmslay, a witty Dominican friar of Newcastle-on-Tyne, was roundly censured when he argued that the decree applied only to hermaphrodites – who had reached 'the age of discretion' to confess their sins once a year to their parish priest or, with his permission (subsequently popes withdrew the need for this permission), to another priest. Many theologians thought that annual confession was only necessary if a grave or 'mortal' sin had been committed, but grave sin was interpreted widely so that only the very devout were thought likely to pass a whole year without committing such a sin.

Attendance at the sacrament, however, did not necessarily mean an exhaustive confession. The encounter normally took place in the parish church, often with others awaiting their own meeting with the priest, and in public, as the *Confessionale* (anonymous, though widely attributed to Bonaventure) suggested, 'in an open place (within the church) where there will be no grounds for suspicion and where the priest can be seen by all but not heard'. Confessional boxes were uncommon before the sixteenth century. Manuals for priests underlined the need for caution on the part of confessors: it was better to leave sins uncovered than to probe too hard or too imaginatively and thus to educate the penitent in sin rather than salvation. Lest confession foster intimacy, priests were enjoined to be especially careful with women and enquire with caution only into common or well-known sins. The degree of confession was thus more at the discretion of the penitent than the confessor, and discussion might often remain at a formal level if the penitent so wished. That such was often the case became a source of concern as contrition (sorrow) on the part of the penitent was increasingly emphasized as necessary for true confession and absolution. Remigio de Girolami, a Dominican friar living in northern Italy in the late thirteenth century, lamented that confessions were frequently superficial as 'many people confess with their mouths but not in their hearts'; his fellow friar, Giordano of Pisa, added that 'many men and women come to confession without giving any thought to it beforehand'.

The Lateran IV canon threatened those who failed to confess annually with excommunication. How far this punishment was

enforced is difficult to answer and surely varied. The findings of
Jacques Toussaert (1960, pp. 109–10, 121, 435–6) regarding late
medieval Flanders are instructive if tentative. He drew attention
to an anonymous monk of the region who wrote that excommunication was incurred if Easter duties, which included annual
confession, were neglected for several successive years. The monk's
statement is supported by diocesan statutes of the region, which
prescribed that the names of those who had failed to fulfil their
Easter duties were to be sent by the parish priest to the dean, and
from him to the bishop. If they had persisted in their recalcitrance
for ten years, their names were to be cited before the provincial
council. This lengthy and cumbersome procedure left many
loopholes, not least that its enforcement required the cooperation
of the very parish clergy among whom Toussaert detected some
hostility to the Lateran canon. In northern Italy, Friar Remigio de
Girolami complained that many people did not confess at all for
ten or twenty years at a stretch, apparently without effective action
being taken.

The importance of the Lateran canon cannot be dismissed
since it established an obligation that generated some friction. The
encounter between penitent and priest in confession was delicate
and potentially intrusive. Nevertheless the results were probably
less dramatic than has often been allowed: the annual rite could be
fulfilled in a rather perfunctory manner, and studies suggest that
refusal had to be persistent or coupled with more serious forms of
dissidence to warrant penalty.

The sacrament of the *Eucharist*, or the Mass, brought two
obligations for the laity: annual reception of the Eucharist (or
communion) at Easter, and attendance at church on Sundays
and certain feastdays. The Lateran canon that mandated annual
confession also required annual reception of the Eucharist during
the Easter season, again under penalty of excommunication;
though it permitted individuals not to receive communion if 'they
think, for a good reason and on the advice of their own (parish)
priest, that they should abstain from receiving it for a time'. In
visitation records from late medieval England, accusations of
failure to comply were relatively infrequent. When they were
recorded, such as during the 1397 visitation of Hereford diocese,
they were typically coupled with other charges, suggesting that

enforcement was primarily an issue only when other obligations were already being ignored.

The more onerous duty was attendance at Mass on Sundays and feast-days. The main feast-days requiring attendance were the same throughout western Christendom, but there were considerable regional variations regarding others. In some legislation the duty was specified more precisely: that the entire Mass had to be heard or that it must be at the parish church, rather than in the churches of mendicant orders or in private chapels. How far the legislation was observed is unknown and probably varied considerably by region and in time, but available evidence suggests that non-attendance was common and fairly widespread. Contemporaries could be quite pessimistic. Humbert of Romans, prior-general of the Dominicans, accused substantial sections of late thirteenth-century society of hardly attending church at all; and in the fifteenth-century Nicholas of Clamanges, admittedly an inveterate pessimist, reckoned that on feast days 'few go to church and even fewer listen to the Mass'.

Lay people, too, could show concern when parishioners absented themselves from Mass. At the 1492 visitation of the parishes in Norwich, the lay jurors brought charges against nine people for not attending their parish church on Sundays and feast-days. Three others were accused of keeping open taverns during services and one woman was said to observe 'an evil custom with various people from neighbouring households, who sit with her and drink during the time of service'. Practicalities meant that a level of non-attendance was tolerated. Moralists admitted, albeit grudgingly, that there existed many legitimate or semi-legitimate reasons to excuse attendance: Humbert of Romans, for example, acknowledged that domestic servants were often prevented by their masters or mistresses from attending church. Another complaint was that people went to church to socialize or be entertained rather than for religious reasons. One parish priest in fifteenth century England lamented of his parishioners, 'they come not thrice in a year ... they jangle, they jape, they kiss women, and hear no word of the service, but scorn the priests, saying that he sleepeth in his Mass and tarries them from their breakfast'. Irregular attendance, for whatever purpose, was probably sufficient to ward off accusation and potential coercion, despite a few decrees such as those of the council of Lavaur in France in 1368, which prescribed that the priest should threaten with excommunication those who miss Mass on two consecutive Sundays without good reason.

Marriage, the fifth sacrament, has been the focus of much recent study. The twelfth and thirteenth centuries brought some important clarifications on basic questions about how a marriage was created, whether it was a sacrament, and the role of local customs. Marriage was enacted by the parties themselves, even after canon 50 of Lateran IV decreed that a priest should be present at the marriage. Aiming to reduce arguments over invalid or disputed marriages, ecclesiastical authorities increasingly proclaimed that marriage should be public, 'in the presence of the church', and numerous warnings were issued against priests who officiated at clandestine weddings. Even so, clandestine marriages continued to be regarded as valid until the council of Trent in the sixteenth century, and would even be upheld over subsequent marriages in church. Parties testified that marriages frequently occurred where the moment might seize them. A variety of such places were mentioned in the course of litigation in later medieval England: under an ash tree, in a bed, in a garden, in a small storehouse, in a field ... in a blacksmith's shop, near a hedge, in a kitchen, by an oak tree, at a tavern, near the king's highway, as various parties testified (Helmholz, 1974, pp. 29 and 49).

While many tried to follow the church's directives, and indeed often demonstrated a complex understanding of their requirements, they were also willing to defy them when they proved too inconvenient. Clarification was generally the goal of the ecclesiastical authorities. But where correction was desired, penalties for fornication were usually fines, and efforts were made to regularize long-term living arrangements into marriage. If the partners proved unwilling to marry, they were abjured to separate, under the understanding that future sexual relations would themselves constitute marriage. In short, both ecclesiastics and laity generally sought to steer a judicial course through the difficulties of marriage, and while the church tried to call attention to moral discipline, it primarily defined its role as arbiter of individual claims and of communal complaints against long-term or scandalous abuses.

The final sacrament pertaining to the laity was *last anointing* (extreme unction). It had emerged as a distinct sacrament only in the ninth century and although highly recommended by writers and councils, it was never regarded as obligatory or as necessary for salvation. Practice appears to have varied. The rite seems to have been almost unknown in upper Ariège, France, in the early fourteenth century; and there is evidence of resistance to it in some regions, though not in others such as Flanders. In England, from the mid-thirteenth century onwards, church authorities are recorded as both urging the laity to act with reverence when the host was being carried in procession to the sick, and impressing upon priests the duty to attend, even in the middle of the night, when called to a sick person – last anointing was commonly accompanied by reception of communion. While the church tried to foster the call for extreme unction, enforcement was directed more at the clergy than at the laity, to ensure that when the sacrament was requested it would be forthcoming.

Minimal requirements: tithes; Sundays and feastdays; fasting and abstinence

Canon 54 of the fourth Lateran council stated that *tithes* – that is, payment normally to one's parish church of a tenth of income or produce – took precedence over all other financial impositions, 'since the Lord has reserved tithes unto himself as a sign of his universal lordship'. Tithes may have been the most intrusive and onerous non-sacramental obligation imposed upon the laity by the Church. Mentioned frequently in various forms in the Old Testament, the payment of tithes had become an obligation for Christians during the early Middle Ages. The obligation was backed by severe penalties, both spiritual and civil. Evidence regarding the extent to which paying tithes was accepted or opposed by the laity is somewhat mixed. Many tithes had fallen into lay hands in the early Middle Ages, as lay people established themselves as patrons of parish churches. Despite attempts of reform movements of the eleventh century onwards to wrest them back to the Church, in many regions of Europe the laity remained closely involved in the system in the later Middle Ages both as possessors of tithes and as collection agents for the Church. As a result, some of the opposition to the payment of tithes was to lay people profiting from the system. Disputes often concerned the rights to receive revenues, and how the sums of money and produce should be calculated, rather than to the principle of payment. As

Richard Helmholz and William Pantin, wrote succinctly, 'there was never a golden age of obedient tithing', and 'it must have required the tact of a saint to make the system run smoothly' (Helmholz, 1974, p. 434; Pantin, 1955, p. 204). Some compromise was required of all parties.

There is some evidence that resistance to the payment of tithes was increasing towards the end of the Middle Ages. In Italy, the towns of Parma, Bologna, and Reggio openly revolted against their payment, while other towns passed legislation that limited the powers of tithe-owners. However, these do not seem to have been revolts about the concept or principle of tithes; rather they were directed against the local lay magnates who collected the tithes or against the wealth of Cathedral chapters in receipt of them. Where there were clashes over payment, the laity were frequently arguing for a return to a stricter and more evangelical, less temporal, use of the tithe. The citizens of Bologna preferred to pay their tithes directly to the poor, while those of Reggio agreed that no one 'was to be compelled to pay tithes in the future except as his conscience dictated ... but that they were still binding upon believers as part of the divine law'. In England, of 140 parishes inspected during a visitation of Salisbury diocese, only seven produced cases of non-payment of tithes. In the same country, a degree of flexibility is indicated by testamentary bequests to parish churches 'for unpaid tithes', which became common in wills in the late Middle Ages. In late-fifteenth century Norwich, for example, prosecutions for non-payment of tithes were rare, yet testamentary bequests 'for unpaid tithes' were common, although the amount of money was usually nominal. The device suggests that citizens had practised in life a measure of freedom in calculating their payments. Importantly and more positively, many people surely appreciated that the parochial system, which they generally supported, depended upon the payment of tithes.

The obligation to abstain from work on *Sundays and feast-days* also developed from biblical precedent. The early Church had been cautious about transferring observance of the Old Testament Sabbath to the Christian Sunday, but the prescription was recognized gradually, finding its way into the emperor Justinian's *Corpus Iuris Civilis* (*Codex*, 3.2), pope Gregory IX's *Decretalia* (2.9.1), and other legislation. By the thirteenth century, the obligation was far-reaching, encompassing all Sundays and almost the same number of feast-days. The legislation prohibited 'servile' work, a category that was difficult to define. It had originally meant activities that made the doer a slave (*servus*) to sin and by extension it became work that was prone to involve sin, principally work for earthly gain, or was proper to slaves or servants, namely manual work. In a ruling subsequently incorporated into the *Decretalia* (2.9.3), pope Alexander III (1159–81) had exempted necessary labour – to protect crops, for example, or to catch fish during a limited fishing season – and the canonical interpretation of 'necessary' subsequently became relatively broad. Legislation not only allowed the purchase of necessary food and drink but was relatively indulgent towards recreation and amusements on Sundays and feast-days.

Failure to abstain from work on prescribed days appears as a charge at various parochial visitations in the late-fourteenth and fifteenth centuries. In England, it occurred in visitations in the diocese of Lincoln, and more prominently in the dioceses of Canterbury, where butchers were notable offenders, and Hereford. In Flanders, it seems, frivolity and licentiousness, not work, were the problem; the obligation to abstain from work became a serious problem only when there were particularly inquisitive authorities. Feast-days, indeed, seem to have been generally welcomed by villeins and labourers who pushed for additional days and even celebration on the vigils of feasts; landlords and sometimes synodal legislation may have worked instead to limit the number of days applicable. Such holidays were welcome at least in part, and a certain laxity about definition meant that it was commonly only the most openly and repeatedly dissident who were prosecuted.

Regarding *fasting and abstinence*, lack of biblical precedent could render the obligations problematic. Christ had surpassed Old Testament prescriptions and declared all foods clean (Mark 7.14–19). Nevertheless, fasting and abstinence assumed a major role in the asceticism of the early Church and this continued to be the case throughout the Middle Ages. The legislation appears formidable. There were considerable regional variations, but the basic minimum was fasting on the weekdays of Lent, the twelve Ember days, and the vigils of major feasts, and abstaining from meat on these fast-days and on all Fridays except those falling on major feast-days. In theory, infringement might incur excommunication. There were, however, a wide range of official exemptions and, increasingly, a general relaxation in interpretation and practice. Fasting had originally meant only one meal a day, but this meal was brought forward from the evening to midday or the afternoon and a light evening meal, or 'collation', was permitted. Many were exempted from even this legislation: the old and the infirm, those not yet adults, and in cases of necessity. The last category might be interpreted quite widely to include travellers and even all those who performed manual work.

The reception of this legislation remains a matter of debate. Toussaert (1960, pp. 428–34) considered that the obligation, at least in late-medieval Flanders, was genuinely popular. He thought it fitted the popular mentality, particularly the idea that fasting was the wages of sin, and was appreciated both as healthy in balancing large-scale eating at other times and as enabling the conservation of meat and other foods in short supply. His assessment may be overly optimistic, and may be less applicable to the countryside than to towns. Even so, the legislation may not have been as disruptive as it initially appears. Records of parochial visitations in England suggest accusations in the matter were rare. No cases were mentioned at the extensive visitation of Hereford diocese in 1397, and only one case at the later visitations of Lincoln diocese, apparently due to the curate forgetting to remind his parishioners about an Ember day. Fast-breaking could be used to identify heretics and the charge was brought against suspected Lollards. Behaviour in these cases was allegedly more provocative: assertive attacks on fasting, sometimes in the form of shared ritual meals where meat was consumed, and active denials that fasting was an obligation. Flexibility within the legislation regarding fasting and abstinence and some measure of sympathy for its aims probably rendered the obligations tolerable for most people, and the indications are that church authorities troubled to prosecute only blatant or persistent offenders or those who were also suspect on other grounds.

Optional devotions

Beyond the basic requirements, there existed a wide range of religious activities open to lay men and women, who enjoyed a good measure of choice regarding them. This section, accordingly, outlines the participation of the laity in many of the religious devotions and lifestyles that were open to and indeed, in large measure, created by them. Others are discussed elsewhere, principally in section iv 'Religious orders and beguines' and section vi 'Liturgy, prayer and mysticism'.

This will be the approach, though it should be remembered that to begin by focusing on particular activities is somewhat misleading. Life was more in the round and integrated than today, so that religion was part of life rather than a compartment of it. In principle, therefore, it might be better to begin with life as a whole, which for most people was influenced by Christianity at almost every turn, and then to see particular religious activities as intensifications within this general context. The final section of the chapter, 'Relaxation sport and enjoyment', will attempt this more holistic approach, by looking at some areas of life which today would be considered largely separate from religion but in the Middle Ages were regarded as integral parts of it.

Eucharist. Two basic duties regarding the Eucharist – receiving communion at least once a year and attending Mass on Sundays and feastdays – have been outlined. Receiving communion remained a rare occurrence for most laypeople during the Middle Ages. Few of them, it seems, received communion more than three or four times a year, while only the very devout approached the sacrament weekly or in rare cases – such as Catherine of Siena or Margery Kempe of Lynn in England – daily. A sense of modesty and unworthiness prevailed: daily communion for the laity became common only with its recommendation by pope Pius X in the early twentieth century.

Eucharistic devotion centred upon belief in Christ's presence in the eucharistic bread; a strong interpretation of the words spoken by Christ over the bread, 'This is my body'. Two events in the thirteenth century gave momentum to the development. First, the fourth Lateran council in 1215 formulated the doctrine of 'transubstantiation': that in the Mass the bread and wine are changed (Latin *transubstantiatis*, changed in substance) into the body and blood of Christ. Secondly, pope Urban IV in 1265 established the feast of 'Corpus Christi' (Latin for 'the body of Christ'), which celebrated Christ's presence in the Eucharist and was to be observed annually throughout the western Church. Through these and other official declarations, as well as much popular devotion, the eucharistic bread, in which Christ was believed to be truly present, came to be preserved in a tabernacle or hanging pyx – situated in a clearly visible location in the church – for adoration and prayer by the people, as well as to be carried in procession on the feast of Corpus Christi and on other occasions.

Participation at Mass on weekdays, when attendance was voluntary, was a popular and widespread form of eucharistic devotion. Such participation both expressed gratitude for God's generosity – the word 'Eucharist' means 'thanksgiving' – and brought to the individual an abundance of divine grace. It was also a means of promoting community and healing divisions.

Chantries – the 'chanting' (singing) or at least 'saying' of masses principally to mitigate the sufferings of people in purgatory – were a well established institution by 1300 and they grew in size and complexity in the later Middle Ages. They ranged from a priest celebrating a limited number of Masses to a sizeable college of clergy. The priest's principal duty was to say Mass daily for the benefactor (in life and after death) and usually for other people, principally the deceased, such as family members and friends and other individuals to whom the founder felt indebted, often too for 'all the faithful departed' who were still detained in purgatory. Chantries combined prudent self-interest with generosity towards others, a rich sense of the communion of the faithful. While they required clergy to celebrate the Masses, most of the initiative in founding and organizing them came from the laity. They formed a prominent and imaginative feature of lay piety. Wills provide plenty of evidence of testators establishing small-scale chantries for a certain number of Masses. Chantry chapels, which survive today inside many cathedrals and parish churches, attest to 'perpetual chantries', for which the benefactor gave money or property to provide for a succession of priests to say daily Mass 'in perpetuity'. All Souls College in Oxford represents the top end of the scale. It was founded by the archbishop of Canterbury in 1438 for forty priests, with the dual purpose of their offering Mass and praying for the souls of king Henry V and the Englishmen who had died in the wars in France, and their forming an academic institution.

Eucharistic processions, around the streets and squares of a parish or town, led by a bishop or priest carrying the Eucharist (the consecrated host), were a notable feature of late medieval piety. They followed directly from the establishment of the feast of Corpus Christi in 1265 and were held principally on this feast-day, which was kept in the early summer (on the Thursday following Trinity Sunday). Sometimes the procession was organized by the parish, sometimes by the local monastery or friary, sometimes by a lay confraternity or craft guild. The initiative and support of the laity was crucial to the event. The painting by Gentile Bellini (1429–1507) of the Corpus Christi procession around Piazza San Marco in Venice, replete with both laity and clergy, brings to life this dimension of eucharistic devotion at the end of the Middle Ages.

Pilgrimages. Jerusalem, the site of Christ's passion, death and resurrection, remained the archetypal focus for Christian pilgrimage. The city was under Muslim control throughout this period except for a short time following the successful first crusade in 1098, yet many pilgrims made the difficult journey to this supreme location for Christian devotion. Margery Kempe, who journeyed from England in the early fifteenth century, described her feelings thus, as well as the good treatment she received from the Muslim inhabitants:

> *And so we proceeded into the Holy Land until we could see Jerusalem. And when I saw it – riding, as I was, on the back of an ass – I thanked God with all my heart; and I prayed that just as he had brought me to see this earthly city of Jerusalem so, of his mercy, he would give me the grace to see the city of Jerusalem on high, the city of heaven ... I was full of holy thoughts and meditation, full of devout contemplation of our lord Jesus Christ's passion, full of the holy intimations that our lord Jesus Christ made to my soul – so much so that I could never put these things into words once they were over, for they were so high and holy. Great was the grace which our Lord showed towards me during my three weeks in Jerusalem ... Afterwards I rode to Bethlehem on an ass, and when I came to the church of the Nativity I went inside to see the crib where our Lord was born. I was overcome with deep devotion and I received many words and intimations in my soul and a great sense of inner consolation ... The Saracens also feted me, they escorted me and guided me to all the places I wanted to visit throughout the country, and I found everyone good and kind*

to me except my own countrymen. (*Book of Margery Kempe*, chapters 28–30)

Pietro Casola, canon of Milan cathedral, wrote a detailed account of his pilgrimage to Jerusalem in 1494, when he was approaching seventy years of age. The warm send-off he received illustrates the popular support for pilgrimage on the part of both laity and clergy:

> *I begged his most reverend Lordship (the archbishop of Milan) to bless the emblems of my pilgrimage – that is, the cross, the stick or pilgrim's staff, and the wallet – and to bestow his blessing on me, according to the order and the ancient institution to be found written in the Pastoral ... When the benediction was over, his Lordship embraced me with no ordinary tears, and kissing me most affectionately, he left me with the peace of God, surrounded by a great crowd, from which I had some difficulty in separating myself, for everyone wanted to shake hands with me and kiss me.* (Newett 1907, p.117)

Rome and Compostella were the two other pre-eminent destinations for pilgrims of the western Church. The first ever 'jubilee' for Rome was declared for the year 1300 by pope Boniface VIII. Huge numbers of pilgrims flocked to the city to gain the plenary indulgence – remission of all the punishment still due for forgiven sins – offered by the pope to those who visited St Peter's and other principal churches in the city. Thereafter jubilee years were proclaimed at diminishing intervals of fifty, thirty-three and twenty-five years, for which large numbers of pilgrims came, though never again quite on the scale of 1300. Even outside these special years, Rome was a major centre of pilgrimage. The surviving records of St Thomas's Hospice (now the Venerable English College), which gave lodging to English pilgrims in Rome, listed an average of some two hundred pilgrims a year between 1479 and 1514: substantial numbers for a medium-sized country distant from Rome. The shrine of the apostle James at Compostella in Spain remained a major centre for pilgrimage throughout the Middle Ages, though the Black Death and the long papal schism, as well as other difficulties both within and beyond the town of Compostella, adversely affected the number of pilgrims during the fourteenth and fifteenth centuries.

Geoffrey Chaucer immortalized pilgrimages to the shrine of Thomas Becket in his *Canterbury Tales*. Laity, clergy and nuns were pilgrims together. Wills of the inhabitants of late medieval Norwich provide other graphic examples from England. Thomas Oudolff, priest of the city, instructed his executors to hire two men to make pilgrimages to local shrines in atonement for his sins: one was to go barefoot to Our Lady of Walsingham, the other 'naked in his shirt' to the Holy Rood at Beccles. In 1429 Robert Baxter, former mayor of Norwich, bequeathed the large sum of £40 (multiply by a thousand or more for the value today) to Richard Ferneys, who lived as a hermit in the city, 'to make a pilgrimage for me to Rome, going round there fifteen times in a great circle, and also to Jerusalem, doing in both places as a true pilgrim does'. Equally ambitious, Edmund Brown, a wealthy merchant of the city who made his will in 1446, instructed his executors to hire three men to make pilgrimages on his behalf: one was to go on foot to the shrine of Thomas Becket at Canterbury, another was to make a pilgrimage to Saint James of Compostella during the next 'year of grace', and the third was to travel 'to Zeeland or beyond, over the sea, to the pilgrimage of the blood of our Lord Jesus Christ, called the Holy Blood of Wihenhak' – probably the shrine at Wilsnack in Germany (Tanner, 1984, pp. 62, 87).

There was, however, the other side of the coin. Pilgrimages were widely condemned by English Lollards; John Hus particularly condemned those to the shrine at Wilsnack in Germany. Many of the orthodox, too, had their reservations. Thomas à Kempis had these sharp words in *De Imitatione Christi* (Imitation of Christ): 'They that go much on pilgrimage seldom grow in sanctity' (Book 1, chapter 23); 'Many run to sundry places to visit the shrines of the saints ... Often such pilgrims are moved by human curiosity and the quest for novelty, and carry home with them small fruit of amendment, especially when they run so gaily from place to place without true contrition' (Book 4, chapter 1).

Craft guilds and pious confraternities. These organizations made an important and varied contribution to popular religion, mainly in the towns and principally during the later Middle Ages. In their group activities, the communal aspect of medieval religion was realized, also the appeal to the senses. The members of each craft or trade in a town – especially in the larger towns – would organize themselves into a 'guild' (usually called a craft guild) which had a variety of responsibilities for the economic, social, political and religious arrangement of the craft or trade. Or groups of like-minded people within a parish, or associated with a friary or other religious house, would form a confraternity for the purposes of prayer and various religious and charitable activities that went beyond what the parish could offer. Both craft guilds and pious confraternities depended upon the clergy: they needed them for the conduct of their religious services, especially the Mass, and in other ways. Nevertheless, guilds and confraternities were essentially lay-driven: control was largely in the hands of the laity and their concerns were paramount.

For craft guilds, a key event was the annual 'guild day'. It was usually held on the feast-day of the saint, or the event in Christ's life (birth, resurrection, ascension, etc.), to which the guild was dedicated. Celebrations normally consisted of a mixture of religious activities, principally Mass for all the living and deceased members of the guild, and a meal together. In addition, all the guilds of a town might come together on one or more days in the year for a joint celebration, a mixture of religious and social activities: a procession through the town, with the members of each guild often dressed in the livery of the guild, followed by Mass or other religious service, and a communal meal. The distinction between 'religious' and 'social' was much less obvious than today; the two dimensions blended into each other. Guilds were normally responsible, too, for providing charitable assistance to members in need. Many of the larger and grander guilds owned their own guild-hall – some still to be seen today, notably in the Low Countries – which provided a centre for the guild's social, religious and charitable activities.

Mystery plays were special features of craft guilds in late medieval England. Cycles of between a dozen and fifty plays, based on the 'mysteries' (events) described in the Old and New Testaments, survive for half a dozen towns, including York, Coventry, Chester and Norwich. All the plays were normally staged on a particular day, usually the feast of Corpus Christi, each one performed by the members of a single guild, or of several guilds together, and often staged on a cart or moveable float, so that the same play would be performed in several places while making, as reported of the Norwich cycle, 'a great circuit of the city'. Plays based on Christ's passion and on the lives of saints survive for other countries, notably France, but organizationally they appear to have been linked with cathedrals or monasteries rather than with craft guilds.

Pious confraternities were more consciously religious bodies than craft guilds, more private too, for the most part. They responded to the particular needs of groups of people within a parish or locality, rather than being based on a craft or trade. Their purpose was more directly the religious growth of their members and they reached out to others through prayer and works of charity. They normally lacked the clear economic functions of craft guilds, though some were socially conscious so that membership was confined to a particular group in society. Some confraternities were linked closely to the town government, with membership more or less restricted to the governing body. Indeed, the distinction between craft guilds and pious confraternities was sometimes blurred, both as terms and in reality: there was a measure of overlap between the two.

Flagellant confraternities were specially popular in Italy. The flagellant movement, in which groups of men, usually hooded and in procession, would scourge themselves in public, came to the fore in central and northern Italy in the second half of the thirteenth century, as a penitential response, aimed at averting the divine anger, to wars and famines in the region as well as to the prophecies of Joachim of Fiore regarding the imminent end of the world. The movement spread across the Alps to France, Germany and the Low Countries and received new impetus from the horrors of the Black Death plague beginning in 1347. Pope Clement VI in 1349 called for the suppression of the movement, but in Italy and some other regions it was allowed to continue within the more regulated framework of officially authorized flagellant confraternities.

Guilds and confraternities varied greatly in size and complexity. They ranged from large, powerful and public institutions in major cities to small confraternities attached to parish churches in the countryside. However, the key fact remains that these institutions, in their various forms, enjoyed exceptional popularity in the later Middle Ages and were vigorous expressions of lay Christianity. Significantly, they were not abolished in the sixteenth century. Many Protestant reformers recognized their importance and sought to transform rather than to abolish them: the Catholic

Counter-Reformation valued them while endeavouring to order them more correctly.

Relaxation, sport and enjoyment

To understand religion in the medieval West, it is essential to appreciate the attitudes of Christians of the time to relaxation and enjoyment. So far this section has focused on particular religious activities, but these individual activities must be considered within the wider, more holistic context of life as a whole. Some relaxation and enjoyment was seen as an essential part of a well balanced life, and therefore as both a religious duty and an integral part of Christianity. The present short section tries, accordingly, to look at various features of the broader context. It must be complemented by the discussion of art and music in section vii. There were, too, aspects of relaxation and enjoyment, both individual and communitarian, in many of the religious activities that are treated elsewhere: prayer, as in both individual and community prayer as well as mystical prayer; singing, as in the liturgy; social gatherings, as at Sunday Mass and within religious communities; pilgrimages; various activities of craft guilds and pious confraternities; and others.

Thomas Aquinas, writing in the mid-thirteenth century, confronted recreation in his discussion of 'Good manners', which comes in *Summa Theologiae*, 2.2, question 168. In article 2 of this question, he asks 'whether there can be virtue in the acts we do in play'. The argument of the early Christian writer John Chrysostom, that 'the devil, not God, sends us to sport', he counters by asserting that it refers to people who play inordinately and especially those who make amusement their main purpose in life. Augustine of Hippo's counsel is quoted with more approval: 'Spare yourself I pray, for it befits a wise person to relax at times and soften the edge of attention.' Then speaking his own mind Aquinas says: 'Man must rest his body for physical refreshment because he cannot work without intermission.' He proceeds to quote with approval from the fourth century *Conferences* of abbot Cassian:

> It is related of blessed John the Evangelist that when people were scandalized at finding him at play with his disciples, he

requested one of his questioners who carried a bow to shoot an arrow. When this had been done several times, the man, on being asked whether he could keep on doing so continuously, replied that the bow would break. Whereupon the blessed John pointed the moral that so, too, would the human spirit snap were it never unbent.

Aquinas's approval of relaxation, so far, may seem to be somewhat grudging, a concession to human weakness rather than approval, and to have in mind intellectual more than physical relaxation. The concessionary nature is emphasized in the next article 3, entitled 'Of the sin of playing too much', where the limits of lawful sport are pointed out. However in the final article 4, entitled 'Of the sin of playing too little', a more positive note is struck.

It is against reason for someone to be burdensome to others, by never showing himself agreeable to others or being a kill-joy or wet blanket on their enjoyment. And so Seneca says: 'Bear yourself with wit, lest you be regarded as sour or despised as dull.' Now those who lack playfulness are sinful, those who never say anything to make you smile, or are grumpy with those who do, Aristotle speaks of them as rough and boorish.

An extensive and more theoretical treatment of enjoyment (Latin *fruitio*) is to be found in Part 2.1, question 11, of the same *Summa*.

Some moral theologians in the Middle Ages may appear excessively negative towards recreation and relaxation, the 'kill-joys' censured by Aquinas, harping on dangers rather than positive merits. But the reality may have been that people were so fond of sport that they needed some check, some direction to their energies, which the clergy tried to provide.

One area in which the clergy were stout defenders of relaxation was their defence of Sundays and feast-days. Fifty-two Sundays and about the same number of feast-days each year were exempt from work, as mentioned earlier, largely thanks to legislation initiated by the Church. It is true that a primary purpose of the legislation was to provide people with the opportunity to attend Mass, but even rigorists did not expect people to spend the whole day in church or at prayer. So the Church's protection of proper human rest and leisure should be acknowledged: a fight for justice, too, defending the vulnerable from exploitation of their work.

In the types of sports engaged in, attention was given to the whole person and thereby – usually more implicitly than explicitly – respect for the mysteries of Creation and Incarnation. Teresa McLean (McLean, 1983) gave the following titles to the eight chapters in her book *The English at Play in the Middle Ages*: Out of Doors; Animal Sports, Hunting and Fishing; Tournaments, Jousts and Tilts; Outdoor, House and Garden Games; Board, Table; Glee, Medieval Music, Singing and Dancing; Medieval Drama; Folk Games. The titles give some idea of the broad range of play and recreation. Much the same would have been true for the rest of medieval Europe as for England, though certainly there were local and regional variations, depending on climate and temperament. Play and games were part of the fabric of life.

The violence involved in many of these activities may horrify us today, yet it was an essential dimension. Partly the activities were forms of semi-institutionalized violence, safety-valves for competitiveness and aggressive drives for which any society is wise to provide some outlets, partly they embraced some useful purpose. People ate meat and fish, so hunting, hawking and fishing made sense. War was part of the fabric of life, people had to defend themselves: so tournaments, jousts and tilts made sense. There was some gratuitous cruelty to animals, as in bear-baiting or cock-fighting, but people were generally tolerant of each others' views in these matters and reluctant to impose their own political correctness upon others.

Most people lived in close proximity with animals. Farm animals, as well as domestic pets, lived under the same roof, often in the same room, as humans. An I–Thou relationship, not of equality but still of some intimacy and understanding, was reached with them. A wide variety of animals – not just dogs and horses – seem to have understood human beings and their needs, in a sense to have loved them even sometimes to the extent of sacrificing themselves for them. Human beings did not reciprocate with the same tenderness and self-sacrifice, to be sure, but at least they gave many animals the pleasure of living with them and sharing in their life, as is well portrayed in much of medieval art, brilliantly by Pieter Bruegel, a little later in the sixteenth century, in 'The Hunters in the Snow'. Much of medieval sport is intelligible only in terms of animals.

In many ways, therefore, sport and recreation pointed to fundamental mysteries of the Christian message: creation, including that of the animal kingdom; the fall of humankind; the Incarnation; the need for human endeavour as well as for relaxation and enjoyment; the mysteries of pain and suffering; the parousia.

The archetypal recreation, in the literal sense of re-creation, was sexual intercourse. Not only was sexual intercourse considered an eminent form of recreation, and in a sense sport, other forms of relaxation and recreation were seen in terms of it. The point would have been taken more or less for granted, without any embarrassment or prudishness, thus revealing a proper respect for both sex and sport. The point is underlined by the way in which the spiritual life, or relationship with God, was also seen in sexual terms. Many writers of the period expressed themselves in such categories, most notably the 'love mysticism' of the beguines Hadewijch and Margaret Porete and the 'spiritual espousals' of Jan van Ruysbroec. This appreciation, too, helps to explain why celibacy was valued by the Church. For, however much married life was valued and enjoyed, celibacy gave a special entry into that still higher state, indeed was a foretaste of it, the very enjoyment (*fruitio*) of God, the Beatific Vision.

iii. Popes, councils and princes

We have already encountered pope Leo IX, whose bull of excommunication initiated the schism between Rome and Constantinople in 1054. He was the first of a series of reform-minded popes in the second half of the eleventh century. At the centre of this reform was the desire to wrest the Church from lay control: especially, to make sure that suitable men were appointed as bishops and parish priests, rather than kings and local lords selecting their relatives and friends, or their loyal officers, for these posts. There was quite widespread conviction, especially in Rome, that only the papacy had sufficient authority to confront powerful secular rulers and to carry out the necessary reforms. The strengthening of papal authority thus became central to the reform movement, but it affected many relationships besides those with lay rulers. One of them was relations with the Orthodox church and the resulting friction partly caused the schism in 1054.

Gregory VII

The most determined of these reform-minded popes was Gregory VII (1073–84). Indeed, the whole movement is usually called after him alone, the 'Gregorian Reform'. He clashed with the German emperor Henry IV on a range of issues, but principally over the appointment of bishops and abbots within the emperor's dominions. Henry eventually backed down and did penance before Gregory outside the castle of Canossa in northern Italy, where the pope was staying at the time. Henry's enmity later rekindled and Gregory died in exile from Rome at Salerno. Nevertheless, Gregory's firm actions remained a benchmark for the papacy for a long time, in some respects until today.

The clearest statement of pope Gregory's thought comes, perhaps, in the so-called *Dictatus Papae*. This famous document, which consists of a list of twenty-seven headings, was written into the papal Register, surely on Gregory's instructions. It therefore carries weight, and is indicative of his mind, even though it was never promulgated as law, and it has much influenced subsequent interpretations of the medieval papacy. It reads as follows:

1. The Roman church was founded by God alone.
2. The Roman pontiff (pope) alone is rightly called universal.
3. He alone can depose or reinstate bishops.
4. His legate, even if of lower grade, takes precedence in a council over all the bishops and may render a sentence of deposition against them.
5. The pope may depose the absent.
6. People ought not to stay in the same house with those excommunicated by him.
7. For him alone is it lawful to enact new laws according to the needs of the time.
8. He alone may use the imperial insignia.
9. The pope is the only person whose feet are to be kissed by all princes.
10. His name alone is to be recited in churches.
11. His title is unique in the world.

12. He may depose emperors.
13. He may transfer bishops, if necessary, from one see to another.
14. He has the power to ordain a cleric of any church he may wish.
15. The person ordained by him may rule over another church ...
16. No council may be regarded as a general council without his order.
17. No chapter or book may be regarded as canonical without his authority.
18. No sentence of his may be retracted by anyone: he alone can retract it.
19. He himself may be judged by nobody.
20. Nobody shall dare to condemn a person who appeals to the apostolic see (papacy).
21. To this see the more important cases of every church should be submitted.
22. The Roman church has never erred, nor shall, by the witness of Scripture, ever err to all eternity.
23. The Roman pontiff, if canonically elected, is undoubtedly sanctified by the merits of St Peter.
24. By his order and with his permission, subordinate persons may bring accusations.
25. Without convening a synod, he can depose and reinstate bishops.
26. Nobody should be considered as Catholic who is not in conformity with the Roman church.
27. The pope may absolve subjects of unjust men from their fealty (loyalty).

Twelfth century

Subsequent popes varied between those who followed the firm attitude of Gregory VII and those who sought a more conciliatory approach. Following the latter approach, a key agreement was the Concordat of Worms, which was reached between pope Calixtus II and the emperor Henry V and was sealed in the city of Worms in Germany in 1122. The concordat concerned the 'investiture' (appointment) of bishops and abbots within the empire – a matter of concern to both emperor and pope since many bishoprics and abbeys were wealthy institutions and their heads exercised considerable social and political authority in addition to their directly religious duties. Both clergy and laity were very much part of the same Church, so it is better to see the conflict as one between two authorities within the Church, lay and clerical, rather than like Church–State relations today, where the majority of state authorities may be non-Christians and, as a result, the two entities – Church and State – are clearly distinct.

By the Concordat, the pope conceded that the election of bishops and abbots within Germany should be conducted in the presence of the emperor or his officer, though 'without simony and violence', and 'if any dispute arises between the parties concerned, you (the emperor), with the counsel or judgement of the metropolitan and bishops of the province, shall give consent and aid to the party which has the more right'. The pope also conceded that the man elected should receive from the emperor the 'regalia and sceptre' (symbols of temporal and political authority) and should 'perform his lawful duties' to the emperor. In return, the emperor surrendered to the church authorities 'all investiture through ring and crozier' (symbols of spiritual authority), and he acknowledged that there should be 'canonical election and free consecration' (therefore without political interference) of bishops and abbots throughout his empire.

Not surprisingly, similar tensions existed in other countries of western Christendom and sporadically burst into the open. The quarrel between king Henry II of England and Thomas Becket, archbishop of Canterbury, was one such classic case, which climaxed with Becket's martyrdom in Canterbury cathedral in 1170, at the prompting of the king. In this case the pope, Alexander III, though supporting Becket's grievances against king Henry, generally tried to act as peace-maker between the two men.

Papal concern for the improvement of Christian life showed itself in six reforming councils which popes summoned and presided over during the twelfth and thirteenth centuries. Four of these general councils of the western Church were held in the Lateran palace, the pope's principal residence in Rome: Lateran I in 1123, Lateran II in 1138, Lateran III in 1189 and Lateran IV in 1215. Two more were held in Lyons in southern France, Lyons I in 1245 and Lyons II in 1274.

Lateran IV

The best known and most comprehensive of the six councils was Lateran IV, which was convoked by the energetic pope Innocent III. Its seventy-one decrees mainly concerned practical rather than doctrinal issues. References to the decrees are scattered throughout this chapter and indicate the wide-ranging scope of the legislation: on transubstantiation and the sacraments in the previous section; on religious orders, the crusades and heresy in later sections. Concern for the Christian faith crossed over into intolerance regarding heretics (canon 3), Jews (canons 67–70) and Muslims (canon 71). Yet zeal for improvement in the morals and education of both laity and clergy, and practical proposals to realize these ideals, lie at the heart of the legislation.

This zeal for moral and educational improvement, and attention to detail, are well summarized in canons 10 'On appointing preachers' and 11 'On schoolmasters'. Having noted that 'for the salvation of the Christian people, the nourishment of the word of God is specially necessary', canon 10 ordered that 'bishops are to appoint suitable men to carry out with profit this duty of sacred preaching, men who are powerful in word and need, and who will visit with care the people entrusted to them … and will build them up by word and example'. Canon 11 provided for a range of educational facilities: instruction 'without payment' for clerics and 'other poor scholars' in each cathedral and, if possible, in other churches as well as provision for a 'theologian to teach Scripture to priests and others and especially to instruct them in matters pertaining to the care of souls' in the cathedral of the archbishop.

Boniface VIII

The initiative of pope Boniface VIII (1294–1303) in instituting the first 'Holy Year' in 1300 has been mentioned. His reign, however, was clouded by a bitter dispute with the king of France, Philip IV 'le Bel' (the Fair). The pope attempted to restrict the king's right to tax the clergy of France, thereby potentially cutting off a very important source of royal income. Philip replied by stopping the movement of gold and valuables to Rome and by other threatening measures. Boniface responded in 1302 with the famous bull *Unam sanctam*, which declared in the strongest terms the teaching already indicated in Gregory VII's *Dictatus Papae*, the supremacy of the 'spiritual' over the 'temporal' sword. The bull also contained a strong statement about the impossibility of salvation outside the Church, teaching that Vatican II struggled to reinterpret. The key passages read as follows:

> *We are obliged by the faith to believe and hold that there is one holy, catholic and apostolic Church, and that outside this Church there is neither salvation nor remission of sins ... Of this one and only Church there is one body and one head – not two heads, like a monster – namely Christ, and Christ's vicar is Peter and Peter's successor ... And we learn from the words of the Gospel that in this Church and in her power there are two swords, the spiritual and the temporal. For when the apostle Peter said 'Behold, here, there are two swords', the Lord did not reply 'It is too much', but 'It is enough' (Luke 22.38). Both swords are in the power of the Church, but the material sword is to be used for the Church, the spiritual sword by the Church: the former by the priest, the latter by kings and captain but at the will and by permission of the priest. One sword, then, should be under the other, and temporal authority subject to the spiritual ... Furthermore we declare, state, define and pronounce that it is altogether necessary for salvation for every human creature to be subject to the Roman pontiff.*

Pope Boniface's reign ended in tragedy. Angered by the pope's various measures, king Philip sent a band of soldiers to arrest him at Anagni to the south of Rome, where he was staying, with the intention of bringing him to trial. The soldiers seized and imprisoned the pope, but though he was soon released by Italian troops, he died within a month back at Rome, a broken man. Reaction then set in against Boniface's memory. Many in the French church were already unhappy with his policies and he had alienated elements within the Italian church, notably the powerful Colonna family who were represented by two brother cardinals. He was held responsible, too, for persuading his saintly predecessor Celestine V to resign in 1294, thereby preparing the way for his own election.

Avignon papacy

Boniface's successor, Benedict XI, lasted less than a year. The cardinals who met in Perugia in northern Italy to elect the next pope were divided between those who supported the firm policies of Boniface and those who wanted rapprochement with the French king, who was the most powerful monarch in Christendom. Eventually after eleven months of bitter debate, the latter group emerged triumphant. Bernard de Got, who was archbishop of Bordeaux in southern France and on relatively good terms with Philip the Fair, gained the necessary two-thirds majority and chose the name Clement V. Almost immediately he moved to France and was crowned pope at Lyons in November 1305. After stays in various places in southern France, he settled with the papal Curia in 1309, at king Philip's request, in Avignon.

Avignon made some sense. The city was a papal 'fief' (property owned by the papacy) and was more secure – helped by the protection of the king of France – than the unruly city of Rome. With the Muslim conquest of the eastern Mediterranean world and north Africa, Rome lay on the edges of western Christendom while Avignon was geographically more central. The exaltation of papal power from Gregory VII onwards had emphasized the pope's role as head of the Church, somewhat at the expense of his title of bishop of Rome. Could not this primary role be equally well carried out, perhaps even better in the circumstances, away from Rome? From the mid-thirteenth century onwards various popes had spent long sojourns in southern France. Pope Innocent IV (1243–54) had fled from Rome in 1244 and spent the next seven years in southern France, where he presided over the first council of Lyons in 1245. Pope Gregory X came to the same city in 1274 to preside over the second council of Lyons. Several popes of the second half of the thirteenth century were Frenchmen: Urban IV (1261–4), Clement IV (1265–8) and Martin IV (1281–5). Others had studied at Paris university. Altogether the papacy had acquired a French air, interrupted by Boniface VIII, so the move to Avignon was in continuity with this trend.

The papacy soon became firmly established in Avignon. A huge palace was built, which can still be seen today remarkably intact, to accommodate the pope and his curia. All seven of the 'Avignon' popes were Frenchmen, more precisely from southern France, and most of the cardinals and other curial officials were from the same country. The overtly French atmosphere gave some offence. Criticism came notably from England, which was in the early stages of the Hundred Years War with France. Yet several of the popes strove to mediate in the war and bring it to an end. The papal curia became a model of efficiency, though there was criticism of its greed regarding the payment of fees and favouritism in the appointment to offices. Many good initiatives came from the Avignon papacy, particularly regarding the promotion of learning. Urban V (1362–70) was noted for holiness and was beatified in 1870. Nevertheless, there was widespread feeling that the pope ought to return to his proper city, Rome. Pope Urban was partly of this mind. He journeyed to Rome in 1367 and remained there for three years, before returning to Avignon in September 1370 where he died two months later. His successor, Gregory XI, was of a similar mind. Urged on by Catherine of Siena, who visited him in Avignon, he reached Rome in January 1377 but died there later in the same year.

Papal schism and conciliarism

The disputed election that followed the death of Gregory XI resulted in the longest papal schism in the history of the Church. There was pressure from the Roman populace upon the electing cardinals to choose an Italian as pope, lest if another Frenchman were chosen he would return to Avignon. But was the pressure from the crowd so great as to invalidate the election? The archbishop of Bari in Italy was eventually chosen and he took the name Urban VI. At first he was recognized as pope both by his electors and by various secular authorities. His difficult character, however, soon became apparent. According to many accounts, he was rude and insulting towards both the cardinals who had elected him and various lay dignitaries who came to visit him. At least arrogance and imbalance of mind were evident. To the issue of the possible invalidity of Urban's election, due to pressure from the Roman crowd, was now added that of his 'incapacity' for the papal office.

Within a few months almost all the cardinals had deserted Urban, declared his election invalid, and elected in his place cardinal Robert of Geneva, who took the name Clement VII. Urban managed to hold Rome and Clement was obliged to retire to Avignon, where he established an alternative curia. The resulting schism lasted for almost forty years. Europe was almost equally divided in its loyalties. France, most of Spain, and Scotland were the principal supporters of the Avignon popes; Italy from Rome northwards, England, Germany, central Europe and Scandinavia sided with the Roman popes; some countries were divided or switched loyalties. Eventually, in 1409, the two groups of cardinals, with widespread support, deserted their respective popes and called a council at Pisa in northern Italy, to attempt a resolution. The result only aggravated the situation further. Another claimant to the papacy was elected, Alexander V, while the other two popes retained a measure of support.

The deadlock was finally resolved by the *council of Constance*, which met from 1414 to 1417. The German emperor Sigismund was the principal initiator of the council – thereby imitating the practice in the early ecumenical councils which had been summoned by the eastern emperors. The summons had very widespread approval in western Christendom, including the support of most secular rulers, and the council was well attended. John XXIII, who had succeeded Alexander V in the Pisan line, initially supported the summons, expecting the council to confirm him as the true pope. But when he realized that the council was expecting his resignation along with those of the other two candidates, he fled from the council and threatened to dissolve it. In this situation of emergency, the council promulgated its decree *Haec sancta* (sometimes called *Sacrosancta*), which asserted the council's superiority over the pope and therefore its right to proceed in the present delicate situation. The crucial passage of the decree, which was approved on 6 April 1415, reads as follows:

> *This holy synod of Constance ... declares that, legitimately assembled in the Holy Spirit, constituting a general council and representing the catholic church militant, it has power immediately from Christ; and that everyone of whatever state or dignity, even papal, is bound to obey it in those matters which pertain to the faith, the eradication of the present schism and the general reform of the church of God in head and members.* (Decrees, p. 409)

Pope Gregory XII, of the Roman line, was persuaded to resign in July. John XXIII also abdicated, under pressure. Benedict XIII, of the Avignon line, adamantly refused to resign and was eventually deposed by the council. Thereby the path was cleared for a fresh election and in November 1417 Oddo Colonna was duly elected by the council and took the name Martin V. Opposition to his legitimacy was restricted to Benedict XIII, now residing in the castle of Peniscola on the Mediterranean coast of Spain, and a small band of his supporters.

The main focus of the council of Constance was on resolving the papal schism, but it treated quite a wide range of other issues. The council's condemnations of John Wyclif and John Hus are treated in section viii – conciliarism did not mean liberalism in theology or soft treatment for those condemned. Constance sought to institutionalize conciliarism through its decree *Frequens*, which ordered the regular holding of general councils.

Following the requirements of *Frequens*, a council duly met in Basel in 1431 but the newly elected pope Eugenius IV immediately showed himself hostile. A long-drawn struggle ensued and eventually Eugenius ordered the transferral of the council to Florence. The majority at Basel refused to recognize the move and so there resulted two rival councils in session at the same time, one at Basel and the other at Florence.

By this time Muslim advances were threatening the city of Constantinople, while there was renewed desire within the leadership of the Orthodox church for reunion with Rome, partly in the hope that reunion might lead to western aid for the defence of Constantinople. To discuss this reunion, the Orthodox church decided to send its delegation to Florence rather than to Basel. Although the resulting decree of reunion *Laetentur Caeli* was soon rejected by the Orthodox church, within western Christendom it was considered a triumph for pope Eugenius and it helped to take the initiative away from the council of Basel. The latter council elected in 1439 a rival pope, the pious duke of Savoy, a widower and father of five children, who took the name Felix V. This risky move reopened the prospect of papal schism, which few welcomed. The council lingered on until 1449, when it finally dissolved itself and Felix V formally resigned his claims to the papacy.

Thereafter the papacy became more openly hostile to the decrees *Haec sancta* and *Frequens*. No further general council was called until Lateran V in the early sixteenth century and pope Pius II, in the bull *Execrabilis* of 1462, condemned appeals from the pope to a general council. The papacy, however, never attempted to formally rescind the two decrees.

Renaissance papacy

The second half of the fifteenth century saw a transformation in the style of the papacy. The popes lived fairly securely in Rome. There was no serious talk of permanently moving again to Avignon or to anywhere else outside Rome. The challenge posed to papal authority by conciliarism was less menacing. The popes became somewhat identified with the Renaissance, though caution is needed here: the identification was emphasized by later historians and to some extent was their construction. The popes in question had many concerns and interests besides the promotion of art, architecture and scholarship. In many respects they were more medieval than modern or Renaissance figure. Nevertheless, most of them devoted considerable attention, for a variety of motives, to rebuilding the city of Rome and to the patronage of art and scholarship.

Nicholas V (1447–54) is usually reckoned the first of the Renaissance popes. He successfully negotiated the conclusion of the council of Basel and the resignation of pope Felix V. A scholar himself as well as patron of scholars and artists, he is considered the founder of the Vatican Library, mainly thanks to his enormous collection of some 1,200 Greek and Latin manuscripts which came to the library. He was responsible for the construction or rebuilding of numerous churches, palaces, bridges and fortifications both in Rome and elsewhere in the Papal States. He employed many artists to adorn these and other buildings, most notably Fra Angelico. He was co-founder, together with the local bishop, of the university of Glasgow. Following the fall of Constantinople in 1453, Nicholas and his successors tried to rally Christendom by calling crusades. They devoted much attention to this characteristic work of the medieval papacy, but to no avail.

Among them, *Sixtus IV* (1471–84) proclaimed a crusade when the Turks captured and held for a year the Italian city of Otranto. However, pope Sixtus was also the most noted Renaissance pope of the fifteenth century. He continued the work of Nicholas V in beautifying the city of Rome and was responsible for the elegant bridge over the Tiber that bears his name, Ponte Sisto. The Sistine

Chapel in the Vatican and its Sistine Choir remain famous today and still acknowledge his crucial contributions in art and music, by being named after him. Scholarship, too, remains in his debt thanks to his promotion of the Vatican Archives and his munificence towards the Vatican Library.

The Spaniard Rodrigo Borgia, who took the name *Alexander VI* (1492–1503), is the most notorious of the Renaissance popes, indeed perhaps of all popes. He kept a string of mistresses and fathered through them at least ten illegitimate children, including two who were borne by Giulia Farnese while he was pope. Promotion of family interests, and of his illegitimate offspring, and the accumulation of wealth, dominated much of his reign. Yet he was active in other areas too. By the Treaty of Tordesillas in 1494, he assigned the 'New World' of the Americas to the authority of Spain and Portugal, reaching an agreement with the monarchs of the two countries regarding the line of demarcation between the two zones. He was co-founder, together with the local bishop William Elphinstone, of the university of Aberdeen in Scotland in 1494/5. For all the enigmas of his personal life, he was devout after a fashion and defended orthodoxy. He celebrated the Jubilee year of 1500 in style and by granting many indulgences. His quarrels with Girolamo Savanarola, the famous Dominican preacher, ended tragically with Savanarola's condemnation and execution by burning at the stake in Florence. Alexander was an important patron of Renaissance artists and he engaged Michelangelo to draw up plans for the rebuilding of St Peter's Church. He died suddenly in August 1503 when, it seems, a poisoned cup of wine, intended for a guest, was given to him by mistake.

The papacy's promotion of the values that came to be associated with the Renaissance should be appreciated – here our consideration includes the popes of the early sixteenth century. The Reformation tended to see the darker side of these values and used it as one more stick, conveniently at hand, with which to beat the papacy. Catholics of the Counter-Reformation defended the doctrinal orthodoxy of popes in question but their appreciation of the men did not extend much further. The moral failures of some of the popes and their worldly lifestyle provided for later Catholic apologists a convenient explanation for the success of the Reformation without the need to justify its teachings. Yet appreciation of the beauty of creation, and recognition of human achievement, which were central features of the Renaissance, are right in line with the Incarnation, the central belief of Christianity that God came in human form in the person of Jesus Christ, thus setting a divine seal of approval on the basic goodness of creation and humanity. In many ways, therefore, the popes of the Renaissance were promoting a healthy and more positive vision of Christianity, a move away from the rather negative spirituality of excessive emphasis upon suffering and the Cross, and of retreat from the world, which had been widely prevalent for some time – as exemplified in Thomas à Kempis's *Imitation of Christ*.

iv. Religious orders and beguines

Regarding religious orders, or 'religious life' as this deepening of Christian witness came to be called, saint Benedict had provided the foundational *Rule* for monasticism in the western Church in the sixth century. Benedictine monasticism still remained the basic and most widespread form of consecrated life in the West in the eleventh century. Soon afterwards, orders of canons ('canon' meaning a rule) emerged as a result of two principal developments. First, the growth of towns required more clergy to cater for the religious needs of the laity. Secondly, the regulation of obligatory celibacy for all priests in the West, which was enshrined in canon 7 of the first Lateran council in 1123 and later reinforced by canon 14 of the fourth Lateran council in 1215, meant that many priests working in the pastoral ministry preferred to live in community rather than singly.

The two best known new orders of canons were those following the Augustinian and Norbertine rules. The former adopted the Rule which Augustine had written for his cathedral clergy in Hippo, which was strong on essentials, quite brief and sensible regarding the human condition. There was no clear founder of the order, rather communities sprang up spontaneously which adopted the name and rule of Augustine. Saint Norbert (1080–1134) also adopted the Rule of Augustine but he added a good number of extra regulations and austerities, such as complete abstinence from meat. The first house of the order was at Prémontré near Laon in northern France, hence the alternative name of Premonstratensian canons. The order was more centralized and tightly controlled than the Augustinian canons and it spread to many countries in western Christendom during the Middle Ages.

Two other important developments occurred around this time. Saint Bernard (1090–1153) was the key personality in a reform of Benedictine monasticism which resulted in a new order, the Cistercians (named after the first monastery, Cîteaux in eastern France). The austere lifestyle and simplified liturgy in community, as well as the emphasis upon manual labour, principally farming, appealed to many young men. The order spread rapidly throughout western Christendom. Carthusians took their name from the mother-house of the order, 'La grande Chartreuse' which stands high in the French Alps; individual monasteries were called 'charterhouses'. The order's founding figure was saint Bruno (1032–1101), who had been educated in France and Germany. Within the monastery, each monk had his own house – forming part of a large quadrangle – where he prayed, worked and ate alone. For some of the liturgy, and occasionally for meals and the making of communal decisions, the monks came together. The Carthusian lifestyle was essentially that of hermits living in community: a western reinvention of early Egyptian monasticism. The order retained its vigour throughout the medieval period and exercised considerable influence upon the wider Church on account of its witness of prayer and dedicated lifestyle and the monks' various contacts with the wider world – through writing, spiritual direction and in other ways. Thomas More spent some years in the London Charterhouse before he married in 1505, and even as Lord Chancellor of England he would return there for prayer and inspiration. Among writers, especially influential were Ludolph of Saxony (1300–78), whose *Vita Christi* (Life of Christ) provided popular meditations on the life of Christ, and Denys van Leeuwen (1407–71), better known as Denis the Carthusian, who wrote extensively on Scripture, morality, mysticism and Islam.

Four orders of friars

The advent of the four orders of friars in the thirteenth century represented a major development in western Christendom: Franciscans, Dominicans, Augustinians and Carmelites.

Franciscans. The charismatic personality of Francis of Assisi provided the inspiration for the first order. Son of a wealthy cloth merchant of Assisi in northern Italy, Francis underwent a religious conversion and dedicated himself to radical poverty as a sign of complete dependence on God. Soon other men joined him in this religious adventure and there arose the Order of Friars Minor (OFM), as the order was officially known. Francis was ordained a deacon but never a priest – he was unworthy of the priesthood, he said – and there was tension within the order as to whether or not most friars should be ordained priests. Eventually the more clerical and priestly approach largely won the day and the order engaged in an astonishing range of apostolates. Famous friars appear in other sections of this chapter as preachers, missionaries and theologians. One became pope, Nicholas V (1288–92), a fair number were cardinals and bishops, including John Peckham, archbishop of Canterbury from 1278 to 1292. Francis and most friars, however, were wary of such prominent posts. Most communities – called friaries – were situated in towns and the friars, through personal contacts with the citizens and the religious services and sacraments which they administered in their churches, had a huge influence upon urban Christianity.

Dominicans. Dominic was a priest and canon of the cathedral of Osma in Spain. He encountered the Albigensian heresy in southern France while returning with his bishop from a mission in northern Europe. He became convinced that Albigensians could be won back to Catholicism only by a combination of orthodox preaching and austere life-style. The outcome was the Order of Preachers (OP), as the Dominican friars were officially known: a new concept for a religious order, whereby preaching was the primary charism. Despite the differing origins of the OP and the OFM, the results were remarkably similar. Dominican friaries soon spread from southern France to most countries of western Christendom. They were usually located in towns and the friars exercised there a powerful apostolic ministry. In terms of the hierarchical church, there were two Dominican popes, the short-lived Innocent V (1276) and Benedict XI (1303–4), and a good number of Dominican cardinals and bishops, including Robert Kilwardby, archbishop of Canterbury (1272–8). Dominican friars were prominent in the Inquisition, most notably Tomas Torquemada who was head of the Spanish Inquisition from 1483 until his death in 1498. Among theologians, Albertus Magnus (Albert the Great) and the towering genius of Thomas Aquinas are especially noteworthy. Three of the great mystical writers of the later Middle Ages were German Dominicans: Meister Eckhart, Henry Suso and Johann Tauler.

Two other orders of friars emerged in the middle of the thirteenth century. The *Augustinian* friars – distinct from the Augustinian canons – were organized as a religious order by pope Innocent IV (1243–54), principally from groups of hermits living in northern Italy. Their members later included the philosopher Giles of Rome, the English historian John Capgrave and, most famously, Martin Luther. *Carmelites* may trace their origins back to the 'sons of the prophet Elijah' mentioned in the Old Testament (2 Kings 2), but more immediately there were hermits living in the Holy Land who preferred to return to Europe rather than live under Muslim occupation. They, too, were organized into an order by pope Innocent IV.

The word 'friar' comes from the Latin *frater* meaning 'brother', so *frère* in French and *frate* in Italian. Its use underlined communal life and apostolate in a fresh way and the word carried a different tone from 'monk', which means 'alone' (Greek, *monos*) and indicates both a more solitary life and the search for God alone. Augustinians and Carmelites, however, continued to consider themselves hermits as well as friars – as indicated for the Augustinians by their official designation, Order of Hermits of Saint Augustine (*Ordo Eremitarum Sancti Augustini* = OESA). Precise numbers are impossible to come by, but the Dominicans and Franciscans peaked around 1300: an estimated 60,000 Franciscan friars in 1,500 houses, and around half these numbers of friars and houses for the Dominicans. Subsequently the numbers in both orders declined in absolute terms, though possibly not in proportion to the overall population of western Christendom, which was reduced drastically by the Black Death plague and its recurrences. By 1300, Augustinian friars numbered around 8,000 in 350 houses, Carmelites reached several thousand in about 150 houses. The two younger orders, however, continued to grow thereafter in terms of both friars and houses.

Other orders, numbers, and critics

Quite a number of other, smaller orders of friars were founded during this time. Some of them still flourish today, including the order of Servite friars, which was founded by seven merchants of Florence in the mid-thirteenth century. Various other orders of men were founded to meet particular needs of the age. The Knights Hospitallers, who flourish today as the Knights of Malta, were founded in the early twelfth century to care for pilgrims to the Holy Land. The Knights Templar were founded shortly afterwards with the principal task of providing military defence for the Holy Land, but the order was suppressed by the council of Vienne in 1311. The Trinitarian order was founded in 1198, principally to ransom Christians held captive by Muslims. Peter Nolasco founded the Mercedarian order shortly afterwards for similar purposes. The order of Canons Regular of the Order of the Holy Cross, better known today as the Crosier Fathers, was founded in the early thirteenth century for a variety of apostolates including preaching and good liturgy. We have already noted the double-monastery of Whitby governed by the abbess Hilda in the seventh century. Another 'double' order was founded in England in the twelfth century, by the long-lived Gilbert of Sempringham (1083–1189). The men (canons) were to provide spiritual direction and liturgical services for the nuns. At Gilbert's death there were nine double monasteries of the order, and four for men only, all in England. The total number had risen to twenty-five when the order was dissolved by king Henry VIII.

Although the new orders tended to capture the limelight, especially in the early years after their foundation, the older Benedictine order remained important throughout the central and late Middle Ages. The monastic life was essentially a hidden one, but particularly noted among theologians was saint Anselm, who was a monk at Aosta in Italy and Bec in France before becoming archbishop of Canterbury in England in 1093.

The combined numbers in the four main orders of friars around the year 1300 amounted to some 100,000 men. It is estimated that there were then around 150,000 more in the other male religious orders. Therefore a total of 250,000 – and roughly the same number of diocesan priests – in a total adult male population of perhaps twenty million. Why was life in these religious orders so popular? It is important to remember the religious ideals of the various orders, but also important to remember more mundane considerations. Most young men, it seems, joined the religious house that was closest to their home; companionship combined with a religious, worthwhile and sensible way of life were surely influential in their choice.

Religious orders had their critics. Canon 13 of the fourth Lateran council in 1215 forbade the foundation of new orders 'lest too great a variety of religious orders leads to grave confusion in God's church'. Yet the canon, by attempting to control expansion, was implicitly acknowledging the popularity of these ways of life. Soon the papacy was granting dispensations from the canon, so that the new orders of Carmelite and Augustinian friars, and others, came to be founded. Monks and friars fared badly in portrayals of them in three influential literary masterpieces of the thirteenth and fourteenth centuries: *Roman de la Rose* (1237/80), Boccaccio's *Decameron* and Geoffrey Chaucer's *Canterbury Tales*. It is noticeable, too, that religious orders were swept aside with remarkably little protest in those countries that accepted the Protestant Reformation. Why? The thirteenth century had marked a high point for religious orders, while there were no major foundations of new orders in the two centuries that followed. There are signs of tiredness and lack of creativity during this later period. Nevertheless, male religious orders remained at the centre of the late medieval church and popular religion cannot be understood without them.

We have seen that the early development of religious life, in third- and fourth-century Egypt, was largely a lay movement. Saint Benedict was never ordained a priest, it seems. For long in Benedictine monasteries, as well as in Celtic monasticism, enough monks were ordained priests as to satisfy the liturgical needs of the community, not more. There were tensions between lay and clerical approaches in many of the religious orders founded in the central Middle Ages, but the more clerical approach came to predominate especially in the later Middle Ages. Religious orders, nevertheless, kept close links with the laity. Many people indeed criticized them for being too close – criticisms that were levelled particularly against the Dominican and Franciscans friars – so that it would be wrong, once again, to exaggerate lay *versus* clerical tensions within the medieval Church.

Most of the orders established associations of 'confraters' or 'tertiaries' (members of the third order) whereby lay men and women could participate, to some extent, in the prayers and other activities of the order. Some of the best known personalities of the time were such tertiaries: Raymon Lull, the mystic Angela of Foligno, the penitent Margaret of Cortona, and Pier Pettinaio, the comb-maker of Siena immortalized by Dante, were Franciscan tertiaries; Catherine of Siena was a Dominican tertiary.

Women had much less freedom than men to prefer a religious order to the married state. The number of nuns was much smaller than that of monks and friars. Nevertheless, there were convents for women – usually forming the female branch (called 'second' order) of a male religious order – in all the countries of western Christendom. Some of the nuns achieved renown in their day, particularly in the area of prayer. Hildegard of Bingen (1098–1179) achieved wide fame as abbess of the Benedictine convent of Rupertsberg in Germany and for her mystical writings; Clare of Assisi was the determined founder of the female branch of the Franciscan order, commonly called the Poor Clares. Three nuns in the Cistercian monastery of Helfta in Germany in the thirteenth century composed remarkable treatises on mystical prayer: Mechtild of Magdeburg, Mechtild of Hackeborn and Gertrude 'the Great'.

Beguines

Beguines provided the most innovative movement within religious life for women. The origin of the word 'beguine' is obscure: it may derive from the simple cloth habit (*béguin* = hood, *beige* = cloth in natural colour) which the women wore. Indeed, the description was not used consistently either by the women themselves or by others describing them. Mary of Oignies (1177–1213), who lived a devout life in Flanders and inspired other women, is widely considered the movement's founder. Rather than enter convents, beguines chose to live together, in small groups, in houses and apartments in towns: the communities were called 'beguinages'. Initially the movement received ecclesiastical backing. Pope Honorius III granted it verbal permission in 1216 and pope Gregory IX gave further authorization in the bull *Gloriam virginalem* of 1233. Mathew Paris (1200–59), the English chronicler and Benedictine monk, described the movement in his *Chronica Majora* for the year 1243. Despite the somewhat hostile tone, the description provides precious early evidence of the lifestyle and its attraction for women:

*At this time, especially in Germany, certain ... women have
adopted a religious profession though it is a light one. They call
themselves 'religious' and take a private vow of continence and
simplicity of life, though they do not follow the Rule of any
saint, nor are they as yet confined within a cloister. They have
so multiplied within a short time that two thousand have been
reported in Cologne and the neighbouring cities.*

The movement received important secular patronage when
king Louis IX of France founded a beguinage in Paris in 1264.
Beguines were largely confined to the Rhineland, northern France
and the Low Countries; though there were similar initiatives in
other countries that went under other names. Robert Grosseteste,
bishop of Lincoln (1235–53), in a provocative talk to the student
Franciscans in Oxford, praised the beguine way of life even above
that of the friars because they practised poverty while 'living by
their own labour'. Beguines are known especially for their mystical
writings. Mary of Oignies was one such writer; another was
Juliana of Liège, who inspired pope Urban IV to establish the feast
of Corpus Christi. The mystic Mechtild of Magdeburg lived for
while as a beguine before becoming a Cistercian nun: Hadewijch,
from Flanders, is noted for the 'mysticism of love' which she
developed in her writings.

In the early fourteenth century the movement fell under a cloud.
Margarete Porete, a beguine originally from Flanders, was burnt at
the stake in Paris in 1310 for her allegedly heterodox views on the
soul's union with God through mystical prayer. In the following
year the council of Vienne, influenced by the case of Margarete
Porete, issued a wide ranging censure of beguines:

*The women commonly known as beguines, since they promise
obedience to nobody, nor renounce possessions, nor profess any
approved rule, are not religious at all, although they wear the
special dress of beguines ... We (the pope) therefore, with the
approval of the council, perpetually forbid their mode of life
and remove it completely from the church of God. (Decrees,
p. 374)*

The decree ended with a saving clause: 'Of course we in no way
intend to forbid any faithful woman, whether they promise chastity
or not, from living uprightly in their hospices, wishing to live a life

of penance and serving the Lord of hosts in a spirit of humility.'
Beguinages survived but in sharply diminished number. Records
of property transactions in Cologne indicate 169 beguinages in
the city in 1310, 62 in 1320 and only two in 1400. Much of the
original inspiration was lost. From small apartments and houses,
beguinages developed into the much larger complexes of houses
that can be seen today, mostly dating from the sixteenth century
onwards, in various cities in Belgium and the Netherlands.

v. Intellectual developments

During the central and late Middle Ages, the western Church
achieved intellectual maturity for the first time. It acquired
theological leadership within the Christian world. Among many
theologians, five individuals were outstanding in originality and
influence: Anselm, Peter Abelard, Thomas Aquinas, Duns Scotus
and William of Ockham. During this period, too, canon law
developed greatly in the West both as a practical and an academic
discipline. Universities secured a central place in western intellectual life from the twelfth century onwards, notably for the
teaching of both theology and canon law. Many literary works of
a religious nature were written, including those of Dante, Geoffrey
Chaucer and Christine de Pizan. Remaining to be discussed in
section vi are writers on prayer and mysticism; they played a key
role in intellectual as well as spiritual life.

Five theologians

Anselm (1033–1109) was born and brought up in Aosta in northern
Italy. He became a monk at the Benedictine monastery of Bec in
Normandy, France, and was chosen by king William II of England
to be archbishop of Canterbury, an office he held for the last
sixteen years of his life. Today he is called respectively in the
three countries, Anselm of Aosta, of Bec, and of Canterbury. He
illustrates well the international nature of western Christendom
at the time, which was much helped by Latin being the common
theological language. As a monk Anselm was a man of faith and
prayer, but he wanted to go deeper in understanding the Christian
message: 'faith seeking understanding' (*fides quaerens intellectum*)
is the dictum especially associated with him. In the three works

for which he is principally known, *Monologion, Proslogion* and *Cur Deus homo* (Why God became man), he used reason to delve deeper into Christian doctrine than any of his predecessors in the western Church since Augustine of Hippo. He asked questions, and sought reasonable explanations, regarding the central mysteries of Christianity: the existence of God, the nature of the Trinity, the purpose of the Incarnation. To prove God's existence he elaborated the 'ontological' argument, which moves from the concept of God to the necessity of his existence. In his life and writings, Anselm manifested a balance between faith and reason, between inquiry and acceptance of divine revelation, that has remained exemplary for Christians ever since.

Peter Abelard (1079–1142) was the most famous teacher in early twelfth-century Paris. He was criticized by many, however, as destructive of faith in his exaltation of reason. It was on these grounds that his three principal written works were censured by other teachers in Paris, some jealous of the large crowds that his lectures attracted: *Tractatus de fide Trinitatis* (Treatise on faith in the Trinity), *Sic et Non* (Yes and no), and *Dialogus inter philosophum, Judaeum et Christianum* (Dialogue between a philosopher, a Jew and a Christian). Nobody could deny the penetration of his thought and the breadth of his knowledge. His most persistent critic was Bernard of Clairvaux: 'a censor of the faith, not a disciple, an improver of it, not an imitator' complained William of St Thierry in a letter to Bernard. Abelard's love affair with his attractive and brilliant student Heloise led to castration at the instigation of Heloise's uncle and guardian Fulbert, canon of Notre Dame cathedral in Paris, who lost patience when Abelard would not choose between marriage to his niece and the celibate priesthood. Subsequently Héloise entered a convent where she became abbess, while Abelard became a monk. The two continued to write to each other and their surviving correspondence, with its blend of ardour and sensitivity to the trials of life, forms a classic of romantic literature, well known in the Middle Ages and retaining its fascination today.

Thomas Aquinas (1225–74) is the best known of the five theologians. Indeed after Augustine of Hippo, he is widely considered the most incisive and influential of all Catholic theologians in the West. Born near Aquino in southern Italy, he entered the recently founded Dominican order at a young age. His quite short but extraordinarily productive academic life was spent principally as a teacher at the university of Paris. He wrote extensively on a wide range of topics, including commentaries on much of Scripture, but his most lasting contribution was the *Summa Theologiae* (or *Summa Theologica*). This monumental work, which excels both in clear and orderly presentation and in the depth and orthodoxy of its teaching, covered almost the full course of theological topics. It was interrupted by his early death, which prevented him from treating all the sacraments. The work has justly been called the great 'cathedral' of medieval theology on account of its attention to detail and overall coherence and sublimity. It is notable for its sustained attempt to harmonize faith and reason, to show that God's revelation in Jesus Christ goes beyond what our natural reason can grasp but does not conflict with it.

The reception of Aquinas's writings was somewhat laboured. The archbishop of Paris, Etienne Tempier, judged that his reconciliation of faith and reason was too favourable to the philosophy of Aristotle, whose works were becoming increasingly available in Europe around this time. He censured propositions associated with Aquinas in 1270 and 1277. The Dominican order stoutly defended Aquinas's orthodoxy and gave his teaching preferred status within the friars' curriculum of studies. He was canonized as a saint by pope John XXIII in 1323, when Tempier's censures were lifted. Later, in 1567, he was declared a Doctor of the Church by the Dominican pope Pius V. The elevation of his teaching to privileged status within the Catholic church came about in two stages: first during the sixteenth century, due especially to papal endorsement of his teaching and the masterly commentary on his *Summa Theologiae* by the Dominican cardinal Thomas Cajetan; secondly, from the late nineteenth to the mid-twentieth century, when a succession of popes, beginning with Leo XIII, in cooperation with the Dominican order, gave strong support to his teaching.

Both *Duns Scotus* (1265–1308) and *William of Ockham* (1285–1347) came from the British Isles: Scotus from the village of Duns in Scotland, Ockham from the village of that name in Surrey. Both became Franciscan friars and teachers at Oxford university. Scotus also taught for a while at Paris university and possibly at Cambridge. Both men were portrayed in later historiography as undermining Aquinas's synthesis of faith and reason. Is the criticism justified? We have already seen that Aquinas's archbishop in Paris thought his synthesis was too close, that faith was being undermined and subjected to reason. In England, too, similar condemnations issued by successive archbishops of Canterbury – Robert Kilwardby in 1277 and John Pecham in 1284 – appear to have had Aquinas in mind. Unease with Aquinas's synthesis was quite widespread.

Scotus and Ockham certainly regarded their intent as eminently positive. Scotus emphasized the primacy of love over knowledge, of will over intellect, both in God and in humankind. Our response, therefore, should be one of love even more than of knowledge; Aquinas's order of importance was subtly altered. Scotus introduced, too, a fresh and fuller interpretation of Christ's work of redemption. This work was seen as an expression of God's love for humankind more than as settlement of debts due to sin, and it was accomplished throughout Christ's life on earth, not just by his death on the cross. Somewhat different emphases were given by Ockham. He stressed the freedom and transcendence of God and individuality within creation. He struggled against what he saw as the dangers of reducing God to human categories of thought, and of exaggerating the similarities among humans at the expense of their uniqueness. He sought to simplify both philosophical and theological discourse: 'Beings (and therefore explanations) should not be multiplied unnecessarily' (Latin, *entia non sunt multiplicanda sine necessitate*) was the dictum attributed to him – 'Ockham's razor' as it came to be called. An intellectual ascetic, Ockham exercised enormous influence in university circles in the fourteenth and fifteenth centuries, more so than any of the other four men mentioned: a fascination comparable in both content and extent to that of Ludwig Wittgenstein in Anglophone countries in recent times.

Canon law

The twenty canons of the first council of Nicea in 325, as well as other canonical collections of the second to fourth centuries, show clearly the importance given to church order, and therefore to canon law, by the early Church. Most other ecumenical councils of the first millennium issued some canons alongside their better known doctrinal statements. Indeed, creeds were then considered an integral part of canon law, partly because they were used as tests of orthodoxy. The sharper distinction between canon law and theology entered the Catholic church mainly through the codes of Canon Law promulgated in 1917 and 1983.

John Scholasticus (+577) and Dionysius Exiguus (+526/556) are considered the two 'fathers' of canon law, for the eastern and the western Churches respectively. Both of them published collections of the most important canons, including those of the first council of Nicea. John Scholasticus became patriarch of Constantinople and his collection, known as *Nomocanon*, became normative for the eastern Church. Dionysius's *Corpus* contained much the same conciliar material as is to be found in *Nomocanon*, but instead of the ecclesiastical legislation of the eastern emperors that is to be found in *Nomocanon*, Dionysius included a selection of papal decrees. The work is entirely in Latin, either reproducing the original text or, principally for the councils, providing translations from the Greek. Dionysius knew both languages. Regarding later additions, the 102 canons of the council of Trullo in 692 were particularly important for the eastern church: they still remain fundamental for Orthodox canon law.

The schism of 1054 proved decisive for the development of canon law in the Catholic church. The canons of the first millennium were retained, but subsequent legislation was almost exclusively western: principally the decrees of popes and general councils. There were six main collections of this legislation. First, the *Decretum* (English 'Decrees') compiled by the monk Gratian, who taught at Bologna, around 1140. This monumental work preserved for the western Church the conciliar and papal canon law of the first millennium while seeking to reconcile divergences between the various canons – hence the fuller title of the work *Concordantia Discordantium Canonum* (Concordance of Discordant Canons). Secondly, the *Decretalia* (Decretals) issued by pope Gregory IX in 1234, which contained legislation subsequent to the publication of Gratian's *Decretum*, principally papal decrees and the legislation of the general councils of the period, notably Lateran IV. Four smaller collections, all western in their contents, took the work down to the end of the fifteenth century: *Liber Sextus* (published in 1298; 'sixth' because *Decretalia* was arranged in five books),

Liber septimus papae Clementis V (1314), *Extravagantes papae Joannis XXII* (1325), and *Extravagantes communes* which included various canons promulgated between 1261 and 1485. All six collections were first published together in 1499 and soon thereafter they became known collectively as *Corpus Iuris Canonici*.

The six collections exercised huge influence upon the medieval West, regarding both church affairs and society more widely. They represented the legislation that was valid for all Christians in the Catholic church. There was, besides, canon law of a local nature which pertained to a particular group, such as a religious order, or to a particular country or region. There were complaints at the time that the Church was becoming too legal in mentality, but most Christians could see the wood from the trees, so to speak, and that canon law was always subject to the demands of the gospel. William Lyndwood's *Provinciale* (1430), which contains the canons promulgated by bishops, councils and other authorities in the English church, represents a particularly good example of canon law at the national level. Lyndwood allows legitimate adjustments for the national situation but he always recognizes the superior authority of popes and general councils.

Universities

The school of theology in fourth century Alexandria in Egypt may be considered the oldest Christian university, while other cities in north Africa and western Asia might claim to have housed universities in the first millennium. However, the word 'university' is western, deriving from the Latin *universitas*, which means 'the whole body of people' or 'corporation'. The term was sometimes applied to various groups of people besides those forming an academic institution.

The earliest universities in the West, as seats of learning, emerged distinctly in the twelfth century: in Bologna, Paris and Oxford, in that order. The institutions were recognized as being larger than schools, and the word *universitas* came to be applied to them. There were fifteen further foundations in the thirteenth century, including Cambridge in England; some twenty-three in the fourteenth century and thirty-four in the fifteenth century (the exact figures are debatable because of mergers and changes of location), including in the fifteenth century St Andrews, Glasgow and Aberdeen in Scotland. They varied greatly in size, from Paris with several thousand students and Oxford with a peak of some 1,500 around the year 1300, to much smaller institutions with a hundred or so students. By the fifteenth century universities were to be found in almost all countries of western Christendom.

The principal function of universities was the education of priests: most students were preparing for the priesthood, some were recently ordained. Perhaps the closest equivalent today is the Gregorian University in Rome, with some 2,500 students most of whom are seminarians or recently ordained priests. The three main subjects taught were *philosophia*, theology and canon law. *Philosophia* (philosophy) comprised a wide curriculum, including the *trivium* (three subjects) of grammar, rhetoric and dialectic, followed by the *quadrivium* (four subjects) of music, arithmetic geometry and astronomy. Those who passed the BA or Licence in Philosophy might then pass to the 'higher' faculties of Theology or Canon Law. A few universities – notably Montpellier in France and Salerno in Italy – possessed a faculty of Medicine, in which most students were laymen. We know that Héloise attended some of Abelard's lectures shortly before the schools of Paris graduated to university status and it is clear that female students were occasionally to be found attending university lectures at a later date in Paris and elsewhere.

The basic format for teaching was the lecture. Books, which were in manuscript form until the invention of printing in the mid-fifteenth century, were another important source of information. Particularly well preserved is the single room of the late medieval library of Oxford University, which survives today as 'Duke Humphrey' room within the Bodleian library. Frequently books were chained to the wall or to a shelf to prevent theft, and many read standing rather than seated. Popular too were 'Disputations', which involved staff and students debating topics on the syllabus in a lively yet controlled way. In *Quodlibet* (Whatsoever) exercises, capable students had to prepare themselves to answer any questions 'whatsoever' within their field of study. Both learning and inquiry were altogether encouraged in students.

Accommodation was to be found either individually, as paying guests in the houses of townspeople, or in small halls often presided over by a teacher, or in larger colleges which can still

be seen particularly well in Oxford and Cambridge. Many of
the religious orders had residences providing accommodation for
their own students. Worcester College in Oxford, which housed
Benedictine students, and the Dominican friary in Bologna survive
today as witnesses to their living conditions.

The effects of universities are to be found writ large throughout
this chapter. Three of the five best known theologians were
university students and professors: Thomas Aquinas, Duns Scotus
and William of Ockham. Many other notable figures featuring
in this chapter studied, and some of them taught, at a university.
Equally important were the numerous graduates – whose names
and careers are largely lost to us – who served the Church in
parishes and religious orders and in various other capacities.
Much of the success of the medieval Church, as well as some of its
weaknesses, may be ascribed to the universities of the time.

Works of literature

The development of national languages from the thirteenth
century onwards resulted in widely read literature that influenced
Christianity at many levels. Frequently one person would read
aloud from a book to a group; a popular and pleasurable form of
learning.

In the thirteenth century, particularly influential was *Roman
de la Rose*, which was written by two French clerics Guillaume de
Lorris and Jean de Meung. Its tone may be secular, even profane,
yet in treating human love it was confronting an issue at the heart
of the gospel message. The popularity of the work shows that
it struck chords in the hearts and minds of many Christians.
Raymond Lull (1233–1315), a married man from Majorca, wrote
several influential works in Catalan which touched on themes
important to Christianity: 'Book of the Gentile and Three Sages',
a work on inter-religious dialogue; *Blanquerna* took the form of
a romance in which Lull hoped for the conversion of both Jews
and Muslims, 'so that in the whole world there may be no more
than one language, one belief, one faith' (chapter 94); 'Book of
Contemplation' was written in Arabic, in which he was fluent, and
translated into Catalan. Lull also wrote extensively in Latin.

Dante Alighieri (1265–1321), a layman who was born and lived
for much of his life in Florence, was the most profound religious

author writing in the vernacular, principally on account of *Divina Commedia*. In this work, which proved seminal for the development of the Italian language, Dante described the three realms of the world to come, hell, purgatory and heaven, with close reference to real persons and events in this life. The reflections that are intertwined in the narrative represent both philosophy and theology, yet they surpass in expression and vividness the scholasticism characteristic of the universities. The outlook is deeply Christian and generally loyal to the institutional Church while at the same time fiercely critical of various individuals, including churchmen and some popes, whom he places in hell. *Divina Commedia* was completed towards the end of Dante's life and it quickly established itself as a major European classic. It remains today probably the best known work of medieval vernacular literature. *Decameron*, written in Italian by Giovanni Boccaccio (1315–75), enjoyed wide popularity yet it is altogether a lighter work than Dante's masterpiece. *Il Canzoniere*, written in Italian by Francesco Petrarch (1304–74), forms a fascinating collection of poems revolving around the themes of life and death. The work reflects a man struggling with his humanity and eternal destiny, with mysteries central to Christianity.

Canterbury Tales, written in English by Geoffrey Chaucer (1343–1400), rivals *Divina Commedia* in renown today but the treatment of religion is less profound. The focus is upon men and women in all their diversity and complexity in this life. In these respects the work is remarkable. Plenty of church personalities appear among the pilgrims – a monk and a friar, two nuns, and a parish priest – and in the tales they tell, but the tone for the most part is somewhat hostile and anticlerical: the sympathetic treatment of the parish priest is an exception. Also written in the vernacular, *Piers Plowman* by William Langland (1330–1400), a priest from northern England, is a powerful and moving account, in the form of an extended poem, of life's journey as represented by a peasant ploughman who gradually comes closer to God and Christ. Langland, too, was fearless in criticizing abuses in the Church of his day.

Christine de Pizan (1364–1430) was exceptionally learned and prolific as a writer. Born in Italy, she lived from a young age in France and wrote in medieval French. Her works reveal a wide range of knowledge and interests, touching on many modern concerns. She wrote on political theory, composed poems of courtly love, and wrote books in defence of the rights and dignity of women, an autobiography *La Vision de Christine*, also *Livre de Paix*, a passionate plea for peace in her war-torn country, and *Ditié de Jehanne d'Arc* in celebration of Joan of Arc's relief of the siege of Orléans in 1429. A moralist in the broad sense, Christine reveals the complexity of medieval thought and behaviour as well as the impossibility of drawing a sharp distinction between Christianity and the secular or profane.

vi. Liturgy, prayer and mysticism

Liturgy, in the sense of prayer that was both public and communal, remained central to Catholic practice throughout this period. The Mass, or Eucharist, in which Christ's saving work was celebrated and realized anew, lay at the heart of the liturgy. Its crucial importance has featured frequently in this chapter. The same mystery was celebrated even while the rites (the precise wording and other observances) varied somewhat: Gallican rite in France, Mozarabic rite in Spain, Ambrosian rite in Milan and Lombardy, Sarum and some other rites in England, Dominican rite for the Order of Preachers, Carthusian rite for Charterhouses, and other variations. The 'Roman rite' became more widespread in the course of the Middle Ages, helped by its adoption by the Franciscan order. The other six sacraments – baptism, confirmation, penance or confession, marriage, orders, and last anointing – remained integral to the liturgy. Here too there was both continuity with the first millennium and some development and regional variation. The divine office, with its eight 'hours' of matins, lauds, prime, terce, sext, none, vespers and compline, remained fundamental for religious orders, especially the monastic orders, and in the later Middle Ages an increasing number of laity were praying some or all of the hours.

A near-contemporary account of the life of Cicely, duchess of York, mother of kings Edward IV and Richard III of England, provides a vivid description of the daily order of this devout woman in the late fifteenth century. The details of liturgy, prayer and spiritual reading are revealing of late medieval lay piety, though the arrangements partly depended upon lady Cicely's aristocratic status. The account reads as follows:

Me seemeth it is requisite to understand the order of her own person concerning God and the world. She used to arise as seven of the clock, and had ready her chaplain to say with her Matins of the day and Matins of our Lady. And when she is full ready, she has a low Mass in her chamber. And after Mass she taketh somewhat to recreate nature; and so goes to the chapel, hearing the divine service and two low Masses. From thence to dinner, during the time whereof she has a reading of holy matter, either (Walter) Hilton of Active and Contemplative Life, Bonaventure De infancia Salvatoris (Infancy of our Saviour), the Golden Legend, St Maud, St Katherine of Siena, or the Revelations of St Brigit.

After dinner she gives audience to all such as have any matter to show unto her, by the space of one hour. And then she sleeps one quarter of an hour. And after she has slept, she continues in prayer unto the first peal of Evensong. Then she drinks wine or ale at her pleasure. Forthwith her chaplain is ready to say with her both evensongs, and after that she goes to the chapel and hears Evensong by note (sung). From thence to supper, and in the time of supper she recites the reading that was had at dinner to those that be in her presence.

After supper she disposes herself to be familiar with her gentle women, to the following of honest mirth. And one hour before her going to bed, she takes a cup of wine, and after that goes to her private closet and takes her leave of God for all night, making an end of her prayers for that day; and by eight of the clock is in bed. I trust to our Lord's mercy that this noble princess thus divides the hours to his high pleasure. (Pantin, 1955, p. 254)

The reading list shows lady Cicely's interest in mysticism, though there is no indication as to whether she was a mystic herself. The mystical state was recognized to be an exceptional gift, given by God to a few – at least in any full or extended form – and in no way to be claimed or expected by everyone. It was recognized, moreover, to be a largely hidden gift, known to God and the individual and partially revealed to others principally through the communications of those who, for various motives and often through intermediaries, attempted to describe their experiences, feebly and very imperfectly, in written works. Mysticism is impossible to define but Jean Gerson, writing in the early fifteenth century, gave a neat description of it as 'knowledge of God by experience reached through the embrace of unifying love' (*Theologia mystica*, consid. 28).

The central and later Middle Ages witnessed an impressive number of people in the western Church who described themselves, or were described by others, as mystics and who left some evidence of this gifted state. The number of women among them is remarkable. Perhaps mystic love for the male Christ is expressed more readily and naturally by women than by men. Some of the individuals have already appeared in this chapter, others are mentioned here for the first time.

In the twelfth century, the German abbess Hildegard of Bingen brought a new level to the description of mystical experience through her writings, most notably *Scivias* (Know the ways) in which she sought to describe her visions of the divine. Intimacy with God helped to make Francis of Assisi the most famous saint and mystic of the thirteenth century. He was the first person recorded as receiving the 'stigmata' – wounds in his body representing the marks of Christ's passion. This century brought forth a number of women who wrote remarkable mystical treatises based on their own experiences: Mechtild of Magdeburg, Mechtild of Hackeborn and Gertrude 'the Great', who were nuns at the Cistercian abbey of Helfta in Germany; three Flemish beguines, Mary of Oignies, Juliana of Liege and Hadewijch; and Angela of Foligno, who dedicated herself to a life of prayer after the death of her husband.

The fourteenth and fifteenth centuries witnessed a further flowering of mysticism within the western Church. Among men, particularly notable were the three Dominican friars from Germany, Meister Eckhart, Henry Suso and Johann Tauler; and from England, the English diocesan priest Walter Hilton, the hermit-priest Richard Rolle, and the anonymous author of *Cloud of Unknowing*. The *Cloud* is specially encouraging to those who experience difficulties in prayer and separation from God. Notable, too, was the Spaniard Raymond Lull, whose writings included a number of works on mysticism.

Among late medieval women, *Catherine of Siena* was the best known mystic, indeed the most famous saint, of her time. The daughter of a prosperous dyer of Siena, her intense and prolonged prayer began at an early age. She declined marriage and continued to live in her parents' home, where many came to visit her. Catherine was willing to intervene in public affairs when necessary: her visit to Avignon to persuade the pope to return to Rome has been mentioned, and she gave advice and measured support to pope Urban VI. She intervened, too, in various disputes between the city of Florence and the papacy. But Catherine was known principally for her life of prayer and the spiritual direction she gave to many people. This prayer, both intercessory for others and mystical, is reflected in various publications: letters written or dictated by her (almost 400 survive); the synthesis of her teaching called *Dialogo* (Dialogue); and various 'prayers' which were compiled by her followers from what she was heard to utter during her meditations and mystical experiences. Catherine was the first woman recorded as bearing the stigmata. She died at the young age of about 33 in 1380 and was canonized by pope Pius II in 1460. Also from Italy, the remarkable mystical experiences of Catherine of Genoa (1447–1510) were subsequently published in 1551 as *Vita et doctrina* (Life and Teaching). Catherine combined this prayer life with caring for the sick in a hospital in Genoa, in which work she was joined by her husband.

Margarete Porete, who was probably a native of Hainault in modern Belgium and who became a beguine, was one of two well-known mystics who ran into mortal trouble with the Church authorities. That Margaret was so exceptional in this respect is indicative of the wide support of the medieval Church for mysticism and prayer. She was burnt at the stake in Paris in 1310 – after being condemned by the Inquisition, she was handed over to the secular authorities for punishment – for continuing to promote her mystical treatise, *Le miroeur des simples âmes* (The Mirror of Simple Souls). Despite the beauty and depth of the work in many respects, there were the twin perils that its teaching led to pantheism – mystical union was so close that absorption in God led to loss of the individual's human identity – and the belief that the mystic was invulnerable to sin, so close was the mystical union with God. Jeanne d'Arc is best known for her military achievements in liberating France, yet she was evidently a young woman closely in touch with God through prayer. The divine 'voices' she claimed to hear were central to her life and mission as well as to her fame.

Her visions were declared 'false and diabolical' at her trial in 1430 and they were one factor among many that led to her execution the following year. However, her reputation was subsequently restored and she was canonized as a saint in 1920.

For England, *Julian of Norwich*, who lived as an anchoress in the city, recorded her visions in *Revelations of Divine Love*, and *The Book of Margery Kempe* provides lively descriptions of the mystical experiences of this citizen of Lynn. Julian's emphasis on the love of God, her description of the motherhood and feminine nature of God and her optimistic tone, epitomized in the words revealed to her, 'All shall be well and all manner of things shall be well', which seem to offer the hope of salvation for all people, accord well with modern concerns. She suggests, too, how heaven is becoming our true selves, how our deficiencies are transformed into good rather than destroyed, how there is an element of the playful lover in God, how people living amid the difficulties and dangers of life can come close to God. In her lifetime Julian had a local reputation for holiness but her *Revelations* became well known only in the twentieth century. Today the work, translated into modern English and many other languages, is perhaps the most widely read of all medieval mystical treatises.

Mystical prayer was a notable feature of late medieval religion, though perhaps it receives more attention today than it did at the time. Most mystics were cautious regarding the importance of this exceptional gift. For the large majority of people, prayer meant the Mass, the divine office, other spoken prayers and meditative or contemplative prayer.

vii. Art, architecture and music

Regarding visual culture – that broad concept – the central and later Middle Ages are remembered now above all for cathedrals of the twelfth and thirteenth centuries and paintings of the early Renaissance. Though much of the medieval heritage has disappeared, it is remarkable how much survives. The second council of Nicea in 787 had defended religious art. In part, therefore, the present section surveys the western fruits of this crucial conciliar decree. The word 'Gothic' is used today to describe the art and architecture of the medieval West, though it was introduced in the late fifteenth century as a derogatory term: art that might be associated with the primitive Goths who had destroyed the Roman Empire, as distinct from the noble classical art of the empire which the Renaissance sought to imitate. When medieval art came to be appreciated anew in the nineteenth century, the description 'Gothic' was retained and 'neo-Gothic' was coined for the new art that resulted from this revival of interest. Altogether the central and later Middle Ages brought crucial cultural developments which have profoundly influenced Catholicism, and Christianity more widely, ever since.

Churches and other buildings

The cathedral church of Chartres, lying some fifty miles south of Paris, was built and decorated between 1130 and 1230. It is widely regarded as the finest early building in the new 'Gothic' style. Pointed arches replaced those rounded in the Romanesque style, as architecture of the preceding period came to be called. There is both elevation and majesty in the construction of the cathedral, crowned by its fine hill-top position. Equally impressive is the brilliant and deeply religious art in the statues and stained glass windows that adorn the building. Other cathedrals and churches of outstanding quality soon followed in this new style elsewhere in northern France. Most notable are the cathedrals in Rouen, Rheims and Amiens; in Paris, Notre Dame cathedral and Sainte-Chapel, which was commissioned by king Louis IX; and, roughly at the same time as Chartres cathedral, the abbey church of Saint-Denis to the north of Paris, which contains the tombs of many kings of France.

Elsewhere, too, the new style caught on. The splendid cathedrals built in England were influenced by developments in France, though they retained distinctive insular characteristics. The stained glass windows in York Minster, and the west front of Wells cathedral which contains some three hundred figures of angels, saints and royalty, are fine examples of the artwork. Most of the parish churches in England were rebuilt in the new style, sometimes called 'English perpendicular', during the fourteenth and fifteenth centuries. Many of them survive today largely intact. Equally impressive for people at the time were the churches and houses of religious orders built in the Gothic style; though the dissolution of religious orders in Protestant countries, and various disturbances in those that remained Catholic, means that far less of this architecture survives. This work can be glimpsed, for example, in the Dominican friary in Norwich, which was converted at the time of the Reformation into the city hall and survives today remarkably intact, or in the eighteenth century drawings and the few surviving remains of the church of Cluny monastery in France, which remained the largest church in western Christendom until the rebuilding of St Peter's in Rome in the sixteenth century.

University buildings were much influenced by the new architecture. The best preserved are those at Oxford and Cambridge universities, most notably New College and the university church of St Mary the Virgin in Oxford, and King's College with its exquisite chapel in Cambridge. From late fourteenth century Cracow in Poland, the elegant original courtyard of the Jagiellonian University remains in excellent condition. In Paris, the redesigning of the city by Baron Haussmann in the nineteenth century swept away almost all the remaining buildings of the medieval university. For Bologna university, too, we must rely on drawings and other records relating to the period rather than on surviving buildings.

Notwithstanding the prevalence of 'Gothic' architecture in its various forms, it is important to keep in mind the architecture of two earlier ages: that which remained from the late Roman Empire and its aftermath and, secondly, buildings in the Romanesque style. In medieval Rome, for example, all the four main 'basilicas' – St Peter's, St John Lateran, St Mary Major (Santa Maria Maggiore) and St Paul's outside-the-Walls – remained essentially buildings of the fourth and fifth centuries, until a fire in the late fourteenth century destroyed most of St John Lateran. Elsewhere much more of this early architecture survived than catches the eye today. Outstanding Romanesque architecture, mainly from the twelfth century, can still be appreciated in the cathedrals of Lund in Sweden and Durham in England as well as in the cathedral of St Magnus on Orkney island to the north of the Scottish mainland.

The Renaissance in fifteenth-century Italy brought a revival of interest in the architecture of the Roman Empire. Filippo Brunelleschi was the undisputed initiator of this return to 'classical' architecture and the cathedral in Florence his most famous monument. Also working in Florence was Leone Battista Alberti. Renaissance architecture entered the sixteenth century with Donato Bramante and Michelangelo and its centre moved to Rome.

There was the other side of the coin, a distaste for architectural grandeur. Hostility seems to have focused principally upon the huge buildings of some religious orders and was often linked to disgust at their extensive lands and property. It helps to explain why the dissolution of religious orders, and the confiscation or destruction of their property, incurred relatively little opposition in those countries that accepted the Reformation. Especially in the late Middle Ages, wealthy religious houses and their large buildings could be singled out for attack. During the Peasants' Revolt in England in 1381, for example, the buildings of St Albans and Bury St Edmunds monasteries were targeted; Norwich cathedral priory was assaulted in 1272 and 1453. Sometimes opposition extended more widely and on principle to church buildings, especially to their ornamentation. At the Lollard trials held within the diocese of Norwich between 1428 and 1431, various individuals admitted to holding that 'material churches be but of little avail and ought to be of little reputation, for every man's prayer said in the field is as good as the prayer said in the church'; bell-towers in churches also came in for attack, on the grounds that the only purpose of ringing the bells was to 'enable priests to collect money'. In the widely read *De imitatione Christi* by Thomas à Kempis there is little attention to church buildings or to services in church; the focus rather is upon interior devotion. On architectural issues, as on many others, there was considerable diversity of outlook among Catholics of the time.

Painting and sculpture

The initial and crucial role of *Ambrogiotto di Bondone* (1267–1337), commonly known as *Giotto*, in the history of Renaissance art was quickly recognized. The exceptional quality of the Florentine painter's art was acknowledged by his contemporaries, including both Dante and Petrarch, and he was regarded as the seminal figure by Giorgio Vasari, whose *Lives of the Artists*, written in the mid-sixteenth century, dominated the interpretation of Reniassance art for several centuries. The details of Giotto's life are sketchy, but a remarkable amount of his art survives, all of it in Italy and almost all is of a religious nature. He moved beyond the somewhat rigid formality and stereotypic formulae prevalent in the art of the time, which was influenced by Byzantine art, to a new sense of dramatic realism. His genius for naturalism and characterization, whereby persons and scenes come vividly alive, are best seen in the cycle of paintings of the life of Christ in the Arena chapel in Padua. His work is also well represented in the chapels of the Peruzzi and Bardi families in Santa Croce church in Florence and possibly – the identity of the painter is disputed – in the frescoes depicting the life of St Francis in the basilica dedicated to the saint in Assisi.

Giotto was not immediately succeeded by artists of comparable talent. Works of good quality in the older, more traditional styles continued to be painted. Good examples are the frescoes of the life of Christ in the main parish church of San Gimignano in northern Italy, which were painted by Barna da Siena around 1380, or the 'Wilton diptych' which portrays king Richard II of England surrounded by Jesus and Mary, three saints and a host of angels. There was the *Danse macabre* or 'Triumph of Death' genre of paintings, which emphasized the proximity of death and developed in the mid-fourteenth century following the horrors of Black Death plague. Vivid examples in Italy are the frescoes by Francesco Traini in the 'Camposanto' cemetery building next to the cathedral in Pisa, or those in the Sacro Speco church within the Benedictine monastery in Subiaco. Art of an earlier age, too, continued to be influential, as instanced by the evocative Byzantine-style 'Last Judgement' which was painted around the year 1200 to adorn the rear inside wall of Chaldon parish church in Surrey, England.

In the early fifteenth century Flemish artists took the lead in quality paintings. Notable among them were the brothers Hubert and Jan van Eyck and Roger van der Weyden. Their paintings combine religious devotion and attention to the divine with warm sympathy for the trials and triumphs of men and women, together with high artistic quality. They are also characterized by attention to detail and symbolism. The altar-piece in St Bavo church in Ghent, painted by the van Eyck brothers, with its many panels centring on the triumph of Christ as the Lamb of God, is perhaps their finest work. Flemish artists were also responsible for a very important technical development, the abandonment of 'tempera' – finely ground colour pigments 'tempered' (mixed) with diluted egg yolk – which had hitherto been the favoured medium, in favour of combining the pigments with oil. This new combination allowed for richer and brighter tones as well as finer attention to detail. The second half of the fifteenth century saw the sensitive work of Hugo van der Goes and Hans Memling, both painting in Flanders, and the imaginative creations of the Dutchman Hieronymus Bosch, most notably his 'Garden of Delights', which is now in the Prado Museum in Madrid.

Italy provided the other most fertile centre in the fifteenth century and gradually leadership moved back to this country. Antonello da Messina (1430–79), who knew Flemish painters certainly through personal contacts and possibly also by visits north, combined both schools well in his own work, including fine portraits of St Mary and St Sebastian. He was the first Italian artist of note to paint with oils, having learnt the new technique through his Flemish contacts, and he ushered in a revolution as other Italian artists followed his example. A galaxy of other important Italian artists of this time were, in roughly chrono-logical order, Massaccio, the Dominican friar Fra Angelico, Filippo Lippi, Paolo Uccello, Piero della Francesca, Andrea Mantegna, Giovanni Bellini, Sandro Botticelli, Domenico Ghirlandaio and Piero Perugino. Perhaps the most famous work is Fra Angelico's intense and lyrical 'Annunciation', depicting Mary and the angel Gabriel, which was painted for the Dominican friary in Florence. Botticelli's 'Birth of Venus', another masterpiece, reminds us of the abiding interest in pagan mythology and warns against an overly Christian interpretation of late medieval Europe. The full flowering of Italian Renaissance art was well under way by 1500. The walls of the Sistine Chapel in Rome were painted in the early 1480s, princi-pally by Botticelli, Ghirlandaio and Perugino. Leonardo da Vinci had painted many of his best known works before the end of the century, including 'Adoration of the Magi', 'Virgin of the Rocks' and the 'Last Supper'.

For late medieval art, Italy and Flanders provided the two most famous centres. The brilliance and depth of the work produced there may help to explain why the two countries remained predom-inantly Catholic thereafter – such fine and evidently Catholic art was instructive and had to be appreciated.

Closely allied to painting were *stained glass and manuscript illumination*. For stained glass the compositions in Chartres and York cathedrals, already mentioned, are outstanding examples. Manuscript illumination had a long history. The apex of the art was reached in the fifteenth century, before the advent of printing produced radical changes of format. Perhaps the finest examples come from the illustrations in the *Très Riches Heures du Duc de Berry*, which were executed by three Flemish brothers, Pol, Jean and Armand de Limbourg. The brothers had trained in Paris, also perhaps in Italy, and were active at the court of Duke Jean de Berry in Bourges, France. For this liturgical prayer book, they produced a series of exquisite panoramas of human life within the setting of nature and following the seasons of the year. The result is both secular and religious – 'incarnational' might be a better description.

Almost as dramatic as developments in painting were those in *sculpture*; though these were largely confined to Italy, principally to Florence, and to the fifteenth century. The twelfth and thirteenth centuries had been a golden age for religious sculpture in Europe, as exemplified by the designs in the cathedrals of Chartres and Wells. This 'Gothic' tradition continued to be creative, for example in the early fourteenth century carvings by Lorenzo Maitani which adorn the façade of Orvieto cathedral. But alongside it there developed a more realistic style of sculpture, paralleling the developments in Renaissance painting. An early masterpiece came with the scenes from the Old and New Testaments on the bronze doors of the baptistery next to the cathedral in Florence, which were carved by Lorenzo Ghiberti. Donatello (1385–1466), an apprentice of Ghiberti and a prolific worker, is best known for the gruesome scene that portrays John the Baptist's head being brought to king Herod, sculpted for the baptismal font of Siena cathedral, and for his bronze David, which he made for an unknown patron.

Donatello's sculpture of David revealed an exaltation of the human body that had not been seen in western art since classical times. The nude adolescent exults in his body as much as in his conquest of Goliath and the onlooker is invited to do the same. For many years it remained the only work of its kind. Exaltation of the nude body reappeared in Michelangelo's majestic statue of the young David, which he carved in marble between 1501 and

1505, and it remained a basic theme of Renaissance art thereafter. Many thought it took the 'incarnational' aspect of Christianity too far. But the religious motivation of this more positive approach to the human body, in reaction to what was regarded as the prevalent over-wary approach, should be appreciated.

Both Donatello and Michelangelo sculpted their statues of David while they were living in Florence and the city remained the undisputed centre of Renaissance sculpture during the fifteenth century. Other artists of high quality working in the city were Luca della Robbia, whose best known work, the marble reliefs for the Singers' Pulpit in Florence cathedral, combines charm with gravity; Bernardo Rossellino; the prolific and versatile Antonio del Verrocchio, who worked in marble, terrarotta, silver and bronze; and Antonio Pollaiuolo.

Music

It will be apparent from various other sections in this and the previous chapter that the medieval Church was very musical. Boys, especially, learnt to sing from an early age. Music was one of the 'Quadrivium' studied at university and often earlier at school. Singing the 'hours' of the divine office was central to the lifestyle of religious orders. Indeed it was called *Opus Dei* (God's work) in the monastic orders because it was such an integral part of the monk's vocation. Monks and friars normally sang the office in the church of their monastery or friary – in the 'choir' of the church – so the laity could participate at least through hearing and sometimes more directly. Sometimes the laity organized their own singing of the office: we have already met Duchess Cicely who heard 'Evensong by note' before supper. Some singing by the congregation in a parish church during Sunday Mass was common. Plenty of fine hymns survive from the Middle Ages, such as *Crux fidelis*, *Pange lingua* and *Victimae paschale* for Holy Week and Easter, and *Veni Sancte Spiritus* for Pentecost. Religious orders formed the primary context for these hymns and they were composed in Latin. But they were also appropriate for the laity, for Masses in parish churches on Sundays and other days. Most of the laity had some knowledge of Latin and singing was an integral part of prayer.

Chantries, which were specially popular in the late Middle Ages, fostered important developments in church music. Mass of the Dead (*Requiem* Mass) was commonly 'chanted' by the priest, wholly or in part, and at least sometimes the laity joined in the singing. It seems likely that the first surviving polyphonic setting for the Ordinary of the Mass, *Messe de Nostre Dame*, which was written in the 1360's by Guillaume de Machaut, canon of Rheims cathedral, was composed for a small lay choir to sing during the chantry Mass which Guillaume had endowed in the cathedral. A liturgical concert in a large church can be imagined, with several chantry masses being sung one after the other or simultaneously.

Other late medieval developments in religious music came from the Low Countries and northern France. There emerged a remarkable group of talented composers and musicians the majority of whom were born and trained in the counties of Hainault, Artois, Flanders and Brabant. An important factor was the court of the duke of Burgundy, who was the dominant noble within the region for much of the period. Successive dukes promoted an elaborate style of court life, within which music was greatly encouraged. Composers associated with the Burgundian court included Johannes Tapissier, Gilles Binchois, Anthony Busnois and Hayne van Ghizeghem. Around 1350 the composer Johannes Chiwagne – better known as Ciconias – from Liége entered the service of pope Clement VI in Avignon and subsequently worked in many cities in northern Italy. In the fifteenth century, Guillaume Dufay, from Cambrai in northern France, perhaps the most acclaimed composer of the century, worked in Italy and at the court of the duke of Savoy as well as in his native city; Johannes Ockeghem worked as a composer almost exclusively for the French royal chapel; Josquin des Prez, also from northern France, spent a long period in Italy, first as a singer at the papal Chapel in Rome, then as composer at the court of the duke of Milan, and he worked for Ercole II Este, duke of Ferrara. As well as the high quality of their music, the musicians in question brought a number of technical improvements that were to have a profound influence upon the development of religious music in the West: elegant counterpoint; compositions that reflected geometric or arithmetic proportions, including numbers that were significant in Christian theology, thus adding a mystical or symbolic dimension; music to stimulate the intellect as well as the ear; the development of polyphony – most notably in

Josquin des Prez's *Missa Pange Lingua* and *Missa Hercules Dux Ferrariae* – and motet as musical forms.

Just as there existed an austere attitude regarding architecture, so with music. Most famously Bernard of Clairvaux, in the twelfth century, censured as over-elaborate the liturgy and singing of the Cluniac monks. He sought to return his Cistercian monks to the primitive monastic liturgy, banishing sung 'Tropes' and 'Sequences' and other later developments. Several popes, most notably John XXII at Avignon, criticized polyphony on the grounds that it was liable to obscure the intelligibility of the text which was being sung. At the close of the Middle Ages, however, it is noticeable that music featured little among the otherwise wide-ranging Protestant criticisms of the medieval Church.

viii. Challenges to western Christendom

The Catholic church faced a variety of challenges from both within and beyond the Christian community. The courage and imagination with which these challenges were met is remarkable, even though some of the approaches and methods cannot be squared with Christian principles today.

Dissident movements within western Christendom

The western Church was confronted within by four major dissident movements during this period: Cathars, also called Albigensians in southern France because the city of Albi lay at the centre of their influence; Waldensians; John Wyclif and the Lollards; Jan Hus and the Hussites.

Cathars. The word 'Cathar' comes from the Greek *katharos* meaning 'pure'. Cathars, accordingly, sought for purity and the spiritual principle, and therefore freedom from the material world, which they regarded as belonging to the evil principle. This dualist teaching, which has obvious similarities with Manichaeism and other heresies in the early Church, and quite probably had more direct links with them through the Bogomil movement in the Balkans, came to prominence in western Europe in the middle of the twelfth century. Its centres were mainly in northern Italy and German-speaking countries as well as in France and the Rhineland.

Many of its outward forms and practices were similar to those of Catholicism, yet the central tenets of the teaching, with its radical rejection of the material world and therefore of Christ's incarnation, placed it outside rather than alongside orthodox Christianity. The Church reacted to the movement with vigour, through the Inquisition and crusades, and through various internal developments – most notably the success of the Franciscan order – which cut much of the ground from under the Cathars' criticism of worldliness and other failures in the Church.

Catharism survived into the later Middle Ages in a somewhat fragmentary manner, principally in southern France. Jacques Fournier, bishop of Pamiers, who later became pope Benedict XII, recorded in minute detail his investigations into Catharism in the parts of his diocese that lay within the French Pyrenees, principally the village of Montaillou and surrounding districts, between 1318 and 1325. His findings, which Emmanuel Le Roy Ladurie summarized in his study *Montaillou*, make fascinating reading. They reveal a mixture of bizarre beliefs and serious theology, members of a harassed and threatened community. By this date Catharism as an organized movement appears to be in terminal decline, accelerated too by bitter internal divisions; though its memory and teachings continued to exercise some influence upon religion in the West, for the most part in an indirect and diffuse way, throughout the late Middle Ages.

Waldensians. The Waldensian movement was both similar to and different from Catharism. The movement emerged later than Catharism and with a definite founder. It survived through the late Middle Ages, to resurface during the sixteenth century Reformation. It shared some of the puritanism and austerity of Catharism but was much less extreme regarding the dualism of spirit and matter. Waldensians saw themselves, for the most part, as a reform movement within the Church rather than an alternative to it.

Valdes, or Peter Waldo as he came to be known, was a rich citizen of Lyons who converted around the year 1170 to a life of poverty, good works and preaching. He soon attracted a following among like-minded people, first in Lyons and then further afield. While some of his ideas met with approval from church authorities, they refused to recognize the right of lay people to preach. As a result, Valdes and his followers were excommunicated and the movement moved into schism. Many of their proposals, however, especially regarding poverty and preaching, were taken over by the new orders of friars, principally the Franciscans and Dominicans, and adapted to forms that were acceptable to the papacy and most bishops.

Waldensian communities, in the later Middle Ages, were to be found principally in southern France, northern Italy, and various German-speaking countries. There were divisions within the movement principally between 'moderates', often called 'Poor men of Lyons', who kept more or less to the teachings of Peter Waldo, and the more extreme wing, based in northern Italy and often called 'Poor Lombards', who went further in denying the validity of the sacraments and on other issues. Divisions within the movement, however, appear to have been less bitter than those among the Cathars. As with most persecuted groups, information about Waldensians, and therefore about the nature of their challenge to the Church, remains shadowy and comes to a large extent from the prosecution. While they always remained a minority movement, it seems safe to say that their numbers, adding together the various groupings, ran into tens of thousands.

John Wyclif (or Wycliffe) provided the most formidable intellectual challenge to the western Church in the later Middle Ages. He anticipated most of the teachings of the Protestant Reformation in the sixteenth century, so that with reason he quickly came to be called in English circles 'the morning star of the Reformation'. Wyclif was born around the year 1330, probably in Yorkshire. He studied at Oxford university, was ordained priest, and spent most of the rest of his life as a teacher at the university. There he was widely recognized as the most brilliant teacher of his time in both philosophy and theology. He was a prolific writer. His teaching, crucially on the doctrine of transubstantiation, but also on a range of other issues, gradually came in for censure on the part of various ecclesiastical authorities: those of his own university of Oxford, pope Gregory XI through papal bulls issued in 1377, and the archbishop of Canterbury presiding over two synods held at the Dominican friary in London in 1382. Wyclif had powerful friends, most prominently the king's uncle, John of Gaunt. Because of them and the relatively free atmosphere prevalent in English academic circles at the time, as well as out of respect for his age and status, Wyclif escaped mortal punishment. In 1381 he was obliged to retire from Oxford to Lutterworth in Leicestershire, where he held the benefice of rector of the parish church. He died there three years later, following a stroke.

His teachings received their most solemn condemnation some thirty years after his death, at the council of Constance in May 1415. The forty-five condemned articles revealed the wide range of issues on which Wyclif was held to teach unorthodoxly and why the Church took him so seriously They concerned the Eucharist (articles 1–5), other sacraments (4, 7, 28), predestination (8, 26–27), prayer (19, 25–26), preaching (13–14), indulgences (42), oaths (43), tithes (18), clergy, religious orders and church property (4, 10–12, 15–16, 20–24, 28, 30–36, 39, 44–45), papacy and the Roman church (8–9, 28, 33, 36–37, 40–42, 44), universities and learning (29), and secular authorities (8, 12, 15–17, 29).

The origin of the word Lollard is unclear. Most likely it comes from the Dutch *lollen* 'to mumble' and signifies a vagabond or religious eccentric: a derogatory term that the orthodox applied to those they regarded as disciples of Wyclif. The individuals concerned avoided the term and preferred to call themselves, so far as we can tell, 'true followers of Christ' or 'true followers of the gospel' or perhaps Wycliffites. The closeness of links between John Wyclif and the Lollards is debated among historians.

During his lifetime Wyclif had some close associates, mostly at Oxford university, as well as a much wider audience. Within a decade or so after his death, the first ever English translation of the whole Bible – subsequently known as the 'Lollard Bible' – appeared (in two versions). Wyclif had advocated such a vernacular trans-lation, but probably all or most of the work was done after his death by a group of translators, perhaps under the separate directions of Nicholas Hereford and John Purvey. This English Bible enjoyed notable success until the new translations of the sixteenth century, as evidenced by the many manuscript copies that survive. Some of them, indeed, were owned by individuals otherwise known for their orthodoxy. However, in 1407 the archbishop of Canterbury, Thomas Arundel, prohibited the use of any translation of the Bible made 'in the time of John Wyclif or since' and forbade the making of any fresh translation without ecclesiastical approval. No such approval was given and the Lollard (or Wycliffite) Bible remained the only available – albeit prohibited – English translation of the whole Bible.

William Sawtry, a priest from East Anglia, was the movement's first martyr. He was burnt at the stake as a relapsed heretic – on the grounds that he had been convicted twice – in London in 1401. Over a hundred other individuals – the majority men, but a significant number of women – were executed during the fifteenth and early sixteenth centuries. In this repression, ecclesiastical and secular authorities cooperated closely: heresy was seen as a threat to both Church and State.

Jan Hus was born of a peasant family at Husinec in Bohemia (approximately the Czech Republic today) around 1372. He was a student and then a popular teacher at the recently founded university of Prague. Ordained priest in 1400, he was elected dean of the philosophy faculty in the following year. Alongside his university teaching Hus became well known as a preacher at Bethlehem chapel, a large church with close links to the university. There he preached in the Czech language rather than in Latin or German. Hus was attracted to the teachings of Wyclif, especially those of a more moderate nature, regarding Wyclif's criticisms of excessive wealth and hierarchical structures in the Church, and his emphasis upon predestination and the Church of the elect. He translated several of Wyclif's works into Czech. At first Hus received encouragement from the archbishop of Prague, but soon matters turned sour. He was denounced to Rome in 1407 and in 1415 he was summoned to the council of Constance where he was tried and condemned, despite protestation that his beliefs were not being fairly represented, and, in breach of the safe-conduct granted to him, he was burnt to death at the stake. His close colleague, Jerome of Prague, met the same fate at the council ten months later.

When news of his death reached Bohemia, Hus quickly became a national hero. Four hundred and fifty-two nobles of Bohemia and neighbouring Moravia affixed their seals to a protest to the council of Constance. The university of Prague declared him a martyr. 'Four Articles of Prague' were proclaimed in 1420 in which the Hussites, as they were now called, laid down a programme involving (1) secularization of church lands and property, (2) Utraquism (the word derives from the Latin *uterque*, meaning 'both'), whereby the laity would receive communion in the forms of both bread and wine, (3) use of the Czech language in the liturgy, and (4) various elements of church reform. The Hussite movement was more united in opposition than in success. A basic division soon emerged between Utraquists (as the moderate party was called), that is, those who were largely satisfied with the Four Articles of 1420, together with greater autonomy from Rome, and those who wanted, in addition, more radical religious and social changes.

The council of Basel reached agreement with the Utraquists in the *Compactata* of Prague in 1433: the chalice was permitted to the laity at communion and the confiscations of church property that had taken place in the earlier stages of the Hussite movement were accepted. The more extreme wing, called 'Taborites' (after Mount Tabor in Galilee), achieved considerable military success for some years, led by Jan Zizka, but they were decisively defeated at the battle of Lipany in 1434 by a coalition of Catholics and moderate Hussites. Bohemia remained, however, a centre for theological debate and proposals for church reform.

Peter Chelcicky (1390–1460) emerged as the inspiration and early leader of the *Unitas fratrum* (Unity of the Brethren) movement in Bohemian and neighbouring Moravia. The movement was influenced by both Hussites and Taborites but had its own characteristics. Peter was a pacifist and strongly opposed to the shedding of human blood; he promoted manual work, shunned urban life and encouraged use of the vernacular language. He was a fierce critic of the evils of both Church and State, believing that poison had entered the Church when it was endowed by the emperor Constantine. Property was to be held in common, at least for priests and lay preachers in the movement; the use of oaths was rejected, even in judicial proceedings; and the sufficiency of Scripture was emphasized. There were revisions and divisions within *Unitas fratrum* after Chelcicky's death, but the movement was still a potent force in the early sixteenth century.

The influence of Wyclif and the Lollards and of the Hussite movement upon the Reformation in the sixteenth century appears indirect rather than immediate, yet the influence was real. Some of their concerns influenced, too, the Catholic Counter-Reformation.

Inquisition and the prosecution of heresy

The Inquisition with a capital 'I' must be distinguished from inquisition. As we have seen, inquiry (Latin *inquisitio*) into religion, notably through the enforcement of emperor worship, was a feature of the Roman Empire within which the early Church lived. Christianity took over many features of this religious inquiry when it emerged as the official religion of the empire in the early fourth century, enshrining them most notably in Book 16 of the Theodosian Code (438/9). In the following centuries uniformity of religion, including inquiry and coercion, were features, with varying degrees of intensity, of most communities that became predominantly Christian. Charlemagne, indeed, threatened with death those who did not convert to Christianity during his conquest of Saxony in the late eighth century.

The beginning of the Inquisition (with a capital 'I') is usually dated to the reign of pope Gregory IX, particularly to bulls issued by him in 1231: though his pontificate saw a crystallization of existing trends rather than a sudden change of policy. In a series of measures the pope reserved the investigation of heresy in certain regions to officials appointed by him, thereby withdrawing the matter from the authority of both secular rulers and the bishops of the locality. Part of the context was the growing threat of the Cathar heresy in southern Europe. Dominican and Franciscan friars were usually appointed as the inquisitors, and gradually a body of recognized procedures and penalties grew up. To what extent the Inquisition was a permanent institution, rather than temporary commissions to individuals, is debated among historians. The commissions, from the thirteenth to the fifteenth century, were confined to certain countries, notably France, Germany and northern Italy. In many other countries the Inquisition never functioned and the prosecution of heresy remained primarily in the hands of the local church, principally the bishops but including the secular authorities. It was only in the sixteenth century, during the reign of pope Paul III (1534–49), that the Inquisition became a clearly defined and centralized institution. In Spain a separate Inquisition, known as the Spanish Inquisition, was established in 1478, approved by the pope but under royal control.

The use of torture by the Inquisition, to extract information and confessions, was authorized by pope Innocent IV in 1252, albeit with restrictions. Penalties for those found guilty of heresy ranged from mild penances to imprisonment, scourging and the ultimate sanction, normally reserved for relapsed or obstinate offenders, of being handed over to the secular authorities, which usually meant death by burning at the stake. Church and State normally cooperated closely in the matter. While there was a genuine desire for the conversion of the sinner and mercy was often exercised – indeed the Inquisition protected many individuals from false accusations, especially women accused of witchcraft – nevertheless corporal punishment was frequent and many people were put to death. Partly there was a desire to protect other members of the Christian community from what was regarded as the infection of heresy, partly there was a sense that the Christian gospel is self-evidently true, so that anyone who has seen the light and then rejects it must be gravely at fault.

The activity of the Inquisition appears to have declined after about 1320. The decline must be explained partly by the Inquisition's early success, especially in dealing with the challenge of Catharism: the need for the Inquisition became less pressing. In the early fourteenth century, some of the investigations into the Knights Templar were undertaken by officials of the Inquisition, but the resulting executions, following the suppression of the order at the council of Vienne in 1311, were largely the responsibility of the king of France. Margaret Porete was condemned by the Inquisition in 1310, but a century later Jeanne d'Arc was tried and executed by the religious and secular authorities of England and France, without the Inquisition intervening. Jacques Fournier investigated the Cathars of Montaillou between 1318 and 1325 as bishop of Pamiers, not as an official of the Inquisition. Waldensians in Berne, Switzerland, were tried and punished in 1399 by the city government.

From the late fourteenth century onwards England and Bohemia were the most significant countries in terms of heresy, yet it was authorities other than the Inquisition that tackled the matter in these countries, wholly so in England and for the most part in Bohemia. Several factors explain the situation in England. The country was largely unaffected by Cathars and Waldensians, so there was little reason for the Inquisition to intervene in the thirteenth century. In addition, hostile feelings towards the French-dominated Avignon papacy would have made papal intervention through the Inquisition difficult in the fourteenth century. The English bishops were capable and well organized, so when Wyclif and the Lollards appeared in the late fourteenth century, they were able to confront the situation themselves, supported by the Crown and other secular authorities and without the immediate need of outside assistance. The challenge, moreover, coincided with the papal schism and the conciliar movement, during which time a divided and weakened papacy had less authority to insist on its right to intervene. Even so, in the condemnation of John Wyclif's teaching, national and central authorities worked in harmony: major contributions to the prosecution in England came, as we have seen, from pope Gregory XI – directly rather than through the Inquisition – and the council of Constance.

The prosecution of heresy was the responsibility of a network of authorities and institutions, for the most part working in cooperation. Complexity within this network will be evident from the prosecutions detailed in this section and elsewhere in the chapter. Within this framework the Inquisition had some kind of an institutional role, though one that is difficult to define. For the most part it was called upon to intervene when and where the traditional authorities proved deficient.

Orthodox and other eastern churches

Hope remained throughout the medieval period that the schism between the Catholic and Orthodox churches, which had begun in 1054, might be healed. Two general councils met in order to resolve the issues: Lyons II in 1274 and Florence in 1439. While formal agreement was reached at Lyons between the council and the Orthodox delegation sent to it by the emperor and the patriarch of Constantinople, the agreement soon failed to find 'reception' within the Orthodox church.

At Florence, agreement was reached on the four principal doctrinal issues separating the two churches. The text of the decree of reunion was published in both Latin and Greek, but it is usually known by the opening celebratory words in the Latin text, *Laetentur caeli* (Let the heavens rejoice). Regarding the contentious *Filioque* clause, which had been added to the Nicene creed by the western Church, there was mutual acceptance. The West would retain it, while the East would keep to the original text without it. Likewise with eucharistic bread, the Catholic church retained the unleavened form while the Orthodox kept leavened bread. Purgatory was recognized, but in a careful and moderate way. Finally, papal authority over all Christians was acknowledged, but this authority was put within the context (*secundum* in the Latin text, *kata* in the Greek) of the 'acts of the ecumenical councils and the sacred canons'.

Despite its serious attention to Orthodox concerns, *Laetentur caeli* failed to find acceptance within the Orthodox communion. Patriarch Joseph of Constantinople, who participated in the negotiations and was a strong supporter of the agreement, died in Florence shortly before the promulgation of the decree. His successor Metrophanos proved hostile to the agreement. The emperor John VIII Palaeologus, who was also present in Florence and favoured the reunion, wavered in his support once he discovered there was little support for it within the church of Constantinople. The capture of Constantinople by the Turks in 1453 effectively terminated the possibility of further discussions between the two churches.

The council of Florence went on to achieve reunions with three other separated churches: Armenian, Coptic (including Ethiopia) and Syriac. The reunions were with small groups within these communities, nevertheless they resulted in churches in communion with Rome which the second Vatican council would later call eastern Catholic churches.

Outside these two councils, the Catholic church's relations with the Orthodox and other separated churches were a mixture of hope and strain, predominantly the latter. Relations with the Orthodox church were severely stretched in 1204 when western crusaders sacked Constantinople, following their attempt to restore a pro-western emperor. There were some individual conversions from Orthodoxy to Catholicism. Notable converts in the fourteenth century were the emperor John V Palaeologus, while he was living in exile in Rome, and the scholar Prochoros Kydones; in the fifteenth century, the theologian Bessarion, who converted to Catholicism during his participation at the council of Florence and was created a cardinal by pope Eugenius IV in 1439. Bessarion bequeathed his library, notable for its large collection of Greek and Latin manuscripts, to the Senate of Venice, where it became the foundation of the Marciana library. He and other scholars who followed him as Constantinople became increasingly threatened, in some cases bringing substantial libraries with them, gave an important impetus to Renaissance studies in the West.

The Orthodox church remained largely confident of its own traditions. However, with the diminishment of the territories immediately subject to the authority of Constantinople, due to Muslim expansion and culminating in the fall of the city in 1453, the Russian church came to play an increasingly important role within the Orthodox communion.

Jews and Muslims

The attitudes of Catholics towards Jews and Muslims were a mixture of esteem and fear, of frustration and the desire to convert them to Christianity, of friendship and hostility. On the whole, Christian relations with both groups deteriorated during this time.

Jews numbered perhaps half a million out of a total population of some sixty million in western Christendom in the thirteenth century. For the most part they lived in small enclaves in towns and cities. Hostility towards them was seen most violently in a succession of pogroms: those that preceded the first crusade of 1098, especially in the Rhineland, and others that accompanied the second crusade in 1146–7; massacres that followed when Jews were accused of crucifying a Christian boy, as at York and Norwich in twelfth century England, and at Rinn and Trent in central Europe in the late fifteenth century; those that occurred, principally in Germany and Switzerland, in the aftermath of the Black Death plague, which was blamed by some on the poisoning of wells by Jews; others that occurred when Jews were accused of desecrating the eucharistic host, as portrayed in ghoulish detail in the series of six paintings by Paolo Uccello (1400–75). In addition, Jews were expelled from various countries in the late thirteenth century, most notably from England and France in the 1290s on the orders of their respective kings – the only Jews who were allowed to remain in England were those who converted to Christianity, for whom a house was established in London – and from various towns and principalities in Germany in the fourteenth and fifteenth centuries. In Spain the Christian 'Reconquest' of the country eventually brought many hardships to the substantial Jewish population; many were pressurized into converting to Christianity and then lived under suspicion, many others left Spain altogether.

There was also appreciation and friendship, though these qualities are less easy to document and sometimes come from unexpected sources. Peter Abelard's *Dialogus* with a Jew has been mentioned. In Spain until around 1250 there was notable *convivencia* (living together) and mutual respect between Christians and Jews. Moses Maimonides (1138–1204), who was born a Jew in Cordoba and eventually settled in Egypt, was highly regarded in the West as both philosopher and biblical exegete. He was quoted with much respect by the Dominican intellectuals Albert the Great and Thomas Aquinas. The council of Vienne (1311–12) ordered the founding of professorships for the teaching of Hebrew at the papal Curia and at the universities of Paris, Oxford, Bologna and Salamanca; though the main purpose of the chairs was to train missionaries capable of converting Jews to Christianity. Pope Clement VI (1342–52) protected Jews in Avignon and preferred for himself a Jewish physician. Both he and the emperor Charles IV sought to defend Jews from the charges of causing the Black Death. Some humanist scholars, notably Giovanni Pico della Mirandola and Johannes Reuchlin, learnt Hebrew and engaged with contemporary Jewish scholarship: the city of Florence was a centre of interest in Kabbala and other forms of Jewish theosophy. Subtly indicative of good relations that existed between Christians and Jews are, paradoxically, the church laws that sought to restrict such contacts. What was prohibited had been occurring, presumably. The council of Basel's 'Decree on Jews and neophytes' in 1434 provides a good example:

> *Renewing the sacred canons, we command both diocesan bishops and secular powers to prohibit in every way Jews and other infidels from having Christians, male or female, in their households, or as nurses of their children; and Christians from joining them in festivities, marriages, banquets or baths, or in much conversation, and from taking them as doctors or agents of marriages or officially appointed mediators of other contracts. (Decrees, p. 483)*

Muslim advances almost everywhere except in Spain, the mortal threat posed thereby to Christianity, and the Christian response of crusades, have been outlined. Crusades dominated this response throughout the period. Their justification was explained succinctly by the fourth Lateran council of 1215, in canon 71 'Expedition for the recovery of the Holy Land' which summoned a new crusade. 'It is our ardent desire to liberate the Holy Land from infidel hands', the canon began, asserting that the crusade was a defensive war, regaining land that had once been Christian. There was, too, the bond of personal loyalty to Christ: 'this concern (Latin, *negotium*) of Jesus Christ' to liberate the land that was uniquely his. The decree granted a plenary indulgence to all who went on the crusade or contributed towards it.

Whereas Jews lived within the lands of western Christendom, few Muslims lived within these borders except in the Iberian peninsula. As a result, most Catholics knew Muslims only distantly, by hearsay and legend rather than as people. As late as the eighth century there was hope that Muslims might convert collectively to Christianity, but any such hopes had vanished by the eleventh century. Islam as a religion was to be confronted rather than accommodated. Duns Scotus, writing shortly after 1300, thought Islam might implode, but his reckoning proved wide of the mark:

> Concerning the permanence of the sect of Muhammad, that sect began more than six hundred years after the law of Christ and, God willing, it will soon be brought to an end, since it has been greatly weakened in the year of Christ 1300 and many of its believers are dead and still more have fled, and a prophecy among them states that their sect is to be brought to an end. (*Ordinatio*, Prologue, 2.1.112)

Accurate knowledge of Islam was quite weak in the West. Even a general council could make the grave error of suggesting that Muslims 'adore' (Latin, *adorent*) Muhammad (council of Vienne, 1311/12, canon 25). There were, however, more positive and friendly indications. Thomas Aquinas, in his *Summa Theologiae*, quoted with appreciation various Arab philosophers and commentators on Aristotle, principally Avicenna and Averroes. In Spain, Christian *convivencia* with Jews was matched by good relations with many Muslims, and Raymond Lull complemented his works of spirituality and mysticism with serious engagement with Islamic thought. The professorships in Hebrew ordered by the council of Vienne were to be matched by the same number of chairs in Arabic, in this case too with a view to training Christian missionaries. The good treatment Margery Kempe received from Muslims during her pilgrimage to the Holy Land in the early fifteenth century, and her appreciation of their kindness, have been noted. The 'infidels' mentioned in 1434 in the council of Basel's 'Decree on Jews and neophytes' surely had Muslims in mind, so the decree implicitly indicates that cordial relations between them and Christians were still common.

Paganism, magic and witchcraft

Paganism. The word 'pagan' conveys a wide and rather derogatory meaning, literally someone from the 'countryside' (Latin, *pagus*), as distinct from the more sophisticated Christians who lived, in the early Church, mainly in the towns. Despite the evidence of minimal standards regarding the knowledge and practice of Christianity in the medieval West, there are few indications of paganism in a more positive sense, as an organized alternative religion to Christianity, during the central and late Middle Ages. Whether considerably more paganism lay hidden but was never openly professed, due to fear of the death penalty that might result, is hard to estimate. Some recent scholars argue that it did, notably Ludo Milis (1998). A very important consideration is the Incarnation: Christ, in taking human nature, proclaimed the basic goodness of creation. Accordingly, there is no sharp distinction between Christianity and the rest of life – in a sense, therefore, between Christianity and paganism. Exaltation of the human was central to the early Renaissance and while critics claimed that the emphasis tended towards paganism, proponents of the Renaissance argued rather that such exaltation represented a better and more authentic Christianity.

Regarding *magic and witchcraft*, the possibility of intervention by persons and forces beyond this world was generally accepted. Often, moreover, there was only a thin line – in terms of verification – between the invocation of good and bad spirits. Whereas paganism was a rather vague label and used only rarely as a judicial accusation, witchcraft and magic were thought to be both identifiable and widespread and, as a result, they appear much more frequently and specifically in court cases and other records. Quite often the ecclesiastical authorities protected women from unjust accusations, but the number of people who were tried for magic and witchcraft, and of those who were sentenced to death as a result, increased notably in the fifteenth century.

One of the most famous of such trials was that of Eleanor Cobham, duchess of Gloucester, in 1441. The revealing account from an anonymous English chronicle, which detailed the doubtful activities of a number of people, reads as follows:

In the month of July (1441), Master Roger Bolingbroke, who was a great and skilful man in astronomy, and Master Thomas Southwell, a canon of St Stephen's chapel, Westminster, were taken as conspirators of the king's (Henry VI) death. For it was said that Master Roger should labour to consume the king's person by way of necromancy; and that Master Thomas should say Masses in forbidden and unsuitable places, that is, in the lodge of Hornsey Park near London, upon certain instruments with which Master Roger should ... use his craft of necromancy against faith and good belief. He (Thomas) assented to the said Roger in all his works. On Sunday the 25th of the same month, the said Roger, with all his instruments of necromancy, stood on a high stage above all mens heads in St Paul's churchyard (in London) while the sermon lasted.

The next Tuesday Dame Eleanor Cobham, duchess of Gloucester, fled by night to the sanctuary at Westminster. Wherefore she was held suspect of certain articles of treason.

In the meantime Master Roger was examined before the king's council, where he confessed and said that he wrought the said necromancy at the instigation of Dame Eleanor, to know what should befall her and to what estate she should come. Wherefore she was cited to appear before certain bishops of the king ... in St Stephen's chapel, Westminster, to answer certain articles of necromancy, witchcraft, heresy and treason ...

And this same time was taken a woman called the witch of Eye, whose sorcery and witchcraft Dame Eleanor had long time used. By such medicines and drinks as the witch made, the said Eleanor compelled the duke of Gloucester to love her and to wed her. Wherefore, and also because of relapse, the said witch was burnt at Smithfield.

Dame Eleanor appeared before the archbishop of Canterbury and others and received her penance in this form: that she should go the same day from Temple Bar with a meek and demure countenance to St Paul's cathedral, bearing in her hand a taper of one pound, and offer it there at the high altar. And the following Wednesday she should go from the Swan in Thames Street, bearing a taper, to Christ Church in London, and there offer it up. And the Friday following she should go likewise from Queenhithe, bearing a taper of the same weight, to St Micheal in Cornhill, and there offer it up. Which penance she fulfilled and did right meekly, so that most of the people had great compassion on her.

After this she was committed to the wardship of Sir Thomas Stanley, wherein she remained all her life afterwards, having yearly 100 marks assigned to her for her findings and costs: whose (Stanley's) pride, covetousness and lechery were the cause of her confusion. (English Historical Documents, 1969, pp. 869–70)

The papacy was generally reluctant to give the Inquisition authority in matters of withcraft; though papal bulls in 1398 and 1484 granted a measure of authority to its officials. Inasmuch as it was thought to involve an overt or tacit pact with the devil, witchcraft was a very serious matter. The fifteenth century saw the production of a number of treatises outlining the diabolical dangers of witchcraft and recommending procedures for dealing with it. The best known, *Malleus Maleficarum* (Hammer of Witches), which was written by the German Dominican friars Heinrich Kramer and Jacob Sprenger and published in 1487, was to remain the most influential work of its kind into the seventeenth century.

Chapter 4
Early Modern Catholicism
1500–1800

Most books until recently have given the title 'Counter-Reformation' to this period of Catholic history, at least to the part of it covering 1540 to 1700. The description 'Early Modern Catholicism' has been favoured of late and it seems to me better, especially for a chapter covering all three centuries. Responding to the Protestant challenge was at the forefront of Catholicism for a long time, but much else was happening within the Catholic church.

The sections in the chapter cover, accordingly, both developments within Catholicism that were responses to the Protestant Reformation and those that depended on other factors. Section i surveys the fortunes of the Catholic church within the countries that made up western Christendom in 1500: the geography of contraction and some recovery. The second to fourth sections focus on the papacy, the council of Trent, and religious orders. Section v turns to missionary work and the establishment of the Catholic church outside Europe. Section vi surveys developments in popular religion and the arts. A brief conclusion summarizes the significance of the period.

i. Extent of Catholicism within Europe

The beginning of the Protestant Reformation is usually dated to the year 1517 when Martin Luther – according to the traditional account – nailed his ninety-five theses to the door of the castle church at Wittenberg in Germany. The theses were primarily an attack on indulgences, in particular those that were being offered by the Dominican preacher Johann Tetzel and his companions in return for suggested money offerings to help pay for the rebuilding of St Peter's church in Rome. To this emotive issue of indulgences Luther soon added many others: the papacy and other aspects of church organization, the sacraments, much of Catholic piety and devotional life including religious orders. At root were his emphases upon Scripture almost to the exclusion of Tradition and church authority, and upon justification by faith almost to the exclusion of good works. Martin Luther was a brilliant preacher and writer, a master of the German language, which he used to great effect in writing hymns and translating the New Testament into his native language. Long before his death in 1546, he was the undisputed leader of the Reformation, with appeal well beyond the German-speaking world.

John Calvin emerged as the second major founder of the Protestant Reformation. He followed Martin Luther in many respects while taking these positions to what he considered their logical conclusions. He was an able organizer and made Geneva (now in Switzerland), where he lived from 1541 until his death in 1564, the centre of his influence. There he established the Genevan Academy, which acted as a college for training Reformed ministers throughout Europe. His *Institutes* provided in a single volume a comprehensive compendium of teaching, whose enormous circulation was unmatched by any other work of the Reformation. Besides Luther and Calvin, there were many other personalities of note, but the third crucial contribution to the Reformation came from England. There the Anglican Church emerged gradually during the sixteenth century, beginning with king Henry VIII's breach with Rome in 1534 over the matter of his divorce and taking more definitive shape during the long reign of queen Elizabeth (1558–1603).

The Catholic church was slow to confront the challenge. Despite many virtues in the Renaissance papacy, worldliness and immorality persisted during the reigns of Leo X (1513–21) and Clement VII (1523–34). As a result, the papacy remained open to many of the criticisms that Reformers were making. Early on Luther appealed to a general council to resolve the crisis, though quickly he moved his appeal to Scripture. The papacy also proved reluctant to call a new general council partly from fear that it might revive the ghost of conciliarism and partly because Lateran V (1512–17), a general council of the western Church, had only recently completed its work. In its final decree, just three months before Luther posted his ninety-five theses at Wittenberg, this council declared as follows, in eerie unawareness of what would soon occur:

> *Finally, it was reported to us (pope Leo X) on several occasions, through the cardinals and prelates of the three committees (of the council), that no topics remained for them to discuss and that over several months nothing at all had been brought before them by anyone.*

Another reason for the slowness of the Catholic church's response to the Protestant challenge was widespread sympathy, even among those who would remain Catholic, for many of the Reformers' criticisms of a more practical nature, while the seriousness of the doctrinal issues became fully apparent only gradually.

Calls for reform had featured within the late medieval Church, as we have seen in the last chapter, and they continued thereafter. As a result, some historians prefer to speak of 'Catholic Reform' throughout the sixteenth century on the grounds that the reforms emerged essentially from within the Catholic community. This analysis is partly correct. Nevertheless reforms especially after about 1540 were much influenced by the Protestant Reformation, as responses to this challenge, so the term Counter-Reformation is also appropriate. Three crucial elements in this Counter-Reformation will be discussed in the following sections of the chapter: the reformed papacy, the council of Trent, and new religious orders. Gradually the Catholic church regained confidence and initiative.

Borders ebbed and flowed considerably during the sixteenth century and the first half of the seventeenth. There were religious wars within Germany and Switzerland; the prolonged 'Wars of Religion' in France during the second half of the sixteenth century; the struggles which brought about the Dutch republic, its independence from Spanish rule and the establishment of a Calvinist church there. The development of the Anglican Church in England was interrupted by the Catholic reign of queen Mary (1553–8). Many were killed on both sides in the various countries, as combatants or casualties in the fighting and some more directly as martyrs for their faith. In England there were between 250 and 300 Protestants martyrs during the reign of Mary and approximately the same number of Catholics in the course of the sixteenth and seventeenth centuries.

When the Thirty Years War ended with the Peace of Westphalia in 1648, roughly half the countries of western Christendom were officially or predominantly Protestant, principally in a Lutheran, Calvinist or Anglican form: much of Germany, all of Scandinavia, the (northern) Netherlands, England and Scotland, much of Switzerland, significant groups in France and in many other countries. Spain, Portugal, Belgium (the southern Netherlands) and Italy remained Catholic; France, too, with the conversion of king Henry IV in 1593 proving a decisive moment – 'Paris is worth a Mass', he is reported as saying – though the Protestant 'Huguenot' communities were accorded a measure of official protection until king Louis XIV revoked the Edict of Nantes in 1685. Ireland remained predominantly Catholic, though the country was ruled mainly by Protestant Anglophiles. Poland and much of eastern Europe, and many of the states into which Germany was divided, also remained officially or predominantly Catholic. In addition, there were Catholic minorities in all the Protestant countries, varying in size and in the toleration which they were accorded; likewise Protestant minorities, though for the most part rather smaller, in Catholic countries.

After 1648, changes in the overall geography of Catholicism in Europe were relatively minor. England briefly had a Catholic king, James II who reigned from 1685 until his expulsion in 1688. Catholic minorities in some Protestant countries grew in size, though for the most part very slowly. Muslim advances continued to impinge upon the eastern frontiers of western Christendom. Vienna was besieged by a large Turkish army in 1683 and relieved only with great difficulty by the Catholic army led by John Sobieski. This was the furthest west into central Europe that Muslim forces would reach, but the slow decline of the military threat from Islam took time to become evident. Within Catholic countries there was some distancing from Rome and the papacy, a move towards national churches: Gallicanism in France, Febronianism in Germany, and similar movements in Spain, Portugal and Austria. Despite the tensions, all these countries remained within the Catholic church.

Towards the end of the eighteenth century much of Europe, including many Catholic countries, was convulsed by the French

Revolution of 1789 and its repercussions abroad. For a time the survival of the Catholic church, almost the continuity of Christianity, seemed threatened. The threat passed, as we shall see in Chapter 5. Regarding population, we have already noted the peak in the Catholic population of around sixty million in 1300. By 1750 the worldwide Catholic population may be estimated to have grown to some one hundred million, the large majority living in Europe, a rise therefore of some 50 per cent or more.

ii. Papacy

The popes of the early sixteenth century retained many of the features of their immediate predecessors, including their patronage of the arts. Regarding the Protestant challenge, pope Leo X took the decisive steps of condemning various of Luther's teachings in 1520 in the bull *Exsurge Domine*, and excommunicating him in the following year after Luther had publicly burnt a copy of the bull. He also bestowed the title *Defensor fidei* on king Henry VIII of England in 1521 in recognition of the book he published in defence of the seven sacraments against the criticisms of Luther, a title that still remains today on British coins in the discreet form of 'F.D'. The pontificate of Clement VII was devastated by the sack of Rome in 1526, when the Catholic troops of Charles V, king of Spain and Holy Roman Emperor, plundered the city and held the pope captive for over a year. During Clement's reign, too, England moved towards schism as the pope refused to annul king Henry's marriage to Catherine of Aragon and thereby allow him to wed Anne Boleyn.

The years of Paul III (1534–49) proved decisive for Catholic reform. In many ways Paul was typical of the Renaissance popes in his patronage of architects and artists, notably Michelangelo, the promotion of his relatives to offices, the lavish style of his papal court and, in earlier life, his moral laxity – he had kept a mistress who bore him three sons and a daughter. As pope, however, his personal morality was austere and he set the tone for a succession of determined and able popes. Very important, too, was his summoning of the council of Trent, which first met in 1545, and his promotion of new religious orders, including the Society of Jesus which he formally approved in 1540. He was responsible for the reorganization of the Inquisition into a Congregation of the

Roman curia, 'The Inquisition or Holy Office' (*Sacra Congregatio Romanae et Universalis Inquisitionis seu Sancti Officii*), thereby increasing the scope of its authority and its direct links with the papacy. A large building to accommodate the Congregation was constructed later in the sixteenth century. It can be seen today, still the office of the Congregation – which was renamed 'The Holy Office' (*Congregatio Sancti Officii*) in 1908 and 'Congregation for the Doctrine of the Faith' (*Congregatio pro Doctrina Fidei*) in 1965 – to the left of the colonnade in front of St Peter's church.

Throughout the following century the papacy bore many of the characteristics of Paul III's pontificate. Popes Julius III and Pius IV maintained the council of Trent in session until it completed its monumental work in 1563. The papacy then played a key role in the implementation of the council's decrees. A succession of popes continued to promote religious orders, both the older orders and some of those newly founded. Missionary work beyond Europe was encouraged. Paul III's establishment of the Inquisition congregation was complemented by a wider reorganization and strengthening of the Roman curia under pope Sixtus V (1585–90), with arrangements that entitle Sixtus to be considered the founder of the modern Curia. An important addition in 1622 was Propaganda congregation (*Congregatio de Propaganda Fidei*), which was established by pope Gregory XV for the Church's missionary territories.

The papacy became involved in various theological controversies within the Catholic church. Clement VIII established a committee (*Congregatio de Auxiliis*) in 1597 to deal with the heated debate between Jesuit and Dominican theologians regarding the relationship between divine grace and human free will. Finally, after ten years of discussion, pope Paul V ruled eirenically that the Dominicans could not be justly accused of Calvinism nor the Jesuits of Pelagianism, and neither side should pronounce the other teaching heretical. Very unfortunate, however, was the condemnation by the Inquisition, acting with papal approval, of Galileo's teaching of heliocentrism (that the earth moves round the sun). A series of judgments, during the pontificates of Paul V (1605–21) and Urban VIII (1623–44), preferred a literal interpretation of some biblical passages to Galileo's observations through the telescope. Only recently has the papacy openly acknowledged the mistaken nature of this condemnation. Widely praised and eventually followed in Protestant countries was pope Gregory XIII's reform of the Calendar in 1582. The core of the reform consisted in dropping ten days (5–14 October 1582) so that the calendar was brought up to date with the reality of the seasons.

In treating with Protestant rulers, popes showed firmness more than accommodation. Pope Pius V's bull *Regnans in excelsis* in 1570 declared queen Elizabeth of England excommunicated on the ground of heresy. More controversially, it declared her right to the English throne forfeit and laws made by her invalid and it encouraged English people to depose her. As a result, Catholics could be regarded as traitors and most of the English martyrs met their fate in this way, suffering the horrible death proper to traitors of being hung, drawn and quartered. The papacy gave encouragement to the king of Spain to depose Elizabeth and to the ill-fated Spanish Armada in 1588. In France, Henry of Navarre had to wait for two years, following his conversion to Catholicism in 1593, before pope Clement VIII would recognize him as the legitimate king.

Popes continued to support Christian crusades against Muslim forces, even though by now the hope of recapturing the Holy Land and Jerusalem was little more than a dream. Pope Pius V contributed both moral and material support to the 'Christian League' which gained in 1571 an important naval victory over the Turkish fleet near Lepanto in the eastern Mediterranean. In the seventeenth century, the papacy supported Catholic countries during the Thirty Years War and refused to accept the concluding Peace of Westphalia in 1648 because it recognized the existence of Protestant countries and governments. However, the Peace proved a turning point for the papacy. Popes thereafter gradually came to terms with the permanence of Protestant countries, yet finding them right outside their authority they turned their attention more exclusively to Catholic affairs.

In important ways the period up to about 1750 saw a strengthening of papal authority within the Catholic church. The continuing and radical criticisms of the papacy on the part of Protestant reformers led most Catholics, in reaction, to emphasize loyalty to the pope and the crucial importance of the papacy within the Church. Important, too was pope Pius IV's establishment in

1564 of a Congregation of the Roman curia (subsequently called *Congregatio concilii*) to rule on any disputed points regarding the interpretation of the decrees promulgated by the council of Trent. In this way the papacy gained an important measure of control over the implementation of this hugely influential council. Doctrinal disputes within the Catholic church were quite restricted, partly as a result of Trent's comprehensiveness and partly because Catholics valued their doctrinal unity in the face of the continuing Protestant challenge. The papacy was considered a central feature of this doctrinal unity. Those doctrinal disputes that occurred were confined to particular groups and did not seriously call into question papal authority as such: the *De auxiliis* dispute and the controversy over Galileo, just mentioned; Jansenism, mainly in France, in the seventeenth and eighteenth centuries: and the Chinese rights controversy in the eighteenth century. Indeed, inasmuch as the papacy was recognized as an arbiter in these controversies, papal authority was enhanced.

Conciliarism remained alive but it did not constitute a serious alternative to papal government, such as it had been in the fifteenth century. The success of the council of Trent meant there was no urgent need of another general council for a long time: paradoxically the success of this council reduced the threat of conciliarism. The college of cardinals never regained the high measure of authority it had held during the papal schism and the ensuing councils of Constance and Basel. Cardinals remained important but more as individuals in the countries in which they resided or in the Roman curia, where they were firmly subject to papal authority. They came together only to elect a new pope.

The papacy entered again into seriously troubled waters in the second half of the eighteenth century. The new threats came principally from Catholic countries. National churches, with a fair measure of autonomy from Rome, had been a feature of much of western Christendom in the later Middle Ages, as we have seen. This pattern continued in many Catholic countries in the sixteenth and seventeenth centuries: the Gallican church in France, for example, or in Spain where the monarchy exercised much control over the church. Events took a more radical turn around 1750. Authoritarian monarchs in France, Spain and Austria wanted further control over the Catholic church within their dominions. Febronianism in Germany took its name from Johann von Hontheim, suffragan bishop of Trier, who acted as ecclesiastical adviser to the three prince-archbishops of Mainz, Trier and Cologne and who wrote under the pseudonym 'Justinus Febronius'. Von Hontheim attacked what he regarded as medieval and later accretions of papal power and sought to restrict papal authority to purely spiritual matters. The three prince-archbishops, joined by the archbishop of Salzburg, formally endorsed these views in 1786 in a document known as the 'Punctation of Ems' – Ems being the city where the document was drawn up. Various Catholic monarchs and their advisers, notably the Marquis of Pombal in Portugal, showed particular hostility to the Society of Jesus (Jesuits) on account of the order's supra-national character and its loyalty to the papacy. Pope Clement XIV was persuaded to suppress the order in 1773.

Following the outbreak of the French Revolution in 1789, events took a still more serious turn for the papacy. Napoleon's army occupied the Papal States and Pope Pius VI was taken prisoner. He was transported to France, eventually to Valence, where he died in 1799. The demise of the papacy seemed a real possibility.

iii. Council of Trent

The council of Trent ranks among the half-dozen most influential councils in the history of the Church. Convoked by Pope Paul III, it first met in 1545 and eventually concluded its work in 1563. The Protestant challenge was the principal reason for convoking the council, even though Luther, Calvin and other leaders of the Reformation were not mentioned by name in the conciliar decrees.

Trent lies within the German-speaking part of northern Italy and was chosen as a compromise between the pope and the German emperor Charles V. The city was a papal fief, so the pope felt he had adequate control over it even though he would have preferred somewhere nearer Rome. Charles V urged that the council take place within the German-speaking world if it was to have credibility in tackling the issues raised by the Protestant Reformation, which had its origins in Germany and still remained centred there. None of the popes attended the council in person but the papacy was directly represented by three cardinal-presidents who, acting in the name of the pope, presided over the conciliar sessions and were responsible for the conduct of business. The decrees emerged from debates within the council. In this way Trent was closer to the ecumenical councils of the early church than to most of the general councils of the medieval period, when decrees were prepared beforehand and the council's role was largely to approve these drafts. The opening of the council and solemn sessions were held in the cathedral, while other meetings were held in various houses and churches in the city. The language of the council, of the debates as well as of the decrees, was Latin.

At first attendance was slight. Some thirty bishops, mostly Italians, were present at the early sessions but gradually numbers built up to over two hundred bishops – a decently representative figure for the Catholic hierarchy of the time. The eighteen years of the council's existence divided into three periods. After two years of work, the council was prorogued in 1547 on account of a plague threatening the city. Four years later the bishops reassembled, first in Bologna and then back in Trent. After a year's work, the council was prorogued again in 1552 when various German princes revolted against the emperor Charles and a Lutheran army drew near to the city. A gap of ten years followed, during which pope Paul IV (1555–9) showed no inclination to recall the council. Finally, Pius IV summoned the council again in 1562 and its work was completed the following year.

The council quickly attended to the key issue of Scripture and Tradition, asserting the role of both in the Church's teaching and thereby censuring the Reformers' almost exclusive emphasis upon the Bible. The central paragraph of the relevant document reads as follows, in English translation:

> *Our Lord Jesus Christ, Son of God, first proclaimed with his own lips this gospel, which had in the past been promised by the prophets in the sacred Scriptures; then he bade it be preached to every creature through his apostles as the source of the whole truth of salvation and rule of conduct. The council clearly perceives that this truth and rule are contained in written books and in unwritten traditions which were received by the apostles from the mouth of Christ himself, or else have come down to us, handed on as it were from the apostles themselves at the inspiration of the Holy Spirit.* (4th session, 1546)

Attention was then directed to the second key issue in the Reformation debates, that of justification. The need for both faith and good works was asserted, and the role of human free will, yet the emphasis upon God's initiative in our justification accords with Protestant teaching:

> *Justification in adults takes its origins from a predisposing grace of God through Jesus Christ, that is, from his invitation which calls them, with no existing merits on their side. Thus those who have been turned away from God by sins are disposed by God's grace inciting and helping them, to turn towards their own justification by giving free assent to and cooperating with this same grace.* (6th session, 1547)

There follows a fine passage on how those already justified can grow further in holiness and in friendship with God and humanity:

> *So those justified in this way and made friends and members of the household of God, going from strength to strength, are – as the Apostle says (2 Corinthians 4, 16) – renewed from day to day by putting to death what is earthly in themselves and yielding themselves as instruments of righteousness for sanctification by observance of the commandments of God and of the church. They grow in that very justness they have received through the grace of Christ, by faith united to good works ....* (6th session, 1547)

Many other topics in the Reformation controversies hinged on the two issues of the relationship between Scripture and Tradition, and that between faith and good works. Trent issued a wide range of decrees on these other topics, justifying teaching and practices that had become traditional in the Catholic church and showing their roots in the early Church, while seeking to purify both teaching and practice of abuses that may have crept in.

There were decrees on each of the seven sacraments: baptism, confirmation, penance or confession, Eucharist, last anointing, marriage and orders. The Eucharist was treated in particular detail. While traditional Catholic doctrine on this sacrament was reaffirmed, attention was paid to some of the Reformers' emphases. The resulting teaching is profound and full of devotion, careful theology and attention to Scripture. The chapter entitled 'The reasons for the institution of the Eucharist' provides a fine summary:

Our saviour, about to depart from this world to the Father,
instituted this sacrament in which he, as it were, poured out
the riches of his divine love towards humanity, causing his
wonderful works to be remembered (Psalm 110.4), and he
bade us cherish his memory as we partake of it (Luke 22.19;
1 Corinthians 11.24) and to proclaim his death until he comes
(1 Corinthians 11.26) to judge the world. He wished this
sacrament to be taken as the spiritual food of souls, to nourish
and strengthen them as they live by the life of him who said, he
who eats me will live forever because of me (John 6.58), and as
an antidote to free us from daily faults and to preserve us from
mortal sins. He further wished it to be a pledge of our future
glory and unending happiness, and thus a sign of that one body
of which he is the head (1 Corinthians 11.3; Ephesians 5.23)
and to which he wished us all to be united as members by the
closest bonds of faith, hope and love, so that we should all
speak with one voice and there might not be division among us
(1 Corinthians 1.10). (13th session, 1551)

Transubstantiation was reaffirmed but, as at Lateran IV, other
fitting descriptions were not excluded.

In addition to doctrinal statements, Trent enacted a wide
range of decrees for the moral reform of the Church. Early on
the council spoke of 'the dual purpose for which the council was
primarily brought together: rooting out of heresy and reform of
conduct' (3rd session, 1546). One important reform decree, known
as 'Tametsi' from its opening word, provided laws for marriage
which still remain largely normative today: 'banns' announcing
a forthcoming marriage, degrees of affinity and consanguinity
within which marriage is not permitted, the presence of the
parish priest at the wedding service. Many of the other reform
decrees concerned the diocesan clergy – the duties and lifestyle
of bishops and parish priests – and religious orders, both male
and female. Particularly important was the decree on seminaries,
which provided for the first time a recognized system of education
for all prospective diocesan priests. It described the academic and
religious formation thus:

The bishop will divide the boys and young men into the
number of classes he thinks fit, according to their number,
age and progress in ecclesiastical learning. Some he will assign

*to service of the churches when he considers the time is ripe,
others he will keep for education in the college. He will replace
those withdrawn with others, so that the college becomes a
perpetual seminary (Latin seminarium) of ministers of God.
In order that they may be more appropriately grounded in
ecclesiastical studies, they should always have the tonsure and
wear clerical dress from the outset; they should study grammar,
singing, keeping church accounts, and other useful skills; and
they should be versed in holy Scripture, church writers, homilies
of the saints, and the practice of rites and ceremonies and of
administering the sacraments, particularly all that seems appropriate to hearing confessions.*

*The bishop should ensure that they attend Mass every day,
confess their sins at least every month, receive the body of our
lord Jesus Christ as often as their confessor judges, and serve
in the cathedral and other churches of the area on feastdays ...
They (bishops) will punish severely the difficult and incorrigible
and those who spread bad habits, and expel them if need be.
They will take the utmost care to remove all obstacles from such
a worthy and holy foundation and to promote all that preserves
and strengthens it. (23rd session, 1563)*

For the establishment of seminaries, particularly important
were various energetic bishops and some of the new religious
orders. Among the bishops, most notable was Charles Borromeo
(1538–84), who established several seminaries in his huge archdiocese of Milan. They became models for seminaries elsewhere.
Among religious orders, the Society of Jesus and the Vincentians
were in the forefront in establishing and running seminaries for
the diocesan clergy. Their work in this apostolate will be treated in
section iv.

During its final session in December 1563, the council issued a
decree which commended indulgences while urging moderation
in granting them. Thus the immediate cause of the Protestant
Reformation was almost the last issue to be treated by Trent. We
can see paradox here but also the fact that the Reformation had
expanded to so many other issues by the time of the council. The
decree taught thus:

*The practice of indulgences should be retained in the Church,
very salutary as it is for the Christian people and approved by*

the authority of holy councils ... But the council desires that moderation be used in granting them, according to the ancient and approved custom of the Church, so that ecclesiastical discipline be not sapped by too easy conditions. (25th session, 1563)

Also at the last session, the council decided that four topics should be entrusted to the pope because it did not have time to discuss them properly: the Index, Catechism, Breviary and Missal. The first 'Index of Prohibited Books' (*Index Librorum Prohibitorum*), listing the books which Catholics were forbidden to read or own, had been published by pope Paul IV in 1557. In the light of Trent's decree, a fuller list was issued by a new congregation of the Roman Curia, *Sacra Congregatio Indicis Librorum Prohibitorum*, which was established by pope Pius V in 1571. This 'Index' was updated regularly until its 'suspension' – in effect its abolition – by pope Paul VI in 1966. The 'Roman Catechism' or 'Catechism of the Council of Trent' was published in Latin in 1566, principally for the use of parish priests. It influenced the many catechisms which were subsequently written at a more popular level in the vernacular languages. The reform of the Breviary led to the 'Roman Breviary', which was promulgated by Pius V in 1568 and remained normative for the daily prayer of diocesan priests, and of many in religious orders, until after the second Vatican council. The reform of the Missal led to the 'Tridentine Mass', which was published by Pius V in 1570 and remained normative for the large majority of Catholics until the liturgical reforms following Vatican II.

The establishment in 1564 of *Congregatio concilii*, for the interpretation and implementation of the council's decrees, has been mentioned (see p. 172). Altogether the council of Trent exercised a huge influence upon Catholicism throughout the rest of the period covered in this chapter and beyond it. Its doctrinal and reforming decrees provided remarkably comprehensive guidance to the Catholic church for a long time and at many levels: theological, sacramental, vocational, devotional and practical. It lies at the centre of the development of post-medieval Catholicism.

iv. Religious orders

Religious orders encountered fierce criticism during the Protestant Reformation. It came partly on grounds of principle, that their lifestyles were elitist and not supported by Scripture. But many of the Reformers had once been members of religious orders, so there was also personal sharpness in their criticisms. Martin Luther had been an Augustinian friar and later married a former nun, Catherine von Bora. In all the countries in which the Reformation took root, religious orders were suppressed – in England the dissolution of monasteries and religious houses took place under king Henry VIII.

The response of the Catholic church was both to justify religious life in principle, as was done at the highest level by the council of Trent, and to encourage religious orders in a variety of ways, both the older orders and the new foundations of the sixteenth century onwards.

New religious orders

Two of the earliest new male orders in the sixteenth century were Theatines and Barnabites, founded in 1524 and 1530. Theatines were called after one of their four founders, Gian Pietro Caraffa, who at the time was bishop of Chieti (*Theate* in Latin) in Italy and later became pope Paul IV. Barnabites took their name from the church of St Barnabas in Milan, which was the first church staffed by the order. Both orders emphasized a strict way of life and the importance of work – especially education, caring for parishes and missionary work. Both orders, too, spread beyond Italy to various countries of Catholic Europe and Theatines established communities further afield in the 'New World'

Oratorians emerged from the group of priests who gathered round Philip Neri (1515–95), an energetic and charismatic priest in Rome. Houses of the order, called 'Oratories', were established mainly in the larger cities of Europe and a few in the New World. Their work consisted principally in offering to Catholics an intelligent and attractive Christianity: good church services, with special attention to preaching and music; hearing confessions; group meetings for prayer, talks and discussion. Some Oratorians became important scholars, notably Cardinal Baronius (1538–1617), the church historian. Pierre de Bérulle, founder and head of the influential Oratory in Paris, was famous as a preacher, spiritual writer and counsellor. The order played a notable and distinctive role in the renewal of Catholic life.

Best known and largest of the new orders of men was the *Society of Jesus*, whose members were known as Jesuits. Ignatius of Loyola (1492–1556), founder of the order, underwent a religious conversion while convalescing from a wound he received as a soldier. There followed deep religious experiences, wanderings, including a pilgrimage to Jerusalem, and years of study for the priesthood at Paris University. At Paris a group of like-minded men gathered round him and together they formed the Society of Jesus, which was approved by pope Paul III in 1540. Ignatius spent the last sixteen years of his life in Rome, guiding and governing the new order. There he finalized *Spiritual Exercises*, a guide and stimulus to living a good life in harmony with God's will, which was based on his own experiences of religious conversion and had great influence within and beyond the Jesuit order.

The best known of Ignatius's early Jesuit companions was Francis Xavier, who came from the same Basque region of Spain as Ignatius. Xavier left Rome in 1541 and embarked upon missionary journeys that took him to India, Sri Lanka, Malaysia, Indonesia and Japan. He died on his way to, and within sight of, mainland China. The extent of his journeys and the number of people who converted to Christianity through him – an estimated 700,000 – are remarkable. He was a vigorous preacher, inventive in his methods of evangelization, and his organization of new converts into Christian communities produced lasting results. Francis Xavier was soon recognized as one of the most outstanding Christian missionaries of all time.

The Society of Jesus expanded rapidly in numbers and influence, growing to some 8,500 members in 1600 and nearly 23,000 in 1773. Work was given much attention, following Ignatius's recommendation that Jesuits should pray as if all depended on God and work as if everything depended on them. The order was flexible regarding the types of work it undertook, trying to select them according to the maxim *Ad majorem Dei gloriam* (For God's greater glory). Education soon became an important apostolate and Jesuits established a network of schools and universities throughout Catholic Europe and beyond. Their pupils came largely from the middle and upper classes and subsequently exercised great influence in many walks of life. René Descartes (1596–1650), the philosopher, was a devoted pupil of La Flèche, the prestigious Jesuit school near Angers in France. The order also established seminaries for training priests, following the council of Trent's decree on seminaries. The best known was the *Collegio Romano* (Roman College) in Rome, which later became the Gregorian University. The college provided for the training of diocesan seminarians from many countries as well as student Jesuits and it came to exercise much influence upon Counter-Reformation Catholicism.

Jesuits worked as writers and scholars – notably the theologians Robert Bellarmine (1542–1621) and Francisco Suarez (1548–1617), the astronomer and mathematician Christopher Clavius (1537–1612), and the Bollandists (called after their founder John van Bolland) who brought scholarly standards to the study of hagiography (lives of saints) – and as preachers and counsellors. They were active as missionaries both in Catholic and Protestant Europe and in the 'new' worlds of America, Africa and Asia. Robert De Nobili (1577–1656) in India, and Matteo Ricci (1552–1610) in China, were persistent and inventive in their efforts at inculturation – that is, in enabling people of these countries and cultures to feel at home in the ways they lived and expressed Christianity – as were the Jesuit missionaries who established villages (called 'Reductions') for the indigenous people of Paraguay in the seventeenth and eighteenth centuries. Numerous Jesuit martyrs – Edmund Campion (1540–81), Robert Southwell (1561–95), John Ogilvie (1580–1615) and some thirty others in Britain, and many others elsewhere – witnessed to the dedication of the order.

Jesuits, nevertheless, were opposed by many Catholics. Some criticized them for being too close to the wealthy and powerful, others for being too flexible in the morality and inculturation they advocated. However, it was their supra-national character and loyalty to the papacy that were the principal reasons for the suppression of the order in 1773. The order survived tenuously in various non-Catholic countries where the papal bull of suppression was never promulgated, notably in Russia and England, but full restoration was granted by the papacy only in 1814.

The seventeenth and eighteenth centuries produced several important new orders of men which remain vigorous today. The Congregation of the Mission (CM) – sometimes called the Vincentian order after its founder Vincent de Paul (1581–1660), and sometimes the Lazarists after the priory of St Lazare which was Vincent's headquarters in Paris – specialized in preaching missions, especially in country districts, and the education of the diocesan clergy in seminaries. By the mid-eighteenth century they were responsible for many seminaries in France as well as others in Italy, Poland, Spain and Portugal. Paul of the Cross (1694–1775) founded the Passionist congregation for giving missions and retreats to the laity, while members of the order led a strict contemplative life when not engaged in apostolic work. Alphonsus Liguori (1696–1787) founded the Redemptorist congregation, also for the preaching of missions. He is perhaps the most famous Catholic moral theologian and members of the order continued his tradition of studying, teaching and writing on moral theology.

For women, the early modern period saw the foundation of several important new orders. The Ursuline order, named after the martyr Ursula, was founded at Brescia in Italy by Angela Merici in 1535. Originally the lifestyle was somewhat similar to that of beguines, but gradually the order was required by the papacy to become more institutional and convents replaced private houses for living. The education of girls became the main apostolate. Schools were established principally in Catholic Europe, but in the seventeenth and eighteenth centuries two were founded in North America, in Quebec and New Orleans. Also focusing on female education was the Institute of the Blessed Virgin Mary, whose founder was Mary Ward (1585–1645) from England. The order of 'Sisters of Charity' was founded in France jointly by Vincent de Paul and Louise de Marillac, for the care of the sick and the poor. It came to have an enormous influence upon the charitable work of the Catholic church. The Visitation order ('Order of the Visitation of the Blessed Virgin Mary') also originated in seventeenth century France, with Francis de Sales and Jane Frances de Chantal as its joint founders. A contemplative order, its most renowned saint was Margaret Mary Alacocque (1647–90), whose visions had a decisive influence upon Catholic devotion to the Sacred Heart of Jesus. In addition, both the Passionist and Redemptorist congregations had associated orders of nuns.

Reforms of medieval orders

The Counter-Reformation had a deep influence upon all the religious orders that survived from the Middle Ages. Many of them were able to reform themselves and to adapt to the changed situations of the early modern period. Tertiaries of these orders, too, continued to play an important role in the life of the Church. Particularly remarkable was Rose of Lima (1586–1617), who led a saintly life as a Dominican tertiary in Peru.

There were a number of splits in these older foundations, resulting in new reformed orders that have greatly influenced the Catholic church. Already in the medieval period there had been tension among Franciscan friars regarding the character of the order, between clerical and more charismatic approaches. In 1517 the order was formally divided into two: the Conventual Franciscans and the Order of Friars Minor (OFM). Shortly afterwards another reform, introduced by Matteo di Bassi, led to the establishment of the Capuchin friars (called after their pointed cowl, *capuche*), whose Rule was drawn up in 1529. The order was temporarily suppressed following the conversion to Lutheranism in 1541 of its third minister-general Bernardino Ochino, but it was restored again and received full recognition as a religious order in 1619. The enthusiastic preaching and missionary work of the Capuchin friars received wide popular support and made them a potent force in the Catholic revival in Europe and the New World. There were many further splits within the Franciscan family. Reunification into the three branches of Conventual, OFM and Capuchins was only achieved in the late nineteenth century and confirmed by pope Leo XIII in 1897. Yet the divisions were in many ways creative, reflecting tensions that lie at the heart of human endeavour to live the Gospel message: the Franciscan family acted as a kind of fulcrum for the entire Christian community.

Two remarkable Spaniards, Teresa of Avila (1515–82) and her disciple John of the Cross (1542–91), initiated the Carmelite reforms. After some years as a Carmelite nun, Teresa felt the call to a stricter way of life and to found a house where the original rule of the order would be better observed. As a result, despite strong opposition, she founded a reformed convent in the town of Avila in 1562. Much of the rest of her life was devoted to establishing other convents in the reformed order. At the same time Teresa devoted herself to long hours of prayer, during which she experienced the closeness and friendship of God in an exceptional way. She wrote down these experiences in a series of works that make Teresa one of the most important authorities on prayer in the Christian tradition: her *Life* (autobiography), *The Way of Perfection* (written for her nuns), *Foundations*, and, perhaps most popular, *The Interior Castle*.

John of the Cross studied theology as a Carmelite friar at Salamanca university and was ordained priest in 1567. He came to know Teresa of Avila and, becoming dissatisfied with the laxity of his order, tried to introduce her reforms to the Carmelite friars. He met with much opposition and was held for almost a year in a prison of the order, from which he managed to escape. Soon afterwards the reformed Carmelite friars were established as a separate religious order. John's sufferings continued as he was partly disowned by other leaders of the new order, and he died more or less in exile from his order after severe illness. He wrote some beautiful and very influential works on prayer, much of it in the form of poetry: *Spiritual Canticle*, *Ascent of Mount Carmel*, in which he describes the 'dark night of the soul' through which a person intent on God must normally pass, and *Living Flame of Love*. The two reformed orders of Carmelites grew thereafter and they have had a deep influence upon the spirituality and prayer of the Catholic church. Through their writings, John of the Cross and Teresa of Avila had a major influence upon the development of the Spanish language.

Within the Benedictine family, Armand Jean de Rancé, abbot of La Trappe monastery in France, sought to restore the original Cistercian discipline to his community. Eventually his reforms led in the nineteenth century to the Trappist order, more correctly styled Order of Cistercians of the Strict Observance (OCSO). Also in France, the Congregation of St Maur emerged in the seventeenth century as a reform of the Benedictine rule. Its most famous abbey was St-Germain-des-Prés in Paris and its best known monks were scholars. Jean Luc d'Achery (1609–85), Jean Mabillon (1632–1707), Edmond Martene (1645–1739), Bernard de Montfaucon (1655–1741), Thierry Ruinart (1657–1709) and others, contributed greatly to Christian scholarship through their new and more critical editions of theological, historical and liturgical texts. Subsequently the Congregation was beset by internal divisions and was dissolved by pope Pius VII in 1814. Benedictine reforms did not always lead in the same direction: De Rancé was sharply critical of the Maurists' engagement in scholarly work, provoking Mabillon's spirited response in *Traité des études monastiques*.

Summary

Religious orders played a very important role in Catholicism in the early modern period. Most of the older, medieval orders survived in Catholic countries and they made a major contribution to early modern Catholicism. They were supplemented by new foundations of men and women: both new orders, such as the Jesuits, and reforms of older orders, such as the Capuchins. Whereas most of the medieval orders of women were branches of male orders, new foundations for women in the early modern period were more independent. In addition to full members of the various orders, it is important to remember tertiaries and others with varying degrees of affiliation, as well as the huge number of people who were affected by the orders and their ministries. Notwithstanding limitations and failures, and they were plenty, religious orders contributed greatly to the development of Catholicism both in Europe and in the newly evangelized countries of Asia, Africa and America. Almost every corner of the Catholic church was affected as well as many people outside it.

v. Missionary work and Catholicism outside Europe

We have seen that Christianity flourished in north Africa and western Asia during the first six centuries AD. The expansion of Islam radically altered the situation in north Africa while the schism between Rome and Constantinople, beginning in 1054, meant that most Christians in Asia were separated from the Catholic church. The situation changed again dramatically after the arrival of Christopher Columbus in America in 1492. Christianity reached America for the first time, at least as an organized church. Shortly afterwards there were major developments for the Church in Africa and Asia. As never before Christianity could be described as a world religion. Catholicism is the focus of our attention, but it is important to remember the great contributions of other missionaries, principally those of the Protestant churches.

America, Africa and Asia will be considered in turn, beginning with America where the novelty of Christianity was most dramatic. Australasia, which was discovered by westerners in the late eighteenth century, belongs to the next chapter. The geographical areas were vast and there were huge ethnic and cultural variations between and within all three continents. Yet there was basic unity in the missionary work inasmuch as it was held together by the doctrines and institutions of the Catholic church. Accordingly, the developments outlined in the last three sections of this chapter regarding the papacy, the council of Trent and religious orders had important ramifications for missionary work. The decrees of the council of Trent remained fundamental to teaching and discipline in the missionary countries while much of the work of evangelization was done by members of religious orders – Dominicans, Franciscans, Augustinians, Jesuits and others. Very important, too, was the constant support given to missionary work by the popes of the time; though they had to make difficult decisions in defending faithfulness to the gospel and church traditions while promoting appropriate adaptation and inculturation. Particularly important in this respect was the establishment of Propaganda congregation (above, p. 170).

America

The growth of the Catholic church in South and central America was extraordinarily rapid and the evangelization, despite many difficulties, remarkably profound. For the first time in the history of the Church since the conversion of the western Europe in the early Middle Ages, an entire sub-continent largely converted to Christianity. The early missionaries were mainly Dominican and Franciscan friars and they came principally from the two countries to which pope Alexander VI had granted sovereignty over the New World in 1494: Portugal, to which the vast territory of Brazil was granted, and Spain, which was given almost all the other lands.

By 1515 the Spanish occupation of the West Indies was almost complete. Hernán Cortés entered the Aztec's civilization of Mexico in 1519 and within two years his army had conquered the country. Ten years later Gonzalo Pizarro entered the realm of the Incas in Peru and his forces subdued the people within five years. Brazil was discovered by Pedro Cabral in 1500 and within half a century the Portuguese had stations at intervals along the whole coastline. Further south, the regions of La Plata, now Argentina and Paraguay, were occupied by the Spaniards.

How deep were the mass conversions to Christianity that followed? Enforced conversions are regarded today as particularly repugnant, but we must be careful that present concerns do not overwhelm our judgement of the past. The conversions were encouraged and often imposed by the 'conquistadores', yet most of the indigenous tribes had earlier been conquerors themselves who may have imposed their beliefs upon others – so they probably had some understanding, even sympathy, for the new situation. The aspect of enforcement, moreover, should not be allowed to overshadow other considerations. In particular, the native peoples seem to have possessed a genuine affinity with Christianity at its best. Only thus can such enduring results be explained, making South and central America the most Catholic region in the world today.

In terms of organization, the first bishoprics west of the Atlantic, those of Santo Domingo (Dominican Republic), Concepción de la Vega (Haiti) and San Juan in Puerto Rico, were established in 1511. By 1522 the organization of the Antilles was complete with eight bishoprics. The first diocese in Mexico was Tlaxcala in 1525, to which Mexico City was added in the following year, the latter becoming the metropolitan see in 1548 with seven dioceses under it. In South America, Caracas (Venezuela) was the first diocese. Lima followed in 1541 and by 1575 it was the metropolitan see of an enormous province extending over the countries that are now called Ecuador, Bolivia, Peru and Chile. In the La Plata region, four bishoprics were established, the first Asuncion in 1547, the fourth Buenos Aires in 1582. Brazil received its first bishop in 1552, for the new diocese of San Salvador de Bahia. In these countries parishes were established as well as churches, hospitals, convents and schools. The first university in the Americas was founded in 1553, in Mexico City.

There were many remarkable and holy individuals: Alfonso Toribio de Mogrovejo (1538–1606), the heroic and energetic archbishop of Lima; Francis Solanus (1549–1610), the Franciscan missionary and preacher who facilitated the conversion of numerous Indians of the Chaco region; saints Rose of Lima, Dominican tertiary, and Martin de Porres (1579–1639), Dominican lay brother. There was great reluctance to ordain native Americans to the priesthood – bishops and priests were almost exclusively from Europe or of European extraction – or to depart from western European formulations of Catholic doctrine. But within this framework there were shining examples of sensitivity to the rights of the indigenous peoples. Notable in this respect was the mercurial diocesan priest Bartholomew de Las Casas (1474–1566), who valiantly defended the rights of Indians, by word and in numerous publications, both in his native Spain and in many countries of South and central America to which he travelled.

The most famous attempt to both Christianize and protect indigenous culture came about through the so-called 'Reductions' of Paraguay, which have recently been portrayed in the film 'The Mission'. The settlements were established by Jesuit mission-aries among the Guarani people in Rio de Plata (covering areas now in southern Brazil, Paraguay, Uruguay and north Argentina) between the early seventeenth century and 1768, when the Society of Jesus was expelled from Spanish colonies in America. In the peak period of 1730 to 1740, there were more than 100,000 native people in about thirty missions. European settlers were excluded from them, but the arrangements were approved and generally supported by successive Spanish governors of Paraguay and by the local bishops. The settlements were organized according to a combination of private and collective property. Domestic indus-tries were encouraged and their products, as well as agricultural surpluses, were sold by the Jesuits to the outside world to procure any items needed for the mission economy. At the centre of each mission stood the parish church. The indigenous people were taught Christian doctrine, reading, writing and singing, while their abilities in painting, sculpture and music were encouraged. Notable are the operas which Domenico Zipoli, the Jesuit missionary from Italy, wrote for them to perform. Work and play were generally tied in with communal religious prayers, songs and processions. The arrangements may have been paternal but they seem to have been genuinely appreciated by the Guarani people.

In North America, California and the surrounding areas then formed part of the Spanish colonial empire. Franciscan mission-aries were particularly active there and many of the elegant churches they built, for large congregations, can be appreciated today. The eastern seaboard was colonized by English Protestants dissatisfied with the Anglican church but Catholics were soon present among them. John Carroll, from Maryland, was the first Catholic bishop in the USA, being appointed bishop of Baltimore by pope Pius VI in 1789. A strong supporter of the colonies' independence from Britain and friend of the first president George Washington, he helped to smooth the path for Catholicism in the new republic. He was, too, a gifted administrator who prepared the way for the excellent organization of the Catholic church in the USA. Further north, the traveller Jacques Cartier entered Canada in 1534 and called the country 'New France'. A century later Catholic evangelization of the country began in earnest. Already in 1639 groups of Ursuline and Augustinian nuns had arrived from France to establish a school for girls and a hospital in Quebec. Particularly heroic were John de Brébeuf and seven other Jesuits who suffered martyrdom at the hands of Huron and Iroquois Indians in the 1640s. By the time Canada passed to British rule in the eighteenth century, Catholicism was firmly established in the French-speaking parts of the country.

Africa

In Ethiopia, Egypt and along the north African coast Christianity was maintained during this period, amid many difficulties, through the Ethiopian and Coptic churches. There were very few Catholics in these regions. In other parts of Africa, however, European explorers and colonizers, beginning with the Portuguese, brought the Catholic church to many coastal regions and to some parts of the interior.

Already in the fifteenth century there had been some movement. Bishoprics were established in the small Portuguese enclaves of Ceuta and Tangier, along the north African coast, in 1421 and 1468. To the west, a bishopric was established in the Canary Islands in 1404 and the conversion of the people to Christianity was almost complete by the end of the century; at least two Dominican friars were martyred in the process. Further south, Madeira and the Azores islands were evangelized during the fifteenth century.

A Portuguese expedition reached the mouth of the Congo river in 1482. Soon missionaries from Portugal, principally from the orders of friars, entered the country and the ruler of the ancient kingdom of Congo, Nzinga Nkuvu, was baptized in 1491. Although he reverted to paganism, his son had also been baptized a Christian. During the latter's long reign as king Afonso I (1506–43), Christianity grew in a remarkable way. Churches were built in the capital city, San Salvador, and a number of Congolese men were ordained priests after studies in Portugal, including the king's brother Henrique, who was consecrated a bishop and eventually returned to Zaire. King Afonso was courageous in complaining of the grievous effects of the slave trade. He was not succeeded by rulers of similar authority, nevertheless the Catholic church saw important developments. Pope Clement VIII created the diocese of San Salvador in 1596, though effectively the diocesan centre soon moved to the Portugese colonial town of Luanda. A Jesuit college was opened in San Salvador in 1625 and a catechism in Kikongo was printed around the same time (much the earliest literary work in any Bantu language). A number of local men (mostly of mixed African-European descent) continued to be ordained priests. In 1645 a Capuchin mission, mostly of Italian friars, arrived in the country and for a long time many Capuchins worked in the country. King Antonio I and most of his nobility were killed in a crushing defeat by the Portugese army in 1665 and thereafter the kingdom was much weakened. Christianity, too, suffered as a result. During the eighteenth century the supply of missionaries faded away and it was not replaced by the ordination of local men. Christian life was in serious decline almost everywhere, though it was partly sustained by catechists who led the Church through these difficult years.

Other countries in the west of Africa that were evangelized by Catholic missionaries during this period, though with precarious results, were Angola, Benin and Sierra Leone. Dutch settlers colonized south Africa from 1652 onwards but they were staunchly Calvinist. Along the east coast, the Portugese occupation of Mozambique and neighbouring countries began in 1505 and spread up the Zambezi valley. Dominican, Augustinian and Jesuit missionaries arrived in the course of the sixteenth and seventeenth centuries. The results, however, were limited. The links between the Catholic church and colonialism appear to have been particularly strong there – indicated by the massive 'Bon Jesu' fort which survives today in Mombasa, Kenya – and may have worked against more widespread conversions. In Ethiopia, there was a prolonged missionary effort led by Jesuits and supported by Portuguese authorities in the sixteenth and early seventeenth centuries. However, when king Susenyos announced in 1626 his abandonment of monophysite and other teachings of the Ethiopian church and his conversion to Roman Catholicism, such was the public outcry that the Jesuits were soon forced to leave the country and Ethiopia became almost closed to Catholic missionary work until the nineteenth century.

In the island of Madagascar, French colonization began in the middle of the seventeenth century. Carmelite and Vincentian missionaries were sent to care for the pastoral needs of the colonizers and to evangelize the indigenous peoples. Progress in evangelization was slow. In 1674 the local inhabitants murdered some seventy-five of the colonists and most of those remaining withdrew from the island. There were sporadic fresh attempts at missionary work in the eighteenth century but widespread conversions to Catholicism in Madagascar had to wait until the nineteenth century.

Asia

The vast continent of Asia was even larger than Africa or America and its peoples still more diverse. Asia contained, too, many ancient civilizations which were documented by extensive literatures and clearly visible in many temples and other buildings – far more so than in Africa or America. The dilemma facing Christian missionaries was acute. Should they follow the prevalent approach of missionaries in Africa and America, discounting existing religious traditions and starting afresh with the teachings and practices of Christianity, which in effect meant those of the Catholic church of the time? Or should they regard more positively Hinduism and Buddhism and the many other religions – with Islam some accommodation had been attempted much earlier and largely abandoned, as we have seen – and seek to reconcile them as far as possible with Christianity? While many Catholic missionaries favoured the more confrontational approach, others proposed various forms of inculturation, mainly in terms of techniques of evangelization but in some cases more profoundly in terms of doctrine. During the three centuries under consideration, almost every country of Asia was reached by Catholic missionaries in some measure and at some time, even though in many cases the results were transitory or fragile.

In India, western Christianity arrived with the fleet of Vasco da Gama in 1498. Franciscan friars came in 1518 as the first large group of missionaries. They and their successors worked in various places including Goa and Cochin and parts of Tamil Nadu, with considerable success. Dominican and Augustinian friars were among those who followed. Francis Xavier was the first Jesuit to arrive, in 1542. He laboured for seven years among the indigenous people – especially those engaged in fishing – in Travancore, Malacca, the Molucca islands and Sri Lanka, resulting in many conversions to Christianity. The best known attempt at inculturation in India was made by Robert de Nobili (1577–1656), who joined the Society of Jesus in his native Italy and set out for India in 1596. He adopted the lifestyle of a Brahmin and was respected by many individuals of his adopted caste as well as by others. But objections were made to his lifestyle and teachings by some of his fellow missionaries as well as by the archbishop of Goa. Pope Gregory XV ruled in his favour in 1623 but pope Benedict XIV condemned various of his innovations in 1744, thereby limiting the process of inculturation. Remarkable too was the English Jesuit Thomas Stephens (1549–1619), author of the long epic *Purana Christao* which combines Vedic content and style with Christian inspiration. In the eighteenth century, Capuchin friars established a flourishing church among the Bettiah people in Bihar. Conversions to Catholicism, however, were limited to individuals and groups of people; there was never much likelihood of more widespread conversions. Catholic missionaries had to contend with Muslim rule of the country and later with British colonial government, which preferred Protestant evangelization, as well as with the profundity and relevance of the religions that India already possessed.

In 1549 Francis Xavier had voyaged from India to Japan and established there the first Christian communities. By the early seventeenth century there were more than 400,000 Catholics, principally in the south of the Japan and centred on the city of Nagasaki. Persecution began in 1587 and increased in the early seventeenth century, resulting in many martyrs. Thereafter, until the mid-nineteenth century, Catholics in Japan were almost completely cut off from the wider Church, yet some communities survived in a remarkable way in the Goto islands and other parts of Kyushu region. In neighbouring Korea, some inhabitants were baptized during the Japanese invasion of the country between

1592 and 1599, probably by Christian soldiers in the invading army. During the following two centuries progress was very slow, resulting partly from Korea's isolation from the western world and intermittent persecution. Nevertheless a substantial underground church remained, to provide some basis for the Catholic revival in the nineteenth century.

In China, the fragile presence of Christianity during the Middle Ages has been mentioned. Francis Xavier sought to enter the country but died on the island of Sanchwan, within sight of the mainland. Catholic missionaries succeeded in entering mainland China from 1580 onwards. There followed remarkable achievements as well as disappointments and persecution. Among the Jesuit missionaries, Alessandro Valignano (1539–1606) and Matteo Ricci (1552–1610) recommended extensive adoption of the Chinese language and local religious customs; Giacomo Rho and Adam Schall, assisted by the Chinese Christians Hsii Kuang-ch'I and Li Chih-tsao, elaborated a reform of the Chinese calendar which was approved by the emperor in 1634, thus gaining favour for the missionaries throughout the country. Important, too, were the contributions of Dominican and Franciscan missionaries from the 1630s onwards, and subsequently those of Augustinian friars and the Société des Missions Etrangères de Paris (MEP). However, the extent of religious inculturation proved divisive. In the 'Chinese Rites Controversy', Rome eventually ruled against the adaptations recommended by Valignano, Ricci and others in a series of judgments, culminating in the decree *Ex quo singulari* of 1742. There were also political complications arising from Portugal's claims to sovereignty over parts of the country and therefore to control over the Church. The number of Catholics reached a peak of some 300,000 around 1700. Thereafter persecution, which had been sporadic in the seventeenth century, became more frequent and the attitude of the emperors more hostile, culminating in the prolonged sufferings of Catholics during the reign of Chia Ch'ing (1796–1820).

In most other countries of Asia reached by Catholic missionaries, the results were quite limited; though in some cases seeds were sown that bore fruit later. In the mountainous kingdom of Bhutan, situated between India and China, two Portuguese Jesuits, Stephen Esteuao Cacella and John Joao Cabral, were the first Europeans known to have entered the country, in 1627. They were well received but conversions did not materialize and so the two men departed within a year. Thereafter missionary work was interrupted for several centuries. MEP priests established a seminary for local clergy in Siam (Thailand) in 1665. The work was difficult but today the same seminary – following various migrations – flourishes nearby in Penang, Malaysia. In Indonesia, already visited by Franciscan missionaries in the fourteenth century, the Catholic church became well established in several regions in the sixteenth century. But this promising start was halted abruptly in the following century with the arrival of the Dutch East India Company, which effectively forbade the practice and spread of Catholicism. Many other examples of precarious beginnings could be mentioned.

The greatest success came in the Philippines, which remains today the only large country in Asia that is predominantly Catholic. The archipelago was first conquered by Spanish forces sent from Mexico in 1564 and was named after the king of Spain, Philip II. Royal control over the Church remained strong and the status of native clergy was inferior to that of Spanish missionaries. Nevertheless the extent and depth of evangelization was remarkable. Augustinian friars accompanied the expedition of 1564 and they were followed by members of other religious orders, both men and women. The first bishopric was established at Manila in 1579 and the Dominican university of St Thomas was founded in the same city in 1611. Parishes, schools, hospitals and other institutions were established on a grand scale, local languages were encouraged, and much attention was given to popular religion in terms of both liturgy and devotions. Domingo de Salazar, the first bishop of Manila, represented the colonial church at its best. A Spanish Dominican, he was a missionary in Mexico and briefly in Florida before coming to the Philippines. As bishop, he was responsible for building the cathedral and a hospital as well as for the diocesan synod of 1582 which attempted to clarify, in accordance with Christian principles, many contentious issues regarding the conquest, settlement and administration of the country. He was a stout defender of the rights and dignity of the Philippino people, notably against the oppressive measures of the Spanish governor Gómez Pérez Dasmarinas, and he promoted Catholicism in tune with their desires and aspirations.

vi. Popular religion and artistic developments

The previous sections of this chapter show the wide popular appeal of early modern Catholicism. A key thesis of the Counter-Reformation was that Christianity should be believed and lived in depth by Catholics, and in these respects there was notable success. Was this popular engagement and support new? There were vested interests in proclaiming the novelty, as we have seen. In particular, in order to explain the widespread success of the Reformation, there was a tendency to downplay late medieval religious practices, to argue that popular religion had then been in urgent need of reform. Thereby the appeal – though misguided – and success of the Protestant Reformation could be explained and, more subtly, the arrival of new religious orders of the Counter-Reformation and their methods of evangelization could be justified.

Yet in many ways popular Catholicism in the early modern period remained thoroughly medieval. Almost all the devotional practices and lifestyles that were outlined at some length in Chapter 3, for the central and later Middle Ages, continued into the early modern period: the centrality of the Mass and sacraments, the divine office and prayer in its many forms, religious orders of men and women, pilgrimages and devotions to the saints, guilds and confraternities, and much else. The council of Trent, which remained authoritative in these matters throughout the early modern period, had urged various reforms but the council's proposals were essentially for a return to medieval practices at their best rather than for novelty.

Devotion and doctrine are inextricably linked. Trent's reinforcement of medieval doctrine – regarding Scripture and Tradition, faith and good works, the sacraments, the teaching of councils, and other matters – had the effect of reaffirming medieval devotional practices, even while some purification was enacted. Regarding missionary work beyond Europe, there were some bold attempts at adaptation and inculturation, principally in parts of Asia. But the prevalent approach in these missionary lands was to export western devotional practices and lifestyles, so this approach too entailed continuity with the Middle Ages.

In the visual arts and music – dimensions of life that exercised profound influence upon Catholicism at all levels – continuity between the late Middle Ages and the early modern period is evident. The last chapter outlined in some detail the earlier achievements. For the sixteenth to eighteenth centuries there were changes of nomenclature – from 'late medieval' and Renaissance to Baroque and Rococo, changes which partly reflect the desire of art historians to categorize periods of time – yet continuity was more striking than discontinuity: the foundations had been laid in the fourteenth and fifteenth centuries.

This continuity in *art* is underlined by the three most famous Italian artists of the Renaissance, who were born in the fifteenth century and lived into the sixteenth, all three remaining Catholics: Leonardo da Vinci, Michelangelo and Raphael. The first two were introduced in the last chapter. Leonardo's painting continued with his portraits of St Anne, *Mona Lisa* and St John the Baptist. He also devoted himself to scientific and scholarly work, making creative contributions to such diverse branches as geological research and the construction of guns and air-machines. There is religious genius in his paintings, yet Leonardo's varied activities shows how the Renaissance comprised a wide range of interests beyond the more obviously religious. Raphael (Raffaello Sanzio) came into contact with both Leonardo and Michelangelo in Florence and there he produced several of his best known paintings. From 1508 he worked in Rome, principally under the patronage of pope Julius II, for whom he executed exquisite paintings to decorate the papal apartments in the Vatican. In 1514 Pope Leo X appointed him chief architect of St Peter's church in succession to Bramante. He died, still a young man, in 1520. Michelangelo returned to Rome in 1505, summoned by Julius II to carve the pope's tomb. Under the same pope's patronage, he painted the celebrated frescoes on the ceiling of the Sistine Chapel and later, under pope Paul III, the monumental *Last Judgment* in the same chapel. Subsequently he was appointed chief architect for the rebuilding of St Peter's and he was engaged on this work until his death.

Both artist and architect, and with many other interests, Michelangelo possessed genius that remains undimmed today, alongside his contemporaries Leonardo and Raphael. Italy produced many other notable Catholics artists and architects through the sixteenth to eighteenth centuries. They contributed to the growing confidence of the Catholic church during the Counter-Reformation period, yet more importantly they reflected values that are inherently Christian and Catholic: reverence for the divine together with respect for all that is truly human, work that is both sublime and mundane, humour too and sensitivity to the mysteries of life, enjoyment of colour and the senses, yet also wariness and the recognition of sin.

In the Low Countries (modern Belgium and the Netherlands), the other main centre of late medieval and early Renaissance art, the two best known artists of the early modern period are Peter Paul Rubens (1577–1640) and Rembrandt (Rembrandt Hermanszoon Van Rijn, 1606–69). Their paintings reflect the religious divide that separated the region into a Catholic south and predominantly Protestant north: Rembrandt from the north, Rubens from the south. Rembrandt's many powerful and exquisitely executed religious works, such as his *Return of the Prodigal Son*, reveal God's love and compassion for humankind as well as our sinfulness and fragile condition. The young Rubens, who was born and brought up in Flanders, spent eight years in Italy where he developed his artistic style, influenced especially by the works of Michelangelo, Raphael and Titian. He returned to his homeland and quickly became its most famous artist, principally through paintings but also through his designs for tapestries. Like Rembrandt, Rubens is sensitive to the divine, but he gives full attention to the corporeal. His religious paintings express the new-found confidence of the Counter-Reformation, even aggressively so in his 'Triumph of the Eucharist' in which Protestants are crushed beneath the advancing chariot of Catholicism.

Religious art flourished in all the countries that remained Catholic and the influence of Italian and Flemish artist remained powerful for a long time. The brilliant Caravaggio (1573–1610) worked mainly in Italy, Sicily and Malta; while Velasquez (1599–1660), the leading Spanish artist, paid two extended visits to Italy where he learnt much. The Italian Jesuit lay-brother Andrea Pozzo (1642–1709) well illustrates the worldwide influence of Italian Baroque art. He is best known for his painting of the ceiling of Sant'Ignazio church in Rome but he was directly responsible for many other works of art in Rome and elsewhere in Italy as well as in Vienna, where he resided towards the end of his life. Through Jesuit missionaries stationed in other countries, who asked him for designs or were affected by his work, his influence spread far and wide within Europe and beyond into America and Asia. A master of perspective, he published in 1693 a classic on the topic,

Perspectiva pictorum et architectorum, which was translated into French, English, Dutch and Chinese.

Regarding religious *music*, developments had centred on the Low Countries and northern France during the late Middle Ages. Much of what followed was inspired by these earlier developments and music continued to play a vital role within Catholicism. Papal patronage was key to the career of Palestrina (Giovanni Pierluigi da Palestrina, 1525–94), who was supported by the Oratorians and other ecclesiastics. He was choir-master of various churches in Rome, including St Peter's, and in this city he wrote his most famous compositions, including *Missa Papae Marcelli* (Mass of pope Marcellus) and *Improperia* (Reproaches) for the liturgy of Good Friday. Palestrina's music is suffused with deep spirituality and the polyphony is restrained. It suited well Tridentine Catholicism and won the approval of church authorities: for many it represented the ideal of sacred music, never more so than in the nineteenth century.

Thomas Tallis (1505–1585) and William Byrd (1543–1623) were two very talented composers in the Royal Chapel of queen Elizabeth I of England. Both remained Catholics while enjoying the queen's support and they wrote a wide range of pieces for Masses and other Catholic services. Byrd was particularly diverse in composing scores for string, keyboard and choral music, including madrigals. Both men developed polyphony, elaborating beyond the relatively austere standards of Palestrina. However, as Catholics living and working in Protestant England, their influence was restricted and never compared with that of Palestrina. .

The development of music in the Catholic church beyond Europe is well represented by Domingo Zipoli (1688–1726), missionary in South America. Born in Prato in northern Italy, Zipoli became a well-known composer of music as well as organist at the Jesuit church in Rome, *Il Gesù*. He was in Spain when he entered the Society of Jesus as a novice and almost immediately he was sent to South America, arriving in Buenos Aires in July 1717. Although frail in health, he continued to work as composer, organist and choir-master. His compositions, including operas, were well received by the indigenous Americans in the Jesuit 'Reductions' in Paraguay and Peru. Three of the operas that he wrote for them to sing have survived: *El rey Orontes de Egipto, Los pastores en el nacimento de*

Cristo, and *Felipe IV*. In recent years the operas have been staged again in Rome, the USA and elsewhere.

Within eighteenth-century Europe, the accolade for the most famous Catholic musician must surely go to Wolfgang Amadeus Mozart (1756–91). The son of a respected composer and violinist, Wolfgang was a prolific composer of religious music from his childhood onwards and he continued thus during eleven years, from 1769 to 1781, in the employment of archbishop Colloredo of Salzburg. During this time he composed a remarkable range of scores for Masses and other liturgical settings. Perhaps best known are his Requiem Mass, which was completed by his pupil Franz Süssmayer, and his motets *Alleluia* and *Ave verum corpus*. Mozart left Salzburg for Vienna in 1781 and his writing of church music for Catholic settings virtually came to a halt. His involvement with Freemasonry during this later period influenced his musical work but he continued to consider himself a believing and practising Catholic. The contrast between Catholic and Protestant church music during the eighteenth century is well illustrated by comparing the early Mozart with the brilliant but more sombre and interior music of Johann Sebastian Bach (1685–1750).

vii. Conclusion

The period covered in this chapter is bounded by two momentous events: the Reformation beginning in 1517 and the French Revolution of 1789. The challenges posed by the Protestant Reformation, and the Catholic response through the Counter-Reformation, greatly influenced the development of Catholicism at all levels during the three centuries. Protestant churches replaced the Orthodox church as the principal preoccupation of Catholicism that lay outside the Catholic church but within the Christian community. The council of Trent, and many sharp controversies, show how important the doctrinal, institutional and moral issues were considered to be. Prolonged wars, which certainly had religious content even if many other factors were involved, revealed the profound personal and practical effects of these controversies, especially in the sixteenth and seventeenth centuries.

However, many factors besides responding to the Protestant Reformation were involved in the history of the Catholic church during this epoch. There existed a variety of tensions – some creative, others limiting – within the Catholic community. New religious orders of both men and women gave fresh impetus to early modern Catholicism, both through the members themselves and through their wide and varied apostolates. Intellectual developments, as well as those in liturgy and prayer, and in art and architecture, were influenced by both Reformation and Counter-Reformation, but also by late medieval developments and by other factors in early modern Europe. Finally and crucially, the discovery of the New World projected Catholicism for the first time into a truly world religion.

Chapter 5
Nineteenth and Twentieth Centuries

i. Introduction

The French bishops at the first Vatican council (1869–70), in a revealing comment, reckoned the world's population then stood at around 1,200 million. Of this total, they estimated, some seventy million were Orthodox, ninety million were Protestants, and two hundred million were Catholics (*Collectio Lacensis*, vol. 7, cols. 845–6). The number of Catholics grew substantially during the nineteenth century and much more during the twentieth century. Catholics today number over a billion: 1,166 million or 17.4 per cent of the world's population according to the most recent Vatican statistics (*The Tablet*, 27 February 2010, p. 31) out of a total Christian population of somewhat more than two billion.

Regarding these figures, two qualifications should be noted. First, the total population of the world has grown some fivefold since the late nineteenth century, so the proportion of Catholics in the total has remained fairly static. Secondly, expansion in the Catholic population has occurred principally outside Europe, in the four continents of Africa, America, Asia and Australasia. Within many countries of Europe there has been a decline in the number of Catholics since around 1970. Overall, therefore, the growth in the number of Catholics during the nineteenth and twentieth centuries was remarkable, but it is less striking in terms of the dramatic increase in the world's population during this time.

Qualitatively, too, there have been major developments. From a predominantly Europe-centred body, the Catholic church has become far more worldwide in terms of both membership and outlook. The first Vatican council was attended by bishops from all five continents, but almost all of them were either Europeans or missionary bishops of European descent. A century later, at the second Vatican council, bishops with roots outside Europe were much more numerous and they played a significant role. The sixteen decrees promulgated by the council represented an expansive Catholicism that had never been seen before, and the ensuing 'reception' of the council involved the worldwide Catholic community still more. In recent years the dynamism of the Church, and its contribution to the wider world, has been thoroughly international.

Despite this expansion, the nineteenth and twentieth centuries were stormy times for the Catholic church. The period began with the aftermath of the French Revolution, when the institutional Church was widely attacked in France and many other countries. Pope Pius VI died a prisoner of the French authorities in Valence in 1799 and his successor Pius VII (1800–23) suffered exile and many indignities before he was finally able to return to Rome in 1815. The capture of Rome by the troops of the Italian Risorgimento in 1870 and the ensuing loss of the Papal States – except the Vatican city within Rome, which was secured for the papacy by the Concordat reached with the Italian state in 1929 – proved another harsh trial. However, the liberation of the papacy from temporal preoccupations and its resulting concentration on more spiritual and directly Christian objectives came to be seen as beneficial in many respects.

Attacks upon the Catholic church occurred in many countries around the world and in a variety of forms. They cannot be compared with the persecutions of the early Church in terms of persistence, yet they have affected many more Catholics overall and have been intense in numerous countries and often for long periods of time. They have taken place both in traditionally Catholic countries, mostly in the western world, and in those countries where the Christian gospel arrived more recently. Motives have been more mixed than during the persecutions of the early Church. Sometimes the structures of the church, as well as its property and political influence, have been the primary objects of attack, rather than the beliefs and practices of Christians; though the various facets of the Catholic church are often hard to distinguish, and those persecuted have suffered nonetheless.

In addition to the persecutions in many countries spilling over from the French Revolution, there were bloody persecutions during the Spanish Civil War (1936–9), in various countries under Nazi occupation, and in many countries governed by Communist regimes. Mexico in the first half of the twentieth century experienced sharp tensions between Church and State, resulting in bitter even though less bloody persecution. Innumerable persecutions which are less well known yet involved great suffering for many Catholics should also be remembered vividly, as too should those involving Christians of other churches.

One major difference between the period of this chapter and the preceding centuries was the marked decline – almost demise – of persecutions and wars among Christians. As outlined in Chapters 2 and 3, there had been tensions between Catholics and Orthodox, sometimes resulting in bloodshed, as well as persecutions of dissenting groups such as Waldensians, Cathars, Lollards and Hussites, while in the sixteenth and seventeenth centuries religious wars between Catholics and Christians belonging to churches of the Reformation were frequent and fierce, and persecution of dissidents within the Catholic community continued. During the nineteenth century, tension remained between Catholics and Protestants and it extended to their missionary work especially in Asia and Africa. Nevertheless only rarely did these tensions lead to warfare or violent persecution on religious grounds. This hugely positive development needs to be appreciated.

The twentieth century witnessed the two most deadly wars ever fought – the First and Second World Wars – in which Christian countries lay at the centre of conflicts. There were, however, important differences compared with earlier times. The reasons for the conflicts were not directly religious or Christian and in both wars Catholics and Protestants fought and died alongside each other in the same armies, navies and air forces, as well as suffering and dying together as civilians. The mutual respect and religious understanding that resulted, at this intimate and personal level, is widely recognized to have been a crucial factor in the development of ecumenical relations in the second half of the twentieth century. The large number of priests and pastors who served as chaplains to the forces also contributed notably to this ecumenical development.

A fine reminder of inter-Christian communion was provided by the twenty-two Ugandan martyrs who were put to death by their ruler Mwanga between 1885 and 1887. They were canonized by Pope Paul VI in 1964 and while the majority of the young men – mostly pages of the ruler – were Catholics, it was soon discovered that their number included several Anglicans. Providentially, the canonizations occurred in the middle of the second Vatican council, which set the seal on improved relations between Catholics and other Christians through its decree on ecumenism, *Unitatis Redintegratio*.

A second significant difference for the Catholic church in the nineteenth and twentieth centuries, compared with earlier periods, was the much greater contact with non-Christian religions and other forms of thought and practice. We have already noted the courage of the early Church in confronting the prevalent Greek and Latin cultures of the time. During the Middle Ages western Christians retained an interest in the two other religions that most impinged upon them, Judaism and Islam. Much greater opening of the Catholic church to the wider world from the sixteenth century onwards brought further knowledge and interest in non-Christian beliefs and practices. In some regions, too, this wider awareness produced notable attempts at inculturation, especially in Asia. Even so, the nineteenth and twentieth centuries brought to Catholicism a new level of knowledge and interest in the wider world, as Christianity developed further into a world religion. Here, too, Catholics benefited greatly from the labours, insights and publications of other Christians, most notably Protestant missionaries.

The resulting interest in other ways of thinking and acting gradually and subtly influenced the Catholic church itself, especially as the number of Catholics in the newly evangelized countries increased and the balance of the Church moved beyond Europe. Once again Vatican II proved a milestone, this time with its declaration on non-Christian religions entitled *Nostra Aetate*. By this document positive appreciation of the richness and insights of the major world religions – Judaism, Islam, Hinduism and Buddhism were singled out for attention – was mandated for Catholics. The half century since the council has brought both opportunities and difficulties for Catholics in their relations with other faiths, and crucially too with subtle forms of materialism and godlessness which influence modern culture.

ii. Intellectual challenges

The Catholic church, to its credit, faced up to a very wide range of intellectual challenges during this period. The process of understanding and responding was arduous, unsurprisingly so in view of the novelty and sophistication of many of the ideas proposed. In the nineteenth and early twentieth centuries the challenges were well defined, for the most part, often deriving from a single author or movement. From around 1950, they became more anomalous and subtle, more difficult to pin down, and as a result more difficult for the Church to confront openly, to distinguish between the good and the dangerous in them. Catholics varied in their responses, ranging from general hostility towards new and foreign ideas to appreciation of the better elements that may be found in them and an attempt to incorporate these elements into Catholic teaching and practice. Many difficulties remained. Nevertheless the strenuous efforts undertaken by many Catholics, aided by many other people, have enabled the Catholic church to remain intellectually credible into the twenty-first century.

From the huge number of intellectual challenges to the Catholic church during the two centuries, those presented by three individuals may be singled out: Charles Darwin (1809–92), Karl Marx (1818–83) and Sigmund Freud (1856–1939).

Charles Darwin was fascinated by botany and natural history from his youth. After short spells of studying medicine at Edinburgh University and for the Anglican ministry at Cambridge, he developed into a self-made scientist, helped by his independent wealth and his contacts with other geologists and botanists. For five years (1831–36) he was the official scientist aboard the 'Beagle', a ship sponsored by the British government to explore and map the South American coastline. Assiduous in his explorations of the natural world in the many islands visited by the Beagle, Darwin's researches eventually resulted in his most famous work *Origin of Species*, which was published in 1859. Some churchmen immediately charged that the book's central thesis of natural selection and evolution challenged the literal biblical interpretation of creation as expounded in the book of Genesis. The Anglican bishop of Oxford, Samuel Wilberforce, became the best known early critic through his public debate with T.H. Huxley, a staunch supporter of Darwin, in Oxford in 1860. Darwin himself gradually moved towards religious agnosticism and even atheism, as expressed principally in his letters.

Although Darwin's theory of evolution caused concern for many Catholics, the Church remained cautious and eventually accepted most of the central tenets. Already in 1869 the first Vatican council, in its decree on faith and reason, taught that the findings of science and revelation are ultimately in harmony. Pope Leo XIII, in his Encyclical letter *Providentissimus Deus* of 1893, wrote that 'whatever they (scientists) can really demonstrate to be true of physical nature, let us show to be capable of reconciliation with our Scriptures' (DS 3287). During the Modernist crisis, the Biblical Commission in Rome, which had been instituted by the same pope Leo, ruled in 1909 that while it favoured a literal inter-pretation of the book of Genesis, nevertheless Catholics are not bound to seek for scientific exactitude of expression throughout the book (DS 3512–19). Later, in 1948, the Biblical Commission noted that its earlier statement 'in no way hindered further truly scien-tific examination of the problems in accordance with the results acquired during the last forty years' (DS 3862). The conclusive step in official approval came two years later when pope Pius XII, in his encyclical *Humani generis*, expressly recognized evolution as a valid hypothesis (DS 3896).

Among Catholic scientists, important support for Darwin's explanations had been provided by the experiments in plant genetics conducted by the Augustinian monk Gregor Mendel (1822–84). The Jesuit scientist Pierre Teilhard de Chardin (1881–1955) advanced further Darwin's discoveries while giving them an explicitly Christian framework; though Rome censured the Jesuit and fuller recognition of his insights came only in the 1960s, princi-pally in the aftermath of the second Vatican council.

Karl Marx was the second of seven children of a Jewish family, whose father embraced Christianity and all the family were baptized as Protestants. After receiving his doctorate in philosophy at Berlin university in 1841, Marx was briefly editor of *Rheinische Zeitung* but his inflammatory views soon persuaded him to move from his native Prussia to Paris. Later he lived for a time in Brussels and then moved in 1849 to London, where he spent the rest of his life, an assiduous reader in the British Museum and a prolific writer. The first volume of his most famous work, *Das Kapital*, appeared in 1867, the second and third volumes were published posthumously in 1885 and 1894, edited by his friend and close collaborator Friedrich Engels. *Das Kapital* was translated into numerous languages and the work, alongside Marx's other writings and those of many other individuals influenced by him, have had a momentous influence upon the course of history in the twentieth century.

Central to Marx's teaching is the thesis that all history is a series of struggles between classes of society for economic power. The exposition is radically atheistic and materialistic. However, both where Marxism has become the dominant political doctrine and where it has not, history has been mainly in sharp contrast with the course that Marx predicted. In the capitalist countries of his time – notably Britain – where Marx most expected the passage from bourgeois to proletariat control, the expected revolutions have largely failed to materialize. Rather it was in 1917 in Russia, where the bourgeoisie was relatively undeveloped, that the revolution first occurred. For the most part, too, in China and various other countries of Asia, Africa and the Americas, the middle class was less developed when Marxist communism was embraced.

As the influence of Marx's teaching grew, the Catholic church initially showed strong opposition on account of its atheistic underpinning and its encouragement to conflict within societies. The papacy was forthright in warning of the dangers. Even so, partly as a result of Marxism, Catholics have become more sympathetic to the plight and the rights of the underprivileged, and some Catholics have sought to apply various Marxist principles more directly to Catholic social teaching. It is noticeable that there was no explicit condemnation of Communism in *Gaudium et Spes*, the document of the second Vatican council that focused most explicitly on social and economic issues, nor indeed in the council's other decrees.

Sigmund Freud, who is regarded as the founder of psychoanalysis, has exercised great influence upon the development of psychiatry, psychology and the social sciences. Brought up by his Jewish parents, and remaining appreciative of Jewish culture, Freud in his writings appears devoid of directly religious commitment. Vienna was the base of his life and work – though he made extensive travels abroad – and he was happily married to Martha Bernays, who bore him six children. Fear of the Nazi regime persuaded him to move to London in 1938, where he spent the last year of his life. Crucial to his teaching are the existence of unconscious mental processes, the genetic origin of motivation in basic drives (instinct theory), the influence of childhood experiences on adult personality (including the Oedipus complex and the basic patterns of 'id', 'ego' and 'superego'), and the belief that all mental or behavioural events, however apparently random, are in fact psychically determined.

As Freud's influence grew, many Catholics remained wary of his psychoanalysis, partly on account of his religious agnosticism and partly because he sought to explain religious belief in terms of childhood experience, thereby relegating the objective truth of Christianity. Moreover, his scientific world view and accompanying determinism threatened human free will. Freud maintained contact with a wide range of associates, who greatly appreciated his insights even while many of them dissented from him on significant points. A mixture of indebtedness and criticism has also come to prevail among Catholics practitioners: appreciation of his psychoanalysis as therapy and, in part, of his psychological theories together with rejection of the determinist and agnostic framework. Counseling, spiritual direction, the religious formation of both clergy and laity, and many other features of Catholic life, have been profoundly influenced by Freud's insights. Some Catholic psychologists and psychiatrists still associate themselves more directly with Freud. As with Darwin's theory of evolution, the Catholic church has been cautious in its official responses, wisely so and recognizing thereby, at least implicitly, the importance and practical implications of many of his insights.

Darwin, Marx and Freud were all familiar, to varying degrees, with the Judaeo-Christian tradition. They were influenced by this tradition in the ways they approached issues, in the language they used, and in some of their proposals. A similar case is Ludwig Wittgenstein (1889–1951), the Jewish philosopher from Vienna, who settled at Cambridge University in England and who has exercised much influence upon the development of philosophy within the Anglophone world, principally through his studies of linguistic analysis. The intellectual impact of non-Christian religions from outside Europe, and the importance of Vatican II's decree *Nostra Aetate* on these religions, are indicated elsewhere in the chapter.

Among Christian scholars, those belonging to churches of the sixteenth-century Reformation have played an active and creative role – especially in the fields of Scripture, liturgy and church history. The attitude of the Catholic church towards Protestant scholarship has been both critical and supportive. The most difficult period was the early twentieth century, during the 'Modernist' crisis, when pope Pius X (1903–14) censured Catholic scholars for what in effect amounted to overmuch reliance upon the findings of Protestant biblical and historical scholarship. Appreciation of Protestant scholarship has existed among many Catholic scholars throughout the period of this chapter, while more decisive and official encouragement came through the second Vatican council. Nevertheless, despite courageous engagement with the wider intellectual world, Catholic theology appeared more on the defensive than creative until the second half of the twentieth century. This defensiveness – perhaps caution is a better word – finds some justification in view of the enormity of the challenges presented. Yet it contrasts with the inventiveness of the early Church in creating creeds and other doctrinal formulae which responded in brilliant and memorable language to the intellectual challenges of the day.

John Henry Newman, the best known Catholic theologian of the nineteenth century, appears separately in section iv 'Saints and sinners'. France produced some outstanding theologians in the first half of the nineteenth century but several of them were affected by the traumas of the French Revolution and its aftermath. The somewhat maverick views of Felicité Robert de Lamennais (1782–1854) were condemned by popes Gregory XVI and Pius IX and he left the Catholic church. The liberal political views of Charles de Montalembert (1810–70) were effectively condemned in Gregory XVI's encyclical *Mirari Vos*. Henri-Dominique Lacordaire (1802–61) was a friend of Lamennais and a contributor to the latter's periodical *L'Avenir*, advocating both political liberalism and ultramontane (pro-papal) theology. Subsequently, however, he became a Dominican friar and turned his attention to the revival of the order in France. The Anglo-Irish George Tyrrell (1861–1909) was the most serious casualty in the Modernist crisis. He was expelled from the Jesuit order and eventually excommunicated on account of his opposition to pope Pius X's encyclical *Pascendi*. Other Catholic intellectuals ran into trouble around the same time and for similar reasons, notably Baron Friedrich von Hügel (1852–1925) and Alfred Loisy (1857–1940). The difficulties of Teilhard de Chardin have been mentioned. Those left relatively untroubled were Catholic novelists, who touched on theological issues in a much less direct manner. Hilaire Belloc (1870–1953), G.K. Chesterton (1874–1936), Evelyn Waugh (1903–66) and Graham Greene (1904–91) are examples from England

iii. Popular religion

It has been emphasized, in previous sections on this topic, that the distinction between popular and more intellectual – sometimes termed élite – Catholicisim should not be exaggerated. The large majority of Catholics had a remarkably good grasp of the Christian faith, including an intellectual understanding, even though many of them acquired this knowledge through means other than reading.

Regarding the distinction during the two centuries covered in the present chapter, the situation is somewhat paradoxical. On the one hand, there was a notable increase in the level of literacy, beginning principally in the West in the late nineteenth century and then expanding worldwide during the twentieth century as education of the young became widespread. This rise in literacy applied to Catholics as much as to the rest of the population, indeed perhaps more so. As a result there was a notable increase in the number of books read by Catholics, including those of a religious nature. The increase was greatly facilitated by the burgeoning book trade, which took the opportunity to translate many titles into a variety of languages.

On the other hand, the two centuries witnessed a flourishing of Catholic devotions that were more directly popular, which sought to engage the whole person and to avoid excessive emphasis upon intellectual considerations. There was an emphasis upon Catholic identity especially from around 1850 to 1950, in part a reaction to the Protestant revival during those hundred years. As a result, there was a return to most of the devotions that had flourished during the central and late Middle Ages and had formed an integral part of Counter-Reformation Catholicism. This revival forms an essential background to the present short section, which confines itself to the most significant developments. The last half-century is treated further in section vi.

Pilgrimage shrines formed a notable feature of popular Catholicism from around 1850, thus reviving a practice that had been pre-eminently medieval. Among the new shrines, Lourdes in southern France became the most famous. Its inspiration was the reported apparition of Mary, mother of Jesus, to the young Bernadette Soubirous in the grotto of a rock in 1858. A spring of water appeared in the grotto and miraculous healings were soon reported. The shrine quickly received ecclesiastical approval and two churches were built: one above the grotto and the church of the Rosary nearby. The extraordinary popularity of Lourdes, and the healing powers of its water, have continued virtually unabated. Another Marian shrine in western Europe of enduring popularity is at Fatima in Portugal. Mary reportedly appeared there to three young children in 1917 and delivered a message which emphasized, among other concerns, the importance of penance, the recitation of the rosary, and the conversion of Russia. Half a million pilgrims gathered there when pope Benedict XVI visited the shrine in May 2010.

Many other places of pilgrimage could be mentioned and the number of pilgrims has increased greatly since around 1950, due much to the expansion of public transport – by road, rail, air and sea – and the resulting affordable prices for travel and residence. Rome has retained its pre-eminent position in terms of numbers, especially for Catholics. There, following the institution of the 'Holy Year' by pope Boniface VIII in 1300, jubilees have been held at regular intervals and with large numbers of pilgrims, especially since 1950. Jerusalem retains its unique attraction and Santiago in Spain, the third of the great medieval shrines, continues to draw many pilgrims. Huge crowds were present when pope John Paul II visited the shrines of Knock in Ireland and Czestochowa in Poland. In England, Walsingham has been revived as a pilgrimage centre with both Catholic and Anglican shrines. In Mexico the famous shrine of Our Lady of Guadalupe dates back to the sixteenth century, while in North America the shrine dedicated to the Jesuits martyred on the borders of Canada and the USA in the seventeenth century has become a popular place of pilgrimage. Most recently, Medjugorje has established itself as a major pilgrimage centre as a result of the reported appearances of Mary, beginning in June 1981, to six Croatian youths of the locality. For the most part the many shrines have managed to combine traditional features with the newer recommendations and devotions stemming especially from the second Vatican council.

Daily communion. Another profound influence upon the devotional life of Catholics was the official encouragement given to the laity to receive Communion frequently, even daily. Crucial in this respect was pope Pius X's decree in 1905, entitled *Sacra tridentina synodus*, which encouraged frequent communion The same pope's decree *Quam singulariter* in 1910, which permitted first Communion at 'the age of reason', helped to develop eucharisitic piety in children from an early age. Important too was the reduction in the time of fasting which was required before Communion could be received, from midnight until only one hour – this mitigation was due principally to pope Pius XII.

Popes. The papacy became an altogether more personal institution from around 1850. The long reign of Pius IX (1846–87) coincided with the invention of photography, so that for the first time ever the majority of Catholics had a visual image of the reigning pope. In addition, Pius's strong personality and notable events during his reign – the first Vatican council and the loss of the Papal States – heightened attention to his person. The effects of photography continued and Pius XI inaugurated the Vatican Radio Station in 1931, which enabled both the personality and the teaching of Pius and his successors to become better known worldwide. This personal dimension was furthered by the captivating personalities and eventful reigns of John XXIII and John Paul II. But there are dangers as well as benefits in this attention to personality, as popes themselves have hinted. It can distract from the pope's fundamental roles as guide and teacher, which are rather distinct from his personality, and it can make a good but awkward pope too open to public criticism.

World religion. Alongside these particular developments, the most important change of all was the further development of

Catholicism into a world religion and the massive ethnic, cultural and political diversity that enriched the Catholic church as a result – overwhelmingly for the good but with plenty of ensuing difficulties. The effects will be evident throughout this chapter.

iv. Saints and sinners

John Henry Newman (1801–90) was beatified by pope Benedict on Sunday 19 September 2010, the last beatification or canonization before the completion of the present book. Newman has proved to be one of the most influential Christian theologians of the last two centuries and he is surely the most eminent of them to be beatified or canonized. As a fellow Englishman, I am particularly glad to treat him first in this section.

Baptized and brought up as an Anglican, Newman spent most of his adult life at Oxford University until his conversion to Catholicism in 1845. A student and then teacher of theology at the university, and ordained an Anglican minister, he held the important post of vicar of the university church, St Mary the Virgin. In this post he became famous for his frequent and learned sermons as well as for his wide circle of friends and contacts. He was a prolific writer of books and pamphlets but their tone became increasingly Catholic. Newman resigned as vicar of St Mary's in 1843. Two years later he was received into the Catholic church and was ordained a Catholic priest in Rome. In 1849 he founded the Oratory in Birmingham as a community of the religious order founded by St Philip Neri. He was elected Provost of the community and lived there for most of the rest of his life, apart from four years from 1854 to 1858 when he was rector of the newly founded Catholic university in Dublin. Newman was a national figure, widely respected also within the Anglican church, and he remained a prolific writer. In 1877 he was elected an Honorary Fellow of the college in Oxford which he had attended as an undergraduate, Trinity College, and two years later he was made a cardinal by pope Leo XIII.

Newman's enduring influence remains difficult to pin down. His long life and celebrity, his extensive writings and long periods as both Anglican and Catholic, are obvious factors. His theological and other religious writings covered a wide range of interests, from the dogmatic and historical, as in his *Essay on the Development of Christian Doctrine* and *A Grammar of Assent*, to the poetical and devotional, as in *The Dream of Gerontius*. All three works were written when Newman was a Catholic. He advised against the proclamation of papal infallibility, partly because it was unnecessary and partly because it would damage relations with other churches, yet he accepted the doctrine once it had been defined by the Vatican council in 1870. His extensive knowledge of tradition and theological development, especially in the early Church, his sensitivity to ecumenical relations, his teaching on liberty of conscience, and his insistence upon the important role of the laity – he wrote an influential article in the *Rambler* periodical 'On Consulting the Faithful in Matters of Doctrine' – touched on issues that bore fruit in the decrees of the second Vatican council. He may be regarded as the nineteenth-century theologian who exercised most influence upon this council, and the enormous amount of subsequent writings about him confirm his lasting influence.

Teresa of Lisieux (1873–97) has attained extraordinary popular appeal. She was one of four daughters in the Martin family who joined the Carmelite convent at Lisieux, Teresa entering at the young age of fifteen. She was inclined to volunteer for the new Carmelite foundation at Hanoi in Vietnam, but poor health persuaded her to remain at Lisieux, where she lived until her early death in heroic fidelity to the austere Carmelite rule and amid intense physical suffering. She wrote, under obedience, a short spiritual autobiography, *L'histoire d'une Ame*, which was published soon after her death and immediately became a spiritual classic, translated into many languages. Numerous miracles and 'favours' were attributed to her intercession and caused the remarkable spread of her cult. Teresa was beatified in 1923, canonized as a saint in 1925 and declared patroness of the Missions by pope Pius XI in 1927. She showed people how sanctity could be reached through fidelity to God's will amid the ordinary duties and daily trials of life.

John Bosco (1815–88) was born in Piedmont in northern Italy, the youngest son of a peasant farmer, who died when John was only two years old. He was brought up by his mother in considerable poverty. He entered the seminary and was ordained a diocesan priest in 1841. However, rather than becoming a parish priest, he soon settled into his life work, the education and apostolate of boys and young men, especially those of the working class. He also became involved in similar initiatives for girls and young women.

He had a genius for gaining the support of wealthy benefactors, who helped to finance his initiatives in establishing schools and workshops for the young. His efforts were supported by patrons of different outlooks, notably archbishop Franzoni of Turin and the liberal anticlerical Count Camillo Cavour, first prime minister of the united Italy. A notable preacher and writer, Don Bosco was a man of prayer who possessed remarkable gifts for friendship and encouraging others. He sought to unite the spiritual life of the young with their work, study and play. In many ways he was a forerunner – already appreciated in his day – of modern educational methods, especially of all that is best in Catholic education. His insistence that boys be taught trades made him a pioneer in modern vocational training. He founded the Salesian order for men (naming the order after St Francis de Sales) in 1859, for which he gained papal approval from Pius IX in 1868; also, together with St Maria Mazzarello, the Salesian Sisters in 1872; and a third order, the Salesian Cooperators, to assist in the work. The three orders grew rapidly and internationally, making the Salesian family a hugely important and creative force for the Catholic church worldwide until the present day.

Jean-Baptiste Marie Vianney (1786–1859), better know as the Curé d'Ars, completes the quartet of nineteenth century saints to be considered here. Like Newman and John Bosco, he became famous in his lifetime but otherwise his path was different. Born and brought up in Dardilly near Lyons in southern France, Jean-Baptiste had great difficulties with his seminary studies for the diocesan priesthood, partly because of the troubled times of the Napoleonic era in which he lived and partly because he found studies, especially Latin, difficult. After ordination at last in 1815, he spent three years as assistant priest at Ecully, and then in 1818 he was appointed to the remote village of Ars-en-Dombes. He became the parish priest of Ars in 1821 and held this post for the rest of his life. There he lived a very austere life and succeeded in converting the parishioners to a devout way of life through a variety of pastoral initiatives, notably preaching and hearing confessions. First from the village of Ars, then from neighbouring parishes, then from throughout France, and from other countries too, came men and women of all walks of life to seek his counsel and obtain absolution. Towards the end of his life he was spending most of the day in the confessional, caring for an estimated 20,000 penitents a year. Many came by train from Lyons, where a special booking-office for Ars was set up. He was beatified in 1905, canonized in 1925 and declared patron of parish priests in 1929. Perhaps he can be admired more than imitated.

Saints of the twentieth century are close to us in time and so make objective assessment difficult. The two popes already canonized or beatified, Saint Pius X and Blessed John XXIII, are mentioned in various places in this chapter. Edith Stein (Sister Teresa Benedicta of the Cross) and Maximilian Kolbe were killed amid the horrors of the concentration camps during World War II. Edith Stein converted from Judaism to Catholicism as a young woman and entered the Carmelite order. A noted writer on philosophical and spiritual topics, she was arrested on account of her Jewish origins and was put to death at Auschwitz camp in August 1942. She was canonized by pope John Paul II in 1987. Maximilian Kolbe was a noted Franciscan friar in Poland, engaged in a wide variety of apostolic works principally in the mass media. He spent six years in Japan as a missionary. Back in Poland, he was arrested in 1941 on account of an article he published that was critical of the German occupation of his country. He was deported to Auschwitz camp. There, when the camp authorities selected ten individuals for execution in reprisal for a prisoner who had escaped, and one of them cried out that he was a married man with a family, Kolbe valiantly offered himself in place of the man. His offer was accepted and he died two weeks later after great suffering. He was canonized by pope John Paul II in 1982.

Agnes Gonxha Bojaxhiu (1910–97), better known as Mother Teresa, was born in Skopje, Macedonia, of Albanian parents. She joined the order of Sisters of Loreto and went as a missionary to India, where she taught in St Mary's school in Calcutta. However, she felt drawn to work with the very poor and in 1948 she was given permission to leave the Loreto order. Dressed in a blue-edged sari, she lived in the slums of Calcutta teaching the children of the poor and caring for the destitute and homeless. Others joined her and in 1950 the new Order, the Missionaries of Charity, was approved. Its foundation was followed in 1963 by the Missionary Brothers of Charity and, soon afterwards, by that of the International Co-Workers of Mother Teresa. The three orders grew rapidly and internationally, most prominently the original female foundation. They have kept to their original charism, the care of the poor and destitute, with remarkable fidelity. Mother Teresa became a familiar figure worldwide, fearless in drawing attention to the plight of the needy and in raising money for their assistance. She was awarded the Nobel Peace Prize in 1979 and was beatified in 2003.

All nine saints and blessed of the nineteenth and twentieth centuries who have been singled out for attention were clergy or nuns. Their causes had powerful backing. One should especially remember, therefore, the laity among the other saints and blessed who have been officially recognized by the Church but remain less well known, as well as the countless other lay men and women whose heroic Christian lives have remained largely hidden from the wider world. All nine, moreover, were Europeans; though several of them laboured outside Europe. The canonization by pope Paul VI of the twenty-two young Ugandan martyrs, mentioned earlier, was specially opportune for its recognition of the heroic virtues of the laity as well as of the Church outside Europe.

Saints are also sinners, as most of them were the first to recognize. Other Catholics of the time ranged from the saintly to the seriously sinful. Most of the sins were similar to those committed by Catholics during the eighteen centuries covered in the first four chapters of the book. However, for the period 1800 to 1965, two kinds of sin might be considered new as regards scale: warfare and colonialism. Newer forms of sinfulness after 1965 will be considered in the last section of the chapter.

Wars involving Catholics were mentioned briefly in section i of this chapter. There the more positive results for Catholicism were highlighted. The fact remains, however, that in the two 'World Wars' of the twentieth century, which were unprecedented in the scale of warfare, in the number of deaths of both combatants and civilians, and in the destruction of property, Catholics were involved on a very large scale. This is said despite the strenuous efforts of some Catholics to avert the conflicts, including papal initiatives, and the refusal of many individuals – often at great personal sacrifice – to become involved in the fighting. They were not Christian wars in the sense that the primary motives were directly religious – as had been the case with much of the warfare during the period of Reformation and Counter-Reformation – and many other people were involved in them. Nevertheless the major role played by the Catholics church – more through individuals than through the institutional church as such – has to be acknowledged. In World War I (1914–18) predominantly Catholic France and Italy, as well as many Catholics from the USA, the UK and its colonies, Ireland, and other countries, fought against a coalition of countries in most of which Catholics were numerous: Germany, the Austrian Empire, various countries of central and eastern Europe. In World War II (1939–45) Catholics were involved on both sides in a conflagration of even greater proportions.

Regarding colonialism, the period up to 1965 saw both the apogee of developments and some of the break-up. For a long time most of the world was governed by countries rooted in western Christendom, divided rather equally between predominantly Catholic countries – principally Spain, France, Portugal and Belgium – and countries with a mainly Protestant ethos – principally the UK, the USA, the Netherlands and Germany. In the colonies of the Catholic countries, evangelization and conversion of the people to Catholicism was usually pursued consciously and vigorously, principally through religious orders, and with considerable success. The danger was that an altogether too European and western form of Christianity was imposed, resulting in reactions and difficult transitions especially in the period after 1960. There were notable Protestant missionaries and substantial numbers of conversions, but Protestant evangelization was generally less interventionist. Their governments, too, were usually more generous in allowing the entry and work of Catholic missionaries – as for example in India and in British colonies in Africa – than Catholic countries were in permitting the entry of Protestant missionaries. Even so, and despite various justifiable criticisms, the end result is that the ex-colonies of Europe's predominantly Catholic countries form much of the backbone of the Catholic church today, and likely will provide much of its vigour and creativeness in the coming century. There may be some parallel with the reinvigoration of the Church that was brought about by the tribes who converted to Christianity after the fall of the Roman Empire.

We have limited our discussion to the 'new' sins within modern warfare and colonialism. On account of their novelty they have been highlighted by historians too. But obviously it is essential to remember the sinfulness of Catholics in more traditional forms, which remains sin, and serious sin, nonetheless.

v. Vatican I and II

Two ecumenical councils of the Catholic church took place during the two centuries covered in this chapter: Vatican I in 1869–70 and Vatican II in 1962–5. They were central events in the life of the Church, important for understanding both the development of the Catholic church during this period and how she was viewed by others. They deserve individual attention.

Vatican I

Vatican I took place some three centuries after the conclusion of the council of Trent in 1563. Trent had been remarkably comprehensive in its coverage of both doctrinal and disciplinary matter, as we have seen, so that for long another council of the whole Catholic church seemed unnecessary. However, two important and linked issues were left largely untouched by the council: the papacy and the nature of the church. Both issues were hotly contested between Catholics and Protestants from the time of the Reformation onwards, but they were also controversial within the Catholic community. We have seen the force of the conciliar movement in the fifteenth century, and conciliarism still had many supporters among Catholics at the time of Trent. As a result, from fear of raising the 'conciliar ghost' and of reviving divisions within the Catholic community, Trent decided to abstain from discussing the papacy or attempting to define the constitution of the church.

Besides these issues of church and papacy, several new challenges to Catholic teaching had emerged during the seventeenth to nineteenth centuries: the scientific revolution of the seventeenth century, epitomized by Galileo and Newton; the Enlightenment of the eighteenth century, epitomized by Voltaire; the effects of the French Revolution of 1789 and its aftermath in France and many other countries; new intellectual challenges in the nineteenth century, such as those posed by the discoveries of Charles Darwin. As a result, the Catholic church needed to confront again the relationship between faith and reason.

The summoning of Vatican I was very much the personal initiative of pope Pius IX. It was not widely expected or called for by bishops or other members of the Catholic church beforehand. There were the background issues just mentioned but they were not matters of an immediately pressing nature, such as had required the summoning of Trent or Nicea I or Chalcedon.

The council met from December 1869 to July 1870. Formal sessions were held in St Peter's basilica, Rome's most famous church, which lies within the part of Rome known as the Vatican city – hence the name 'Vatican council'. Members of the council with a vote numbered some seven hundred, principally – following tradition – the bishops of the Catholic church. Those present at the council accounted for some two-thirds of the world's bishops. For the first time at an ecumenical council, all five continents were represented; though the large majority of bishops with sees outside Europe were of European origin – either missionary bishops from Europe or the offspring of families who had emigrated, at varying dates in the past, from Europe. So the flavour of the council was primarily European, yet it was the most worldwide council of the Church to that date, due both to its membership and to the rapid diffusion of news through the developing mass media.

The original intention had been for the council to discuss quite a wide range of issues, including the missions, religious orders, eastern churches, church–state relations and the revision of canon law; though the definition of papal authority, principally papal infallibility, was always regarded – especially by pope Pius – as the council's principal task. The council was curtailed by two impending wars. The reunification of Italy, accomplished by the armies of Garibaldi and others, had already reduced the Papal States to Rome and a small surrounding enclave, which was protected principally by French troops. The imminent outbreak of war between France and Prussia meant both that the French troops defending Rome were likely to be withdrawn in order to defend France, and the bishops from France and Germany would leave the council. As a result of these two military threats, the business of the council was reduced to two relatively short decrees: 'Dogmatic Constitution on the Catholic Faith' and 'First Dogmatic Constitution on the Church of Christ'.

The first decree, on the Catholic faith, was divided into four chapters, with the following headings: 'On God the creator of all things', 'On revelation', 'On faith' and 'On faith and reason'. It was the final chapter 'On faith and reasons' that sought most directly to confront the intellectual challenges of the time. Part of the background was the 'Syllabus of Errors', which had been issued by pope Pius IX in 1864 and concluded with the sweeping condemnation of all those who said that the 'Roman pontiff can and ought to reconcile and adjust himself with progress, liberalism and modern civilization'. The tone of the council's decree is more eirenic, seeking to steer a middle course between the extremes of rationalism and fideism, between exaggerated emphases upon either reason or faith. The decree begins thus:

> *The perpetual agreement of the Catholic church has maintained and still maintains this too: that there is a twofold order of knowledge, distinct not only as regards its source, but also as regards its object. With regard to the source, we know at the one level by natural reason, at the other level by divine faith.*

There is respect for both faith and reason, though the right of the Church to pronounce on disputed issues is maintained. Some would argue that to begin with the distinction between faith and reason is dangerous in its too ready acceptance of a distinction that originated in medieval scholasticism, was developed by Descartes and subsequent western philosophy, and results in a dichotomy which remains difficult to bridge: better rather to begin with the unity of knowledge and life, an approach that is more consonant with the Scriptures and the early fathers of the Church both eastern and western. The overall tone of the chapter is positive and encouraging, though with cautions too:

> *Even though faith is above reason, there can never be any real disagreement between faith and reason, since it is the same God who reveals the mysteries and infuses faith, and who has endowed the human mind with the light of Reason ... Hence, so far is the Church from hindering the development of human arts and studies, that in fact she assists and promotes them in many ways ... May understanding, knowledge and wisdom increase as ages and centuries roll along, and greatly and vigorously flourish in each and all, in the individual and the whole church: but this only in its proper kind, that is to say, in the same doctrine, the same sense, and the same understanding.*

The better known of the council's two decrees is the second, 'First Dogmatic Constitution on the Church of Christ'. Originally the decree was intended to provide a full treatment of the Church – the first time an ecumenical council had attempted such comprehensive coverage of the topic. However, with the threats of the council's curtailment, only the papacy was treated. The decree is thus styled 'first', leaving the possibility that other aspects of the Church would be treated in one or more subsequent decrees. This short decree is divided into four chapters, the first two of which are entitled 'On the institution of the apostolic primacy in blessed Peter' and 'On the permanence of the primacy of blessed Peter in the Roman pontiffs'. The two chapters may be acceptable to almost all Christians, except some fundamentalists or literal interpreters of Scripture who would argue that Jesus never explicitly ordered the Church to elect successors to Peter. Chapter 3, entitled 'On the power and character of the primacy of the Roman pontiff', proclaimed this primacy in strong language which provided difficulty also for some Catholics: 'world-wide primacy', 'full power to tend, rule and govern the universal Church', 'a pre-eminence of ordinary power over every other church'. However, 'this power of the supreme pontiff by no means detracts from the ordinary and immediate power of ... bishops'.

It was the fourth and final chapter, entitled 'On the infallible teaching authority of the Roman pontiff', that was intended to be the kernel of the decree and which caused the most controversy. After an historical introduction, the chapter concludes with the core of the definition:

> *Therefore ... with the approval of the sacred council, we (the pope) teach and define as a divinely revealed dogma that when the Roman pontiff speaks* ex cathedra, *that is, when in the exercise of his office as shepherd and teacher of all Christians ... he defines a doctrine concerning faith or morals to be held by the whole church, he possesses, by the divine assistance promised to him in blessed Peter, that infallibility which the divine Redeemer willed his Church to enjoy in defining doctrine concerning faith or morals. Therefore such definitions of the Roman pontiff are of themselves, and not by the consent of the church, irreformable.*

This final formula was the result of intense debate within the council over several months. Inasmuch as there was a substantial minority of bishops who were opposed to the definition, either in principle or on the grounds of *non expedit* ('not expedient', an elastic term that covered a range of positions), the wording represents something of a compromise. While maintaining the doctrine of infallibility, the terms are refined. The guarantee is restricted to teaching on matters of faith (Latin original, *fides*) and morals (Latin original *mores*, which is best but not perfectly translated as 'morals') that are binding for the whole Church. It does not cover, therefore, other issues – such as historical matters – or indeed moral issues that pertain to a particular locality. The definition does not say directly that the pope is infallible, rather that 'he possesses ... the infallibility that the divine Redeemer (Christ) willed his Church to enjoy', thus placing papal infallibility in an elegant way within the context of the overall guidance that Christ promised to his Church. Vatican II would later define 'Church' more clearly in terms of the people of God as well as the church hierarchy. The phrasing thus allows for individual mistakes even in doctrine, such as pope Honorius's faulty teaching of monothelitism or the condemnation of Galileo (above pp. 62 and 170). No list of doctrines that fall within the terms of the definition is given and there has been much discussion among Catholics as to which doctrinal pronouncements of the popes should be considered infallible. The final sentence 'Therefore ... irreformable' was included at the insistence of pope Pius, to exclude the claim that infallibility was guaranteed to papal pronouncements only after they had been accepted by the church as a whole – a process that could be almost interminable.

At a preliminary vote on the decree on 13 July 1870, four hundred and fifty-one members of the council voted yes (Latin *placet*), eighty-eight voted no (*non placet*) and sixty-two had reservations (*placet iuxta modum*). The large majority, therefore, were in favour but a substantial minority, including bishops of a number of major sees, were opposed or had reservations and some hundred (of the seven hundred) did not vote at all. The final vote, a week later, was five hundred and thirty-three in favour and only two bishops (of Little Rock in Arkansas, USA, and Caiazzo in southern Italy) against; but, as the totals indicate, a substantial number of bishops decided to absent themselves rather than vote against the decree: some left Rome before the final vote. There was, therefore a significant minority against or uneasy with the decree, but surely not enough to invalidate it, especially as only two bishops actually voted against. Here one recalls the serious divisions at Ephesus and some of the other early councils whose ecumenicity nevertheless came to be recognized by the Church. All the bishops who abstained or voted against soon gave their formal recognition to the decree; though a number of individuals, most notably the German church historian Johann von Döllinger, left the Catholic church to join the Old Catholic church (also called the church of Utrecht), which had been founded in the eighteenth century in opposition to papal claims of the time.

On 19 July, the day after the promulgation of the decree, war broke out between France and Prussia, resulting in the departure from the council of the bishops of these two countries and the withdrawal from Rome of the French troops who were defending the city against the surrounding Italian forces. Some work continued to be done during the summer but on 20 September the Italian troops entered Rome and a month later pope Pius formally adjourned the council indefinitely.

Vatican II

The interval of almost a century between the adjournment of Vatican I and the summoning of Vatican II appears providential. Many of the decrees that had been proposed for Vatican I but were never debated, had time to mature into those of Vatican II. Notably, Vatican I's decree on the papacy provided the impetus for the full treatment on the Church in *Lumen gentium*.

Vatican II, like Vatican I, came unexpectedly. The theology of Trent still exercised great influence in the 1950s and Vatican I's definition of papal infallibility seemed to provide a means of resolving future debates. Indeed, not long before the summoning of Vatican II, papal infallibility had been used by Pius XII in 1950 in the proclamation of Mary's assumption into heaven. Another ecumenical council seemed to many people unnecessary. Both Pius XI (1922–39) and Pius XII (1939–58), it is true, spoke on various occasions of resuming the adjourned Vatican I in order to complete its work, but the proposal was communicated in a low-key manner to the popes' close advisers rather than to the general public, as a possibility rather than a definite proposition.

There was considerable surprise, therefore, when pope John XXIII announced on 25 January 1959, three months after his election, that he wished to convoke an ecumenical council. Later he clarified that it would be a new council and not a continuation of Vatican I. Commentators have debated how far the pope had a conscious plan for the council. He spoke of wishing to open the windows of the Church in order to let in some fresh air, but he also said that the purpose of the council would be to strengthen doctrine and improve ecclesiastical discipline: proposals that together offer varying interpretations. Most clearly, in the letter *Humanae salutis* of December 1961, in which the pope officially convoked the council to meet the following year, three principal aims were given: the better internal ordering of the Church, unity among Christians, and the promotion of peace in the world. John was a shrewd man and deeply spiritual; attentive to the Holy Spirit wherever she might blow. He had, too, a good sense of history, being a church historian of some note.

It seems clear that nobody, including pope John, foresaw how the council would develop. The pope established ten preparatory commissions – with most of the heads and many of the members coming from the Roman curia – to prepare draft documents for the forthcoming council. These draft documents, however, quickly proved unacceptable to the council, so new decrees had to be hammered out almost from scratch. Some idea of the resulting long development is given by the dates on which the council eventually approved its sixteen decrees. The titles (which reproduce the initial words of the document) and the dates of approval are as follows:

Sacrosanctum concilium, Constitution on the Sacred Liturgy
(4 December 1963).
Inter mirifica, Decree on the Mass Media (4 December 1963).
Lumen gentium, Dogmatic Constitution on the Church
(21 November 1964).
Orientalium ecclesiarum, Decree on the Eastern Catholic
Churches (21 November 1964).
Unitatis redintegratio, Decree on Ecumenism (21 November
1964).
Christus Dominus, Decree on the Pastoral Office of Bishops in
the Church (28 October 1965).
Perfectae caritatis, Decree on the Renewal of Religious Life
(28 October 1965).

Optatam totius, Decree on Priestly Formation (28 October 1965).

Gravissimum educationis, Declaration on Christian Education (28 October 1965).

Nostra aetate, Declaration on the Church's Relation to Non-Christian Religions, (28 October 1965).

Dei verbum, Dogmatic Constitution on Divine Revelation (18 November 1965).

Apostolicam actuositatem, Decree on the Apostolate of the Laity (18 November 1965).

Dignitatis humanae, Declaration on Religious Freedom (7 December 1965).

Ad gentes, Decree on the Missionary Activity of the Church (7 December 1965).

Presbyterorum ordinis, Decree on the Ministry and Life of Priests (7 December 1965).

Gaudium et spes, Pastoral Constitution on the Church in the Modern World (7 December 1965).

The original intention had been for the council to complete its work during the autumn of 1962. However, with the rejection of the draft documents it soon became apparent that another session would be necessary, and this second session was duly announced by pope John for the autumn of 1963. Pope John died in June 1963, following a week of worldwide mourning as the gravity of his situation became apparent. A few weeks later his successor was elected, pope Paul VI. He then had the onerous task of guiding the council to its conclusion, which he did with great skill. Two further periods of some ten weeks, in the autumns of 1964 and 1965, were necessary to complete the work of the council. As can be seen from the dates above, it was only at the end of the second period that the first two documents of the council were approved; three more were approved during the third session, and the remaining eleven during the fourth and last session.

Full members of the council, principally the bishops of the Church and various heads of religious orders, numbered some 2,400 at any one time (new arrivals replacing the several hundred who died during the course of the council). They had the right to speak during the debates, which were held in the nave of St Peter's church, and to vote on the decrees. Vatican II was thus by far the largest and most international of the twenty-one ecumenical councils of the Catholic church to date. Important, too, were the theologians – officially called *periti* (experts) – who could not speak during the debates but were eligible, alongside the bishops, for the 'conciliar commissions' which composed the new decrees. Most notable among them were the French Dominican Yves Congar, the German Jesuit Karl Rahner, and Monsignor Gérard Philips from Belgium.

Journalists played an important role in bringing news of the council to a worldwide audience. Some indeed complained that the journalists were influencing the council rather than just reporting it. Particularly notable in the English-speaking world was the Redemptorist priest Joseph Xavier Murphy, who wrote regular columns in *The New Yorker* under the pseudonym Xavier Rynne (Rynne was his mother's maiden name). Francophone and German-speaking countries were well served by regular columns in *Le Monde*, *La Croix* and *Frankfurter Allgemeine Zeitung*. Other Christian churches and communities were invited to send representatives – officially called 'Observers' – to attend the meetings of the council. Particularly active were those from the Anglican and Lutheran churches, who contributed significantly to some conciliar decrees, notably *Unitatis redintegratio* on ecumenism. Some Catholics, too, were invited to participate as 'Observers', including some nuns and other women, thus giving the council a minimal female composition.

The sixteen decrees were distinguished by three grades of authority. At the lowest level were the three 'Declarations' – on Christian Education, non-Christian Religions, and Religious Freedom. Despite its importance, education was never intended to be a primary focus of the council. The declaration on Non-Christian Religions developed late in the council and in a tentative manner, yet its positive assessment of other world religions – Judaism, Hinduism, Buddhism and Islam are treated individually – has made it one of the most influential of all the conciliar decrees, leading to a radical transformation in Catholic attitudes towards other faiths and their adherents.

The Catholic church rejects nothing of those things which are true and holy in these religions. It regards with respect those ways of acting and living and those precepts and teachings which, though often at variance with what it holds and expounds, frequently reflect a ray of that truth which enlightens everyone. It therefore calls upon its members with prudence and charity, through dialogue and cooperation with the followers of other religions, bearing witness to the Christian faith and way of life, to recognize, preserve and promote those spiritual and moral good things as well as the socio-cultural values which are to be found among them. (Nostra aetate, no. 2)

The decree on Religious Freedom remained at the level of a Declaration mainly because there was unease among many members of the council that the decree was watering down the ideal of a Catholic society, but it too has turned out to be one of the council's most important and influential documents.

Nine of the documents fell into the middle grade of 'Decrees'. (Note therefore the twofold sense of 'decree': (1) to describe all documents approved by ecumenical (and other) councils; (2) to describe middle-ranking conciliar documents, in the case of Vatican II those of greater authority than 'declarations' but of lesser authority than 'constitutions'.) Many of the nine decrees expanded on individual chapters in *Lumen gentium*. Among them, the decree on Ecumenism has been particularly influential, emphasizing the common ground shared by Christians – that we are much more united than divided – and encouraging further efforts towards reunion at both the doctrinal and practical levels. The decree on Religious Life sought both a return to the original inspiration of each religious order as well as adaptation to the realities and challenges of modern life: a combination that has proved hard to realize.

Four documents were accorded the highest authority of 'Constitution'. *Sacrosanctum concilium* on the Liturgy was the first of the council's decrees to be approved and at the time it seemed to have the widespread backing of the council. There was general agreement on its two principal aims: a return to the sources of the liturgy and fuller participation on the part of the laity. Yet it has proved to be one of the most difficult decrees to implement, not least in the transition from Latin to the vernacular languages. *Dei verbum* asserted the centrality of Scripture in all areas of Catholic life as well as the intimate connection between Scripture and Tradition. It encouraged Catholic biblical scholarship and cooperation with scholars of other Christian traditions. In these and other ways it helped to heal the rift between the Catholic church and the churches of the Reformation, regarding the interpretation and use of the Bible, which had existed since the sixteenth century.

The other two 'Constitutions' concern the Church. *Lumen gentium* focuses on the nature and ordering of the Church, thereby completing and realigning the work of Vatican I on the papacy. Its first two chapters, entitled 'The Mystery of the Church' and 'The People of God', introduce a more humble and people-centred description of the Church. Chapter 3, entitled 'The Hierarchical Constitution of the Church and in particular the Episopate', reasserts the teaching of Vatican I on the papacy but also places the pope better within the context of the other bishops of the Church. Chapters 4, 5 and 7, entitled respectively 'The Laity', 'The Universal Call to Holiness in the Church', and 'The Eschatological Character of the Pilgrim Church and its Union with the Heavenly Church', expand on themes introduced in the first two chapters, emphasizing both the exalted vocation of all Christians and the difficulties of life here on earth. Chapter 6 'Religious', treats of religious orders, a topic that is covered more fully in the decree *Perfectae caritatis*. Finally, Chapter 8 'The Blessed Virgin Mary, Mother of God, in the Mystery of Christ and the Church' provides a full treatment of Mary as a model for Christians and her exalted role in the life of the Church.

Gaudium et spes, the other Constitution on the Church, is more practical, especially its second Part entitled 'Some Urgent Problems'. Here the chapter and section headings outline the range of issues covered: 'Promoting the Dignity of Marriage', 'The Conditions of Culture in Today's World', 'Socio-Economic Life', 'Life in the Political Community', and 'Promoting Peace and Encouraging the Community of Nations'. Some would see *Gaudium et spes* as the crown of the whole council, the last of the decrees to be approved, the one that most closely corresponded to pope John's wish for a pastoral council that would result in *aggiornamento* (updating), and the decree that has had the widest influence upon Catholic activity in the world.

In the final voting all the decrees were approved by overwhelming majorities, thereby fully following the conciliar tradition of 'virtual unanimity'. The central thrust of the decrees is clear. At the same time there is respect for the reservations of minority groupings who were hesitant with various aspects of the teachings. Overall the council may be seen as a miracle of God's grace as well as of human ingenuity, by producing extensive teaching on a wide range of major issues that both respects the Church's traditions and speaks in language that has connected well with Christians and the world at large ever since.

vi. Recent developments: 1965–2010

Reception of Vatican II was the greatest preoccupation of the Catholic church in the aftermath of the council, certainly until around 1980. Thereafter other factors claimed much of the limelight, notably the fall of Communism in central and eastern Europe, and changes in lifestyle resulting partly from developments in communications. This final section covers a huge amount of material in a short space and in a very tentative way – inevitably so, since many of the results still await their unfolding

Reception of Vatican II

The second Vatican council must be counted among the half dozen most influential councils in the Church's history. Its decrees were remarkably comprehensive while both membership of and interest in the council were worldwide on an unprecedented scale, as we have seen. All sixteen decrees were eventually approved by overwhelming majorities and there were no formal schisms at the time. Nevertheless the reception of Vatican II proved difficult.

In a sense this difficulty need cause no surprise. The reception of many other major councils – especially those of the first millennium – proved arduous: Nicea I, Ephesus, Chalcedon, Nicaea II, some of the late medieval councils, even Vatican I. New teaching, or re-expressing traditional doctrines in new language, as well as changes in discipline, are bound to cause soul-searching, especially when conducted on an extensive scale. In terms of the comprehensiveness of its decrees, Trent provides the closest parallel to Vatican II. Yet there were important differences between the two councils. Trent largely succeeded in uniting Catholics in the face of the Protestant challenge, and its decrees had the strong backing of the papacy. Vatican II had no such clear external challenge to unite

Catholics, and much of the hesitation regarding some of its decrees – at least regarding their alleged exaggerated or faulty application – came from within the Roman curia. The councils, moreover, did not enter into much detail regarding the application of its decrees. For a variety of reasons, Vatican II somewhat lacked mechanisms for its execution that were both clear and effective.

Although Vatican II's decree *Gaudium et spes* contained a chapter on marriage, pope Paul withdrew the issue of birth control from the council's agenda. Three years later, in the summer of 1968, the pope issued the encyclical *Humanae vitae* which condemned the use of artificial means of contraception, including therefore the recently discovered contraceptive pill which was in widespread use among Catholics. The encyclical caused a major crisis within the Catholic community with opposition to it coming from both laity and clergy. Indirectly it represented a watershed in the reception of the council's teaching as well as in Catholic attitudes towards the papacy.

Sacrosanctum concilium, Vatican II's decree on the liturgy, permitted more widespread use of vernacular languages in the Mass while also encouraging the use of Latin. In practice, the vernacular quickly replaced Latin almost everywhere and new texts were produced to replace the Tridentine Mass. Similar changes in both language and content were introduced for the other sacraments and liturgical texts. Some Catholics felt the changes had gone too far and too fast, particularly regarding Sunday Mass which affected the majority of Catholics most immediately. These changes more or less coincided with a decline in the number of practising Catholics in the western world, so that blame for the decline might be linked to the liturgical changes. They were a major reason for the schism led by archbishop Lefebvre, starting in 1976. Subsequently more use of both Latin and the old rite was officially sanctioned, culminating in pope Benedict's recent approval of regular celebration of the Tridentine Mass in Latin. The moves have pleased some Catholics while disappointing others.

Despite the council's two decrees on the priesthood – *Optatam totius* on priestly formation and *Presbyterorum ordinis* on the ministry and life of priests – the number of seminarians began to fall soon after the end of the council while the number of priests leaving the priesthood increased dramatically. Likewise, notwithstanding the council's decree *Perfectae caritatis* on the renewal of religious life, religious orders of both men and women were adversely affected by declines in the number of entrants and increases in those leaving. The declines have been partly offset by increases in both priestly and religious vocations in countries outside the western world as well as by the growth of new religious orders and movements, such as Opus Dei, Legionaries of Christ, Comunione e Liberazione, Neo-catechumenate, Fe y Alegría, and many others. In various ways, too, some of the older orders have progressed in recent years. Partly as a response to Vatican II's encouragement to the laity to play a more active role in the Church, some of the works previously done by priests and religious have been taken on by lay men and women and these developments may be seen in a positive light.

In terms of ecumenical relations with other Christian churches and communities, Vatican II's decree *Unitatis redintegratio* produced encouraging fruits in the years immediately after the council. Particularly notable were the joint declarations issued by the Anglican-Roman Catholic International Commission (ARCIC), which was established jointly by Michael Ramsey, archbishop of Canterbury, and pope Paul VI when they met in Rome in 1966. Agreement was reached in principle on Eucharistic Doctrine (1971), Ministry and Ordination (1973), and Authority in the Church (1976); though the agreements were formally ratified by the papacy only in 1991, and then with qualifications. From around 1980 progress in official ecumenical dialogues with various churches became more difficult, partly through the arrival of new obstacles, such as the ordination of women within the Anglican Communion, and partly through what was seen as the firmer approach of pope John Paul II. Even so, much progress has continued at local levels in terms of both mutual understanding and practical cooperation. An important agreement on justification, ratified by the papacy, was reached in 1999 between the Catholic and Lutheran churches.

A significant ecumenical initiative came in the letter written by pope Paul VI in 1974 to celebrate the seventh centenary of the second council of Lyons. The letter referred to this council and its predecessors as 'general councils of the western church' (*generales synodos in orbe occidentali*), rather than using the word 'ecumenical' for them (*Acta Apostolicae Sedis*, 1974, p. 620).

Thereby the pope seemed to accept the possibility of reconsidering the status of the medieval councils – which had been given the firmer label of 'ecumenical' from the time of the 'Roman edition' of the councils (*Editio romana*, 4 vols, 1608–12) onwards – as well as, by implication, the later councils of Trent and Vatican I and II. Several theologians, notably Yves Congar and Victor Peri, had been making similar suggestions shortly beforehand. Later there was a passing reference to the distinction between ecumenical and general council in ARCIC's 'Agreed Statement on Authority in the Church' (1976), no. 19, but pope Paul's invitation remains to be explored more fully.

Much of the momentum of Vatican II's declaration on other faiths and religions, *Nostra aetate*, has been maintained. A major challenge, however, which was largely unseen by the council, has come through the emergence of a more militant Islam.

To some extent the ongoing implementation of the council has been met by the institution of the 'Synod of Bishops', which comprises representatives from the various national episcopates. Its role is to offer advice to the pope and, indirectly, to the wider Catholic community, not to make binding decrees. Beginning in 1968, the meetings have been held in Rome, initially every three years and then every two years. A variety of topical issues have been discussed at the synods.

Important too was the new Code of Canon Law, *Codex Iuris Canonici*, which was promulgated by pope John Paul II in 1983 with the specific intent of including the insights of the second Vatican council. It replaced the first *Codex Iuris Canonici* which had been promulgated by pope Benedict XV in 1917. Thereby the movement in Catholic canon law from a collection or body (Latin *corpus*) of responses to particular cases, to a code of law, was consolidated: the move from *Corpus* to *Codex*. A separate Code for the eastern churches in communion with Rome, *Codex Canonum Ecclesiarum Orientalium*, was promulgated by pope John Paul in 1990.

Tensions and difficulties should not obscure the overwhelming importance and success of the council. As well as enhancing many aspects of renewal within the Catholic community, the council radically transformed Catholic attitudes towards other Christians and other faiths. It has enabled the Catholic church to confront the modern world with both confidence and humility and to expand from its predominantly European base to become a truly worldwide religion.

Independence and peace

The decline of western colonialism, already well advanced by 1962, accelerated further during and immediately after the second Vatican council as more countries, principally in Africa and Asia, gained political independence. The council itself said little about this epoch-making development in the world order: *Gaudium et spes* (no. 9) has only a passing reference to 'nations on the road to progress and recently become independent'. The lacuna may, perhaps, be explained partly by the lack of unanimity on the issue among members of the council, partly because western missionaries had been responsible for much of the growth of the Church outside Europe, so that a mentality of some dependence for these countries was subtly endemic.

Nevertheless the Catholic church was quite quick and positive in recognizing political independence, and its consequences for the Church, once it had been achieved. Already at Vatican II bishops from outside Europe played an increasingly important role during the third and fourth years of the council. Notable among the native African bishops were, for example, cardinal Rugambwa of Tanzania, archbishop Zoa of Yaoundé in Cameroon, and archbishop Malula of Leopoldville (Kinshasa) in Congo, or from Indonesia, archbishops Darmojuwono and Djajasepoetra. Although the contents of most of the council's decrees have the western world most directly in mind – for which they have been criticized – nevertheless indirectly they gave encouragement to many of the better political, social and economic developments that have taken place outside Europe during the last half century.

Within these developments, the Catholic church's advocacy of peace has been very important. We have seen the Church's promotion of crusades during many centuries, and its longstanding justification of religious wars. In the twentieth century, popes Benedict XV and Pius XII appealed for an end to the two world wars, yet Catholics were among those most involved in the fighting, and the Italian army in Abyssinia as well as Franco's forces in Spain received a measure of official Church support in the 1930s. The invention of the atomic bomb, first used in 1945, and later of still more powerful nuclear weapons, changed the nature of warfare and its destructive possibilities. For the Catholic church, a decisive turning point came with pope John XXIII's encyclical *Pacem in terris* (Peace on earth), written in 1963, and the chapter 'Promoting peace and encouraging the community of nations' in Vatican II's decree *Gaudium et spes*. Both documents made passionate appeals for an end to warfare as a means of resolving disputes among nations. The approach has been followed resolutely by the papacy and many Catholics ever since, even while the right to legitimate self-defence has been sustained. Altogether the Catholic church has played an important role in the new advocacy of peace. Catholics, nevertheless, have been participants in much of the warfare that has taken place in the last half century – in Vietnam, Afghanistan, Iraq, many countries in Africa, and elsewhere.

The fall of the Communist government in Poland in 1989, and the subsequent collapse of similar regimes in other countries of central and eastern Europe, curtailed another form of colonialism, that centred upon Moscow and the Soviet Union. The developments came rapidly and unexpectedly and relatively peacefully. The Catholic church played a leading role in the early stages of this revolution inasmuch as it began in predominantly Catholic Poland and the most notable figures in the movement were its two citizens, pope John Paul II and the trade-union leader and devout Catholic, Lech Walesa. In other countries, too, the Catholic church's longstanding opposition to Marxist and Communist principles played a role in the moderation or demise of governments of this character.

John Paul II was the first non-Italian pope since Hadrian VI in the early sixteenth century. His long reign, his charismatic presence and extensive pastoral visits worldwide, his earlier sufferings as a Pole during both German and Russian occupations of his country, and the attempted assassination at the beginning of his pontificate, brought the papacy center stage worldwide. He encountered considerable criticism both within the Catholic church and outside, yet undoubtedly he contributed significantly to post-Vatican II developments in the Catholic church.

Technological revolutions: lights and shadows

Continuing developments in technology, especially in terms of the mass media, have brought both opportunities and challenges for the Catholic church. In many ways the Church has responded well. Vatican Radio was established at an early date and has developed into a large organization broadcasting in many languages to many countries. The papacy has been well aware of its duty to communicate to those within and beyond the Church. Vatican II dedicated one of it sixteen decrees to the mass media, *Inter mirifica*. The document was shorter and less profound than many would have wished, but at least it recognized the importance of the mass media and encouraged Catholics to engage in them. At the national and local levels there have been many initiatives.

Nevertheless the last twenty years have produced something of a crisis for the Catholic church regarding the mass media. The overwhelming majority of the media – radio, television and films, literature of many kinds from books to newspapers, as well as new developments through the internet and allied media – lie quite outside Church control. Individuals must struggle to make the Catholic voice heard as well as to maintain their integrity and Christian principles in their use of the media. Most of the media is secular in tone – sometimes openly so, sometimes more subtly. The speed with which news travels and the powers of investigative journalism have exposed the Catholic church to much criticism. Sexual abuse of minors by Catholic clergy has been particularly shocking in recent years. We can be grateful that grievous sins, very damaging to their victims, have been brought to public attention. Thereby the likelihood of repetition has been reduced. Nevertheless there is the peril that one shocking dimension is eclipsing other areas of sinfulness as well as the good news of the gospel message. Subtly, too, there is danger that the Church will concentrate too much on its public presentation, on the more obvious and easily grasped dimensions of the Christian message, and so come to minimize or forget the wonder and depth of this mystery.

Conclusion

We have come a long way in a remarkable story. How far we are from the conclusion of the history of the Catholic church on earth, who knows? Maybe, at the beginning of the next millennium, after many further developments, readers will see that the Catholic church was still in its infancy, or at most in middle age, in the year 2010. Six points or reflections occur to me by way of conclusion.

First, there has been strong emphasis in this history upon people. Some sections may seem to be little more than a collection of potted biographies. Yet the emphasis upon people, particularly individuals, is surely correct. Most basically the church means the people of God in all their wonder and complexity. Their attempts to live out the gospel message and to allow Christ to enter their lives, amid circumstance that have varied greatly according to time and place as well as according to the characters and situations of individuals, makes a noble and fascinating story. For Catholics the story, in addition to its fascination, is constitutive of Tradition, which means that it forms an essential element in their understanding of God's revelation and a trusty companion on the journey towards the kingdom of God.

Two duets, between Scripture and Tradition, and between God and humanity, make the second and third points. The necessity and complementarity of Scripture and Tradition was declared by the council of Trent and reaffirmed by the second Vatican council, as we have seen. The present history may be seen as an account of how Christians have tried to be faithful to both these elements during the course of some two thousand years. The result has seen both creativity and tensions. Catholics, at their best, have sought to be faithful to the gospel message and courageous in confronting the challenges and opportunities of their time and circumstances.

Scripture and Tradition affirm both God's initiative and human free will. Accordingly, the relationship between God and humanity lies at the heart of the Church's history. The story is so remarkable that it cannot be explained without divine providence. At the same time, human character in all its forms will be apparent in the pages of this short book: heroic sanctity, much faithfulness and sincerity on a daily basis, plenty of sinfulness; remarkable achievements and disappointing failures.

Fourthly, the story is one of both continuity and change. Scripture, albeit often difficult to interpret, the faithfulness of God, and the constant efforts of men and women, form the core of continuity. Tradition and the development of history, including human frailty, make room rather for change. The interplay between continuity and change makes a moving and fascinating story.

Fifthly, and resulting from the previous four considerations, simplifications must be avoided. We have been dealing with a very long period of time and a huge number of complex individuals. Today especially, in our impatient world, there is the temptation to oversimplify, to reduce complex issues to platitudes and soundbites. For the history of the Church such an approach does great violence and injustice to the individuals involved, and is disrespectful to our own intelligence. I hope the present book has at least brought out the complexity of the Church's past and thereby has done some justice to the depth and variety of people who make up the Catholic tradition.

Finally, a word again regarding the shape of the book. For the first six hundred years or so most of the momentum in the Church came from the East and from north Africa. With the rise of Islam and the schism between Rome and Constantinople beginning in 1054, these regions were largely cut off from the Catholic church. Thereafter the centre of the Catholic church moved decisively to the West and the eleventh to fifteenth centuries proved crucial to its development. The third chapter of the book covers this central period in particular detail, both on account of its intrinsic importance and because it helps to explain many of the subsequent developments in Catholicism. The sixteenth to eighteenth centuries saw Europe split asunder, into Catholic and Protestant countries, but it also saw Catholicism recover and develop for the first time into a world religion. The nineteenth and twentieth centuries witnessed a tenfold increase in the number of Catholics as well as a shift in the focus of the Church to the world outside Europe. This wider world brought many challenges to the Catholic church – material, cultural and intellectual. Humbler than before yet still vigorous, the Catholic church today faces the challenges of the twenty-first century with both optimism and caution.

Appendix

List of Ecumenical Councils

The Catholic church gives the status of ecumenical to the twenty-one councils listed below. The first seven are recognized as ecumenical by the Orthodox church and at least the first four are accorded a privileged status by many of the Protestant churches. For the distinction between 'ecumenical' and 'general', see above pp. 232–3.

The word 'ecumenical' comes from the Greek work *oikoumenike*, meaning literally 'where there are houses' (*oikos* = house) and by extension 'the inhabited world'. Applied to councils, the word distinguishes councils of the whole church from those of a regional or local nature. As councils of the whole Church, their authority is regarded as binding; as distinct from the lesser or local authority of other councils.

Until recently, the words 'council' and 'synod' were synonymous. 'Council' (Latin *concilium*) was normally used in the Latin-speaking western Church, 'synod' (Greek *synodos*) in the eastern churches. A formal distinction between council and synod was introduced into the Catholic church only after Vatican II, with the establishment of the 'Synod of bishops' (see p. 233).

Before the East–West Schism	Middle Ages	Modern Period
Nicea I (325)	Lateran I (1123)	Trent (1545–63)
Constantinople I (381)	Lateran II (1139)	Vatican I (1869–70)
Ephesus (431)	Lateran III (1179)	Vatican II (1962–5)
Chalcedon (451)	Lateran IV (1215)	
Constantinople II (553)	Lyons I (1245)	
Constantinople III (680–1)	Lyons II (1274)	
Nicea II (787)	Vienne (1311–12)	
Constantinople IV (869–70)	Constance (1414–18)	
	Basel–Florence (1431–45)	
	Lateran V (1512–17)	

Glossary

barbarian – See p. 42.

basilica – A church of special importance, deriving from the Greek word for king, *basileus*. The best known is St Peter's church/ basilica in Rome.

bull (papal) – Derives from the Latin word for a seal, *bulla*. A lead seal was normally affixed to important papal documents, so the word came to be applied to the document itself.

canon law – Means, in a Christian context, church law or law of the Christian community.

cardinal – Derives from the Latin word for a hinge, see p. 73.

catacombs – Subterranean galleries, see p. 22.

Copt – Derives from the Greek word for Egypt, see p. 71.

diocese – See p. 19.

ecumenical and general councils – See p. 28 and Appendix, pp. 241–2.

fathers of the Church – Major Christian writers before about 600 AD.

Filioque – Means 'and from the Son', see pp. 44 and 68–9.

Gothic architecture – See p. 141.

homoousios – Means 'of the same being' or 'consubstantial', see pp. 29–30.

iconoclasm – Destruction of images.

indulgences – The granting, by an appropriate church authority, of remission of the punishment still due to sins that have been forgiven, normally on condition of specified prayers or good works.

Lent – The season of forty days in preparation for Easter, see p. 31.

liturgy – Means public religious services, deriving from the Greek words *leitos* (public) and *ergon* (work).

money – See p. 101 for the value of pounds sterling in the Middle Ages.

mysticism – See pp. 137–8 for a definition.

orthodox (with a small 'o') – Indicates correct doctrine.

Orthodox (with a capital 'O') church – Church(es) acknowledging the primacy of the patriarch of Constantinople. Used principally after the beginning of the schism in 1054.

pagan – See p. 162.

pope – Among Catholics a title reserved for the bishop of Rome, see p. 18.

popular religion – See p. 76 for a definition.

stigmata – marks in the human body corresponding to the wounds of Christ which resulted from his crucifixion, see p. 138.

synod and council – See Appendix, p. 241.

Theotokos – The title given to Mary as 'mother of God' or 'God-bearer: *Theos* means God, *tokos* means 'bearer' and by extension 'mother'.

Tradition (with a capital 'T') – What has been 'handed down' (Latin *tradere*) by the Church. Tradition accompanies Scripture as authoritative for Catholics, see p. 1.

ultramontane – Pro-papal, deriving from a northerner's perspective of Rome as 'beyond' (Latin *ultra*) 'the mountains' (Latin *montes*) of the Alps.

Bibliography

This selective bibliography lists the most important modern publications in English as well as other works that are referred to in the book. For works that are frequently cited, see Notes and Abbreviations (pp. xiii–xiv).

General works

Dictionaries and encyclopedias

Encyclopedia of the Early Church, ed. Angelo di Berardino, 2 vols, Cambridge 1992.

New Catholic Encyclopedia, 16 vols, 3rd edn, Farmington Hills MI 2003.

The Oxford Dictionary of Saints, ed. D. Farmer, 3rd edn, Oxford 1992.

The Oxford Dictionary of the Christian Church, eds F. L. Cross and E. Livingstone, 3rd edn revised, Oxford 2005.

The Oxford Dictionary of the Popes, ed. J. N. D. Kelly, Oxford 1986.

Collections of sources

Classics of Western Christianity (Mahwah). This fine series by Paulist Press provides the main texts in English translation, together with an introduction and notes, of many spiritual writers and mystics.

The Christian Faith: Doctrinal Documents of the Catholic Church, ed. Jacques Dupuis, revised 7th edn, Bangalore 2001.

Documents of the Christian Church, ed. H. Bettenson, 2nd edn, London 1963.

Readings in Church History, ed. J. Colman Barry, revised edn, Westminster MA 1985.

245

Other general works

Baur, John, *2000 Years of Christianity in Africa*, revised edn, Nairobi 1998.

Cambridge History of Christianity, various authors, 9 vols, Cambridge 2006–8.

Copleston, F., *A History of Philosophy*, 9 vols, London 1946–75.

Duffy, E., *Saints and Sinners: A History of the* Popes, 2nd edn, New Haven and London 2002.

Dussel, E. (ed.), *The Church in Latin America 1492–1992*, Tunbridge Wells and Maryknoll 1992.

Evans, G. R. (general editor), *The I. B. Tauris History of the Christian Church*, 7 vols, London and New York 2006–10.

Hastings, Adrian, *The Church in Africa 1450–1950*, Oxford 1994.

Hussey, J. M., *The Orthodox Church in the Byzantine Empire*, Oxford 1986.

Jedin, H. (ed.), *History of the Church*, 10 vols, London 1980.

MacCulloch, Diarmaid, *A History of Christianity: The First Three Thousand Years*, London 2009.

Neill, Stephen, *A History of Christian Missions*, Harmondsworth 1964.

Tanner, Norman, *The Councils of the Church: A Short History*, New York 2001.

Chapter 1 (and Chapter 2 until 600 AD)

Brown, Peter, *Augustine of Hippo: A Biography*, 2nd edn, London 2000.

Chadwick, H., *The Church in Ancient Society: From Galilee to Gregory the Great*, Oxford 2001.

Grillmeier, A., *Christ in Christian Tradition*, 2 vols, revised edn, London 1975–96.

Hanson, R. P., *The Search for the Christian Doctrine of God: The Arian Controversy 318–381*, Edinburgh 1988.

Kelly, J. N. D., *Early Christian Creeds*, 3rd edn, London 1972.

— *Early Christian Doctrines*, 5th edn, London 1977.

Price, R. and Gaddis, M. (eds), *The Acts of the Council of Chalcedon*, 3 vols, Liverpool 2005.

Stevenson, J. (ed.), *Creeds, Councils and Controversies: Documents*

Illustrating the History of the Church AD 337–461, 2nd edn, London 1989.

Young, Francis M., *From Nicaea to Chalcedon: A Guide to the Literature and its Background*, 2nd edn, London 2010.

Chapters 2 and 3

Davies, Brian, *The Thought of Thomas Aquinas*, Oxford 1992.

Edwards, J., 'Religious Faith and Doubt in Late Medieval Spain: Soria *c.* 1450–1550', *Past and Present*, cxx, (1988), pp. 3–15.

English Historical Documents, vol. 4 (1327–1485), ed. A. R. Myers, London 1969.

Helmholz, R., *Marriage Litigation in Medieval England*, Cambridge 1974.

Knowles, David and Obolensky, Dmitri, *The Christian Centuries*, vol. 2, *The Middle Ages*, London and New York 1969.

Lambert, Malcolm, *Medieval Heresy*, 3rd edn, Oxford 2002.

Le Roy Ladurie, Emmanuel, *Montaillou: Cathars and Catholics in a French Village, 1274–1324*, London 1978.

McLean, Teresa, *The English at Play in the Middle Ages*, Windsor Forest 1983.

Milis, Ludo (ed.), *The Pagan Middle Ages*, Woodbridge 1998.

Morris, C., *The Papal Monarchy 1050–1250*, Oxford 1989.

Murray, Alexander, 'Piety and Impiety in Thirteenth-Century Italy', in G. J. Cuming and D. Baker (eds), *Popular Belief and Practice, Studies in Church History*, viii, Cambridge 1972, pp. 83–106.

Newett, M. M., *Canon Pietro Casola's Pilgrimage to Jerusalem in the Year 1494*, Manchester 1907.

Oakley, F., *The Western Church in the Later Middle Age*, Ithaca and London 1979.

Pantin, W., *The English Church in the Fourteenth Century*, Cambridge 1955.

Reynolds, Susan, 'Social Mentalities and the Case of Medieval Scepticism', *Transactions of the Royal Historical Society*, 6th series, i (1991), pp. 21–41.

Southern, R. W., *Western Society and the Church in the Middle Ages*, Harmondsworth 1970.

Swanson, Robert, *Religion and Devotion in Europe, c. 1215–c.1515*, Cambridge 1995.

Tanner, Norman, *The Church in Late Medieval Norwich, 1370–1532*, Toronto 1984.

— 'Making Merry in the Middle Ages', *The Month*, September–October 1996, pp. 373–6.

Tanner, Norman and Watson, Sethina, 'Least of the Laity: The Minimum Requirements for a Medieval Christian', *Journal of Medieval History*, xxxii, (2006), pp. 395–423.

Toussaert, J., *Le sentiment religieux en Flandre à la fin du Moyen Age*, Paris 1960.

Chapter 4

Duffy, Eamon, *The Stripping of the Altars: Traditional Religion in England 1400–1580*, New Haven 1992.

Jedin, H., *A History of the Council of Trent*, London 1957–. So far only the first two volumes of the five-volume German original have appeared in English.

MacCulloch, Diarmaid, *Reformation: Europe's House Divided 1490–1700*, London 2003.

McManners, J., *Church and Society in Eighteenth Century France*, 2 vols, Oxford 1998.

O'Malley, John W., *The Early Jesuits*, Cambridge MA and London 1993.

Chapter 5

Alberigo, G., and Komonchak, J. (general editors), *History of Vatican II*, 5 vols, 1996–2005.

Breward, I., *A History of the Church in Australasia*, Oxford 2001.

Butler, Cuthbert, *The Vatican Council*, 2 vols, London and New York 1930.

Callahan, W. J., *The Catholic Church in Spain 1875–1998*, Washington DC 2000.

Handy, Robert T., *A History of the Churches in the United States and Canada*, Oxford 1976.

Ker, Ian, *John Henry Newman: A Biography*, Oxford 1988.

O'Malley, John W., *What Happened at Vatican II*, Cambridge MA 2008.

The Papal Encyclicals (1740–1958), ed. C. Carlen, 5 vols, Ypsilanti MI 1990.

Index

This selective index of Persons, Places and Subjects seeks to cover the topics in the most helpful way.